HILARY M. LIPS is an assistant professor of psychology at the University of Winnipeg and is currently engaged in research on the social-psychological aspects of pregnancy.

NINA LEE COLWILL teaches undergraduate psychology and business courses at the University of Manitoba; her current research involves sex-role problems in organizations.

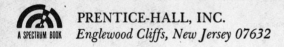

PRENTICE-HALL, INC.
Englewood Cliffs, New Jersey 07632
A SPECTRUM BOOK

THE
PSYCHOLOGY
OF SEX
DIFFERENCES

Hilary M. Lips & Nina Lee Colwill

Library of Congress Cataloging in Publication Data

Lips, Hilary M
   The psychology of sex differences.

   (A Spectrum Book)
   Bibliography: p.
   Includes index.
     1. Sex differences (Psychology) 2. Sex role.
3. Sexism. I. Colwill, Nina Lee, joint author.
II. Title.
BF692.2.L56   155.3'3   78-11328
ISBN 0-13-736561-6
ISBN 0-13-736553-5 pbk.

*To our parents
and to all other parents
who have been more concerned with their children's humanity
than with their femininity or masculinity*

Editorial/production supervision and
interior design by Carol Smith
Cover design by Kay Ritta
Manufacturing buyer: Cathie Lenard

© 1978 by Prentice-Hall, Inc.
Englewood Cliffs, New Jersey 07632

A SPECTRUM BOOK

10 9 8 7 6 5

Printed in the United States of America

PRENTICE-HALL INTERNATIONAL, INC., *London*

PRENTICE-HALL OF AUSTRALIA PTY. LIMITED, *Sydney*

PRENTICE-HALL OF CANADA, LTD., *Toronto*

PRENTICE-HALL OF INDIA PRIVATE LIMITED, *New Delhi*

PRENTICE-HALL OF JAPAN, INC., *Tokyo*

PRENTICE-HALL OF SOUTHEAST ASIA PTE. LTD., *Singapore*

WHITEHALL BOOKS LIMITED, *Wellington, New Zealand*

Contents

Preface

The study of sex differences has a long history in the field of psychology. Early investigators saw sex differences in temperament or behavior as logical consequences of obvious (and not so obvious) anatomical differences. During recent years, however, partially through the impetus provided by the feminist movement, psychologists have begun to reassess the position of their discipline in this matter. Perhaps the strongest feature of this reassessment has been a recognition of the need to examine sex differences within a social context rather than to focus on their anatomical, physiological, or intrapsychic origins. One of the strongest appeals in this regard came from Naomi Weisstein (1971) in a monograph entitled *Psychology constructs the female, or the fantasy life of the male psychologist.* The article pointed out that many of psychology's findings about sex differences could be explained by invoking concepts such as conformity to social pressure, expectancy effects, differential socialization practices for females and males, and experimenter bias. As social psychologists, we share Weisstein's orientation, and we have noted that since her article appeared some years ago, there has been an upsurge of research interest in the social variables underlying sex differences. As a result of this increased interest, psychology's approach to the study of sex differences has become steadily more sophisticated. An appreciation of the complex interplay of forces that produces the behavior our society labels "masculine" and "feminine" can be approached in some areas. It is beginning to be recognized, for example, that even behavior that previously was thought to stem from such a strictly biological basis as pregnancy or the menstrual cycle has social as well as physiological components. In teaching about the psychology of sex differences, we are involved in a constant struggle to keep the complexity of the issue—its social as well as biological nature—in perspective. It is our hope that this book will help the reader with the same struggle.

The first chapter examines sex differences research methodologies and some of their attendant problems. The next five chapters examine various approaches to the study of sex differences. We first look at personality theorists who believe sex differences to be the basis of meaningful personality differences. Some, such as Freud, have had incalculable impact on the beliefs about men and women that we hold today. Next, we explore the process of sexual differentiation, from the moment of conception to the formation of a gender identity. Part of the sexual differentiation process is the acquisition of sex hormones, and the physiological and psychological impact of hormones and hormonal cycles is a third approach to our analysis of sex differences. Fourth, we view sex differences through the eyes of a sociologist: probably the strongest nurture position we will see. And last, we study the concepts of masculinity, femininity, and androgyny. What is meant by these terms, and what do we buy into when we accept them as meaningful concepts?

By the end of the sixth chapter, we hope that you will have a strong basis upon which to analyze the available research in four areas of sex differences: abilities, achievement, aggression, and power. Although throughout the book we examine sex differences in many other attitudes and behaviors, those four chapters serve as an in-depth analysis of four important areas of human activity. With the tools acquired in the first half of the book, you should have no trouble critically evaluating our analyses and generating alternative hypotheses of your own.

In the last two chapters we look at issues and institutions that exist as a function of our population's being divided into two sexes: the complexities of marriage, parenthood, and human sexuality. A myriad of sex roles comes into play as we fulfill the specific roles of husband, wife, mother, father, and lover. With the tools and information you acquire in the first ten chapters, you should be in a good position to examine the origins and implications of these roles.

In teaching our courses on the psychology of sex differences and indeed in writing this book, we have found ourselves constantly emphasizing that which we wish, philosophically and politically, to de-emphasize: the differences between males and females. As Ambert (1976) has pointed out:

> For, in spite of current research trends and ideologies, the sexes are more alike than dissimilar. We are in the presence of a range of human potentialities and qualities and the more important observation resides in the overlap of human traits between the sexes in spite of a socialization process that encourages cleavage. [p. 7]

Yet, Ambert has written of the sociological sex structure of our society, and we have written of the psychology of sex differences. Do our books encourage the very cleavage of which she speaks? We can only hope, as does she, that the effect will be less to remind us of our differences and more to remind us of the great overlap of human traits and the wide range of human potential.

Acknowledgments

Several people have collaborated with us in writing this book. Neena L. Chappell (Ph.D., sociology, McMaster University, Hamilton, Canada) is an assistant professor in the Department of Social and Preventive Medicine at the University of Manitoba. She has taught courses in socialization and the sociology of sex roles and has researched and written in the area of sex roles, with particular emphasis on working women. She was thus an obvious choice as author of the chapter on socialization. Wendy L. Josephson is a Ph.D. candidate in social psychology at the University of Manitoba. She has taught social psychology and has done research in the area of media effects on children's aggressive behavior. This gave her an excellent background to be coauthor of the chapter on aggression. Stephen W. Holborn (Ph.D., University of Iowa) is an assistant professor in the Department of Psychology at the University of Manitoba. His research interests in basic and applied analyses of the principles of human learning, and the fact that he is a trained behavior therapist specializing in problems of anxiety and improved sexual functioning, allowed him to bring special expertise to the sexuality chapter; he also made a major contribution to the development of the first chapter. Anita Myers is a Ph.D. student in social psychology at York University in Toronto. She has researched and written in the areas of sex differences in cognitive style and the measurement and interpretation of psychological androgyny and thus was able to make a valuable contribution to the chapter on abilities. Judy Conn, a graduate student in social psychology at the University of Manitoba, brought her strong interest in the impact of sex roles on society to the chapter on marriage and the family. The expertise of these individuals helped us immeasurably in our attempt to give accurate treatment to a wide range of issues.

We are grateful to the following people for their careful reading of and critical comments on various parts of the manuscript: Robert Altemeyer, Dennis Anderson, Wayne Andrew, Julie Beddoes, Gail Clark, Stephen F. Davis, Loretta Edmonds, Gloria D. Evans, Virginia Hoitsma, Stephen W. Holborn, David R. Humpherys, Wendy L. Josephson, Stuart Kaye, Barry Kelly, Tom Lips, Neil M. Malamuth, Michael McIntyre, Anita Myers, Barrie Noonan, Joseph J. Pear, Daniel Perlman, Deanna Speight, Barry Spinner, Robert W. Tait, Mavis Turner, June Whitbread, and Alexander Wilson. We also acknowledge the other students, professors, and colleagues who, in classroom discussions and coffee-break conversations, helped us to develop so many of the thoughts included here.

On numerous occasions we were rescued from total panic by the competent, energetic, and interested help of Virginia Hart, Linda Lamontagne, and Barbara Latocki, who typed most of the manuscript. Invaluable technical assistance was also provided by Alice Harvey, who copyedited the manuscript, by Carol Smith, who guided the book through to completion at Prentice-Hall, and by Sheila Andrich and Terry Richard who worked patiently and carefully with us on the indexes.

In writing this book we have gathered strength from many sources. In particular we would like to thank, for reasons best known to themselves: Dennis Anderson, Wayne Andrew, Neena L. Chappell, Gail Clark, Todd L. Fay, Joanne Haynes, J. Ronald Edmonds, Wendy L. Josephson, Anita Myers, Daniel Perlman, Mavis Turner, and Gordon Winocur.

1 Nina Lee Colwill

THE STUDY
OF SEX
DIFFERENCES:
Research
Perspectives
& Problems

> With few exceptions, social psychologists regard their discipline as *an attempt to understand and explain how the thought, feeling, and behavior of individuals are influenced by the actual, imagined, or implied presence of others.*
> [Allport, 1969, p. 3]

"You can take the boy out of the country," the old saying goes, "but you can't take the country out of the boy." Assuming this dictum applies to females as well as to males, it probably applies to Lips and Colwill in our writing of this book. We have between us more than two decades of training and teaching in social psychology—somewhat of a guarantee, according to the very tenets of social psychology, that we view the world through social psychological glasses. We believe, as does Allport, that behavior is "influenced by the actual, imagined, or implied presence of others," and the implications of this assumption are necessarily present in everything we write or teach. Thus, whereas the geneticist may look first to heritability and the physiologist to such factors as hormonal influences to explain sex differences in human behavior, we look first at the social factors that influence the way men and women view and respond to their worlds.

Allport (1969) suggests that what we now call social psychology was, until a century ago, considered part of political philosophy. In many ways the psychology of sex differences is returning to a political front in the latter third of this century. The social psychological perspective on sex differences—that our differences are not an immutable fact but a function of the environment in which we find ourselves—has been the basis for many legal reforms in the past decade. Thus, child custody, family property laws, and equal pay for equal work legislation have undergone dramatic changes in the past decade, since the research of psychology has demonstrated the malleability of our long-accepted "sex differences," and the voice of sex-role liberation politics has been heard in the land.

Although social psychology has contributed greatly to the political philosophy of sex-role liberation and although sex-role liberation politics have often had a hand in molding the perspective of social psychologists, we still must be able, as students of sex differences, to recognize where one ends and the other begins. Social psychologists, for the most part, consider their knowledge to be data-based. Their theories are many and often complex, but ultimately those theories must stand the test of empirical research.

By identifying themselves with psychology, social psychologists have committed themselves to an empirical base. Many of the issues dealt with by social psychology are philosophical political issues—racism, sexism, discrimination against homosexuals. Many of the arguments made by social psychologists have been made by political philosophers, but the social psychologist's research perspective allows these arguments to be empirically validated. Although we try throughout this book to indicate where social psychology leaves off and sex-role liberation politics begin, the distinction is not always clear. The goal of this book is to help you to see this distinction and to learn to value the empirical methods of psychology in arriving at answers to social problems.

PROBLEMS IN THE THEORY
AND RESEARCH OF SEX DIFFERENCES

The body of knowledge that we call the psychology of sex differences is only as strong as the theory and research that comprise it. In this section we examine a wide variety of problems, some of which are common to every branch of psychology and some of which are unique to the psychology of sex differences.

The Differences Orientation

Perhaps one of the most obvious problems in both the theory and research of sex differences is that its roots are in an orientation of *differences*. Psychology learns from differences: differences between children and adults, between blacks and whites, between Americans and Canadians, and between males and females. Through these differences we learn about the components of maturation, of race, of citizenship, and of sex. One of the implications of the differences orientation—we might even call it a differences ideology—is that we have few mechanisms within which to examine nondifferences. As researchers, we may find (and, in fact, have found) nondifferences in a particular behavior, but psychology offers few vehicles for airing what we sometimes call these nonresults. And so every time we read of a sex difference, we must remember that the results of a comparable study may be gathering dust in some cupboard, because another researcher was not lucky enough to reach statistical significance. In short, the world of academic publishing gives sex differences a definite edge over similarities between the sexes, a situation that is strongly felt in the emphasis we place on differences.

This problem is not unique to the psychology of sex differences, of course, but it is of particular concern to researchers in this area because of its political implications. Many psychologists and sociologists who do sex-differences or sex-roles research identify themselves philosophically as sex-role liberationists, yet the irony of their work is that it often serves to stress sex differences, a fact that has the potential to retard sex-role liberation. Even more problematic than a sex-differences perspective is a women's studies orientation, which has become very popular in the past few years; many universities have set up entire departments of women's studies. Such an orientation has the potential of reinforcing the stereotype of "the woman problem," which—like "the black problem"—may be a very difficult orientation to discard once it takes hold. The "problem" is clearly not women any more than it is blacks. The problem is the arbitrary assignment of characteristics on the basis of sex or race, and all the attendant horrors.

Does this mean we should give up research and writing in the area of sex differences? Obviously not. If we believe in the worth of eradicating our arbitrary distinctions, we must know what is amenable to change and what is worth changing. Only research and the dissipation of research will provide the proper perspective.

Statistical Significance and Social Significance

A second problem in the study of sex differences might easily be considered a subset of the first. After reading an interesting piece of research, we can easily forget that males and females merely differed on a particular behavior to the point of *statistical significance*. Psychology uses statistics because the manipulation of our variables seldom produces such dramatic effects that we can say: "Under condition X, men will do this, but women will do that." A statistically significant difference, which is the most we usually attain, merely tells us that the difference we have observed is unlikely to have happened by *chance alone*: that two mixed-sex groups chosen at random would be unlikely to differ to the extent that these same-sex groups differed. Finding a significant sex difference may tell us that in this experiment, the variation between sex groups on a particular behavior was greater than the variation within sex groups: that males differed from females more than males differed from each other and more than females differed from each other.

If all males differed from all females on the traits, abilities, and behaviors that we have come to call sex differences—if males and females formed two distinct camps—we obviously would not need statistics. We need statistics in order to be able to speak of sex differences, because on nearly every known behavior, the sexes overlap. Although the animal literature may offer more examples, it is difficult to conceive of a single human behavior, outside of impregnation and childbearing, that is exclusive to males or to females. Although we tend to think of males as aggressive, females as submissive, males as independent and females as nurturant, there is obviously great overlap in the possession of these traits. Some women are more aggressive than some men; some men are more nurturant than most women; and a few men may even be more submissive than all women.

Let us use a simple example provided by Stoll (1974) to illustrate our point. Let us assume that if we were to plot the frequency of eyeblinks in three-day-old infants, we would find that our data approximates the normal curve pictured in Figure 1.

If we were to separate infants into the two sex groups, we might find that the frequency of eyeblinks ordered themselves along a normal curve for both males and females. We might also find that there was a significant difference between the *average* number of eyeblinks for males and for females. As Stoll indicates in Figure 2, however, this might mean many different things. Once one understands the

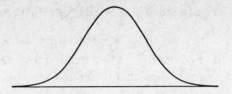

FIGURE 1 The normal curve.

FIGURE 2 Sex differences in eyeblink response. Hypothethical data: Glockenspiel counts eye blinks in 18,346 infants on the third day of life and discovers that on the average the males blink .415 times more often than the females. She reports that this difference is "statistically significant." If we charted the distribution of eyeblink frequencies, we could find any one of the following situations:

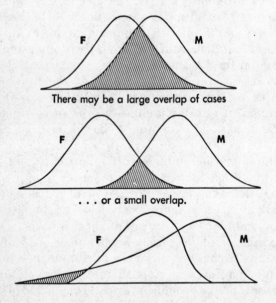

There may be a large overlap of cases

. . . or a small overlap.

There may even be cases of males who blink less frequently than females. Probability statistics are such that any of these situations is often possible. We need to ask Glockenspiel how much *variation* there was in the samples as one clue to identifying the underlying distribution. Also, because the difference is "statistically significant," this does not mean it is "socially significant."*

*From *Female & Male* by Clarice Stasz Stoll (Dubuque, Iowa: William C. Brown Company, Publishers, 1974, p. 8). © 1974 by William C. Brown Company, Publishers. Reprinted by permission of the publisher.

pattern of overlap, the sex difference in eyeblink response becomes a much more complex phenomenon. It would be very difficult to predict, merely knowing that one child was male and another female, which would be the most frequent eyeblinker. In short, the *statistically* significant result has little *social* significance (Stoll, 1974).

Stoll's example was expressly chosen for its simplicity. You can imagine the complexity that is added when we examine such variable behaviors as aggression, submission, independence, and nurturance. It is easy to be lulled into an acceptance of the notion that our sons will *necessarily* be more aggressive than our daughters, because a sex difference in aggression has been demonstrated to be statistically significant in several studies. It is especially easy to overinterpret the social significance of statistically significant differences when they have some commonsense appeal.

Correlation versus Experimentation

Whenever two variables are related to each other without experimental manipulation—whenever it is possible to predict one from our knowledge of the other—we say that these variables are correlated. Thus race is correlated with IQ, and biological sex is correlated with aggression. It is very tempting to believe that one of these variables *caused* the other, but correlational data never allow us that option. There are thousands of other variables associated with being black or white, male or female, in our society, and many of these may contribute to the relationships. Thus, boys as a class may be more aggressive than girls as a class because they are rewarded for aggression by their peers, because they engage in more sports, or because they are allowed to watch more violent television. We have no information that indicates that the biological fact of being male *causes* aggression. To gain that information, we would have to conduct an experiment. We would have to randomly assign children at birth to maleness or femaleness, a clearly impossible task. To conduct an experiment, one must manipulate an independent variable—in this case, sex—and observe the effects on a dependent variable—in this case, aggression. Because we cannot manipulate sex, we are stuck with correlational data in the study of sex differences.

That is not to say that correlational sex-differences data are useless. It is an important starting point to know how the sexes differ. Only then can we begin to explore the reasons why.

As we examine sex differences in a myriad of animal and human behaviors, try to keep these problems in mind, and the sexes may not seem as different as you thought. There are other problems, specific to specific studies, that we will now review, but the three just discussed are always present. Let us now consider separately problems in two classes of sex-differences research: problems in animal studies and problems in human research.

Animal Studies

Much research on sex differences employs nonhuman animals as subjects. Why do we do this? One of the reasons is that we can often move beyond correlational studies with animals. We can conduct experiments with animals that would be unethical, immoral, or impossible to do with humans. It would be unthinkable to inject pregnant humans with cross-sex hormones in order to observe effects on the behaviors of their offspring, yet we can do this with lower animals. Similarly, we cannot isolate human infants at birth in order to observe the effects of nonsocialization of sex-differentiated behaviors, but the social isolation of lower animals is a common research technique. We learn much about lower animals from laboratory animal research, but it is only too tempting to suppose we are learning the same thing about humans. As Weisstein (1971) says, "The most general and serious problem is that there are no grounds to assume that anything primates do is necessary, natural, or desirable in humans, for the simple reason that humans are not non-humans" (p. 5). At best, we are arguing by analogy. At worst, our results may not even apply to animals of the same species raised in the wild.

Fundamental to the use of lower animals for the study of human sex differences is the belief that there is some "truth" about sex differences that can best be found by separating biology from socialization and that this can be done by examining the behaviors of animals, as if they were nonsocialized humans. We would suppose that drawn to its logical conclusion, the argument for the use of lower animals as some "pure" kind of humans would contend that animal research is even better than human research, since we do not have to ferret out that part of behavior due to biology from that part of behavior due to socialization. As Linton (1971) has pointed out, however, animals *are* socialized:

The major factor which is being overlooked is that these primates under observation *live in a social group*. Animal behaviorists have been emphasizing for years the importance of the social group, and the extent to which most primate behavior is *learned*. It is inexcusable to emphasize the importance of this learned behavior in all other contexts, and to ignore it when considering sex-role behavior. [p. 195]

One of the most interesting points Linton makes is that we do not know what cues are used by lower animals to differentiate between males and females and what steps they take to socialize their young and their peers into sex-role-appropriate behavior. It may be, for instance, that smell is a very important component in the animal's ability to differentiate between male and female animals. That would predict that our sex hormone experiments with animals may be confounded. Sex hormone treatments may be disturbing the "sex smell" sufficiently that animals that have received sex hormone treatments are treated very differently from their peers by their peers. If this were the case, we could not draw conclusions about the effects of sex hormones *per se* on animal, let alone human, behavior. Yet, as we see in several chapters of this book (Chapters 1, 9, and 12), sex hormone treatment of pregnant animals or newborn animals has been a popular research method in the study of sex hormonal influence on behavior, and causal inferences are often made on the basis of these data.

One of the problems we meet in every branch of psychology is the problem of operational definitions. How do we define our terms? This is not a trivial issue, for as we will see again and again in this book, our definition of such terms as *aggression, power, nurturance,* and *achievement* greatly affects the conclusions we draw about sex differences. As difficult as it is to agree upon operational definitions in human research, the problem is compounded when we try to generalize from lower animal to human research. In studies of mother nurturance, for instance, can we really equate the mother rhesus monkey picking fleas from her baby with the human mother reading to her child?

In short, let us not confuse humans with nonhumans. As Weisstein has suggested: "It would be reasonable to conclude, following this logic, that it is quite useless to teach human infants to speak, since it has been tried with chimpanzees and it does not work" (p. 5).

Human Research

In this section we explore some of the problems inherent in sex-differences research among humans. Although there are other problems, we focus mainly on social psychological issues. It will be helpful to remember that all these problems are complicated, compounded, and reinforced by the three general problems we discussed at the beginning of this section.

Psychology as a Masculine Noun.   One of the messages that recurs in this book is that of a misogynous society—a society in which women are downgraded and men exalted. So strong is the evidence for our general acceptance of an antifemale prejudice (see, e.g., Broverman, Broverman, Clarkson, Rosenkrantz, & Vogel, 1970) that the message has become almost a truism. This cannot help but have a dramatic effect on the research and theory of psychology. Holmes and Jorgensen (1971) have pointed out, for instance, that approximately two-thirds of subjects in published psychological research are male. Yet we speak of such findings as though they are evidence for the psychological functioning of all people. Thus in spite of the fact that the personality construct, need for achievement, has completely failed to explain female behavior, we refer to it not as "need for achievement in men" but merely as "need for achievement."

In 1971, Naomi Weisstein wrote a short article that captured the imaginations of feminist psychologists everywhere. She called her witty paper *Psychology constructs the female or, the fantasy life of the male psychologist.* In it she pointed out that male psychologists have created a psychology of woman based not on research evidence but on their feelings about how they would like the world to be. "Psychology," she accuses, "has functioned as a pseudo-scientific buttress for patriarchal ideology and patriarchal social organization" (p. 2). Her treatise is not yet dated. The personality theorists she lambasted—Bettelheim, Erikson, and Freud—are still being read and studied, and there is no indication that their works will soon be treated as the quaint writings of some long-forgotten time.

The impact of the personality theorists is discussed in Chapter 2, but one of their major areas of impact is, of course, in therapy. Phyllis Chesler (1972), who has become famous for her book *Women and madness*, has documented the harm done to women by a male-defined psychology translated into a male-defined therapy and administered

10

by male therapists. This phenomenon probably represents the greatest impact of the masculinization of psychology.

Sex as an Artifact. As we saw in our discussion of correlation and causation, sex of subject often masks other variables in psychological research. Thus sex differences may merely be artifacts attributable to the research design of a study. Let us now examine the research of someone who started out looking for sex differences in organizational behavior and concluded that sex was merely an artifact.

Rosabeth Moss Kanter (1976) took her research into an organizational setting to find out what makes females poorer leaders than males and less successful in business. She went armed with a training that had taught her that women were socialized into poor leadership skills, and she merely sought to explore the dynamics of that notion—to isolate variables in the past and present of female workers that might be related to their lower success rate. After several dead ends, she began to wonder if sex were not an artifact. Perhaps some other factor more reliably separated successful from unsuccessful people, and females merely tended to be associated with the "unsuccessful" variable. It was with this hypothesis that she found differences! As we discuss further in Chapter 10, the important variable for predicting low success was the job situation: people in token positions, dead-end positions, and "powerless leadership" positions were likely to make poor leaders and to have relatively unsuccessful careers. Sex was not nearly as good a predictor of poor leadership and low rate of success as was type of job, regardless of sex of the incumbent.

The situation in which Kanter found herself may not be atypical of sex-differences research. Obviously, studies that encompass several variables are more likely to unearth this situation, because the researchers can test the relationship between several factors. We would do well, when reading of sex differences in various psychological measures, to think of factors other than sex that might explain these differences and to always keep in mind that correlation does not imply causation.

The Social Psychology of the Psychological Experiment. Over forty years ago, Rosenzweig (1933), in a pioneer paper on the social psychology of the psychological experiment, mentioned sex as a "personal quality" of the experimenter with the potential of introducing "errors of personality influence" into the laboratory. But the *Zeitgeist* was not in Rosenzweig's favor (Adair, 1973), for it is only within the last decade that his brilliant insights into the psychological problems inherent in the experimental situation have come into vogue. Particularly, for our interests, sex of the experimenter has recently become not only a factor of consideration in experimental design and analysis but a legitimate independent variable in its own right.

As we saw earlier in this section, the majority of subjects in psychological experiments is male. The majority of experimenters is also male. Sex-of-experimenter effects are present in every area of psychological research from hypnosis (Johnson, Smith, Whatley, & DeVoge, 1973) to eyeblink conditioning (Gold, 1969). There are many complex effects, but the most dramatic is that female experimenters tend to disconfirm their hypotheses, whereas male experimenters *confirm* theirs (Rosenthal, Persinger, Mulry, Vikan–Kline, & Grothe, 1964). Yet, in spite of the importance of sex of experimenter, 85 percent of researchers never mentioned sex of the experimenter in the journals reviewed by Harris (1971).

The social psychology of the psychological experiment is rife with other variables (problems) that can interact with sex, causing artifactual findings. We know, for instance, that females are more likely than males to comply with the demand characteristics of an experimental situation (Rosenthal, 1966). Thus a reported sex difference in a laboratory study about nurturance may really reflect the fact that females are more likely than males to respond to the demand characteristics of the experiment: to nurture, as they think the experimenter wants them to, rather than to follow their "natural" inclinations.

As we have seen, the theory and research of the psychology of sex differences is not without problems. Many are not, however, insolvable. As you read through this book, you will probably be as impressed as we were with some of the ways in which these problems have been circumvented and with the soundness of some of the theory and research in our special branch of psychology.

NATURE, NURTURE, AND THE INTERACTIONIST POSITION

There has probably never been an introductory psychology text written or an introductory psychology class taught that did not address the nature–nurture issue. Is human behavior determined by environment or by heredity? More to the point, for our purposes: are sex differences part of our human inheritance, or do we learn to be males and females by interacting with the environment in which we find ourselves?

This is the most basic question in the study of sex differences, the question from which all others stem:

> This is no mere academic exercise of concern only to students of behavior. The planets will move as they always have, whether we adopt a geocentric or a heliocentric view of the heavens. It is only the equations we generate to account for those motions that will be more or less complex; the motions of the planets are sublimely indifferent to our earthbound astronomy. But the behavior of men is not independent of the theories of human behavior. . . . What we believe of man affects the behavior of men, for it determines what each expects of the other. [Eisenberg, 1972, p. 123]

And women, too, we are compelled to add.

We do not study in a vacuum, then. Eisenberg's analysis underscores the potential social consequences of the position we take on the nature–nurture issue. He suggests that there is a latent message in treatises on the innateness of human behavior: the justification of bigotry. He contends, for instance, that writers such as Lorenz (1940, cited in Eisenberg, 1972) were instrumental in the Nazi justification of discrimination and, later, annihilation on the basis of racial impurity:

> In domesticated animals, he argued, degenerative mutations result in the loss of species-specific releaser mechanisms responding to innate schemata that govern mating patterns and that serve in nature to maintain the purity of the stock. Similar phenomena are said to be an inevitable by-product of civilization unless the state is vigilant. [Eisenberg, 1972, p. 124].

But few would accept state vigilance or racial purity in our present social climate. Rather, it has been very comfortable in the past few years for those of us who stress the important role of social factors in the development and maintenance of sex-differentiated behaviors. We have called ourselves sex-role liberationists, and the political, social, and economic climate has been ripe to accept our name and our message. Who would fault freedom in this decade? But even as there are dangers in the pat acceptance of the innateness of human behavior, so are there dangers in the pat acceptance of the socialization of sex differences. Both positions are equally deficient. Incidentally, it is but a short step from "girls and boys tend to be different because of our differential socialization processes" to "girls and boys *must be* different because of our differential socialization processes." Such an emphasis leaves us with no less rigidity than the belief that sex chromosomes alone determine all sex differences. For individual parents faced with what they consider to be the rules of a society, the effect may seem as overpowering as if they were faced with an immutable biological fact. How can I raise my child to be a person, sex unspecified, against the rules of my culture? Do I have the right? Even the ardent feminist, Judy Lamarsh, has been forced to ask herself:

> If I were to have a girl child right now, I don't think I would have the strength of my own convictions to bring her up as a person. Perhaps she would be happier, free of her role. Then too she might be very unhappy, for as a child growing up she would hit so many of the taboos in the world. So perhaps not socializing her in a traditional manner would be a dreadful thing to do.

> I would still be more likely to put the frilly clothes on her, still teach her all the things that I was taught and all my sisters were taught thousands of years before me; because I don't really know what happens when you teach a child otherwise. [Judy Lamarsh, cited in Nunes & White, 1973, p. 48]

Nature or nurture: which should we support? It is one of the goals of this book to provide you with skills to help you make that decision. Toward that end, let us now examine the concepts in some detail.

Nature

Variously called genetics, heredity, nativism, innateness, and instinct, the nature position in its most extreme form states that human behavior can be almost exclusively accounted for by our genetic inheritance. Dating at least back to Plato, the nature position probably reached its most ridiculous heights with the homunculus theory. The homunculus was a little person thought to be present in the head of every newborn, which supposedly carried with it innate sin and basic depravity (Lerner, 1976).

Probably no psychologist writing today believes that psychological traits (even basic depravity) are inherited directly. Rather, we believe our inheritance is a genotype or genetic endowment. Our phenotype, on the other hand, is our observable physical characteristics or behavior. Even the most nativistic among us believe it to be susceptible to environmental influence (Lerner, 1976). It is the relative impact of the genotype on the determination of the phenotype that is the basis of the nature–nurture controversy.

That the phenotype is primarily influenced by the genotype is probably the most extreme nativistic statement one is likely to hear today. This is partly because of the failure of genetics to provide us with clear-cut answers. In any case, extreme genetic positions are very unfashionable in a society sensitized, through the influence of the black movement, to racism and, through the influence of the women's movement, to sexism. Much more fashionable is the equally extreme and equally deficient position that we are what we are and we do what we do solely because of our environment: in short, that nurture is all.

Nurture

Empiricism, learning, or environment: all mean nurture, and all contend, to a greater or lesser degree, that we are ruled by events that take place after conception. In its most extreme form, the nurture position, epitomized by John Locke, an eighteenth-century empiricist, posits that the mind is a *tabula rasa* or blank slate upon which the experiences of life are written.

Probably the most quoted nurture statement is that made by "the first high priest of behaviorism, John B. Watson" (Hirsch, 1970, p. 90):

> Give me a dozen healthy infants, well-formed, and my own specified world to bring them up in, and I'll guarantee to take any one at random and train him to become any type of specialist I might select—doctor, lawyer, artist, merchant-chief and yes, even beggar-man and thief, regardless of his talents, penchants, tendencies, abilities, vocations, race of his ancestors. [Watson, 1930, p. 104]

As Hirsch points out, however, even Watson's position was not as extreme as his quoters would have us believe. His next sentence, which few of us have ever read, was:

> I am going far beyond my facts and I admit it, but so have the advocates of the contrary and they have been doing it for many thousands of years. [Watson, 1930, p. 104]

If the nativists concede to the empiricists and the behaviorists concede to the geneticists, where, then, do we stand? In an attempt to answer that question, let us now examine the third, the interactionist, position.

The Interactionist Position

Throughout this book our analysis of human behavior is, for conceptual convenience, often separated into categories emphasizing genetic influences and environmental influences. However, this in no way should be construed to mean that genetic factors can be considered to operate in isolation of environmental factors, or vice versa—just as in the traditional lyric about love and marriage, "you can't have one without the other." (This is, incidentally, truer for environment and heredity than it is for love and marriage.)

Let us illustrate with a simple example. Assume that the presence or absence of a specific genetic component completely determines susceptibility to allergic reactions to bee stings. Although inheritance either makes one vulnerable or invulnerable to an allergic reaction to bee stings, obviously even the vulnerable will emerge through life unscathed, unless actually stung. Conversely, being stung by a bee, though perhaps annoyingly painful, is insufficient in and of itself to produce an allergic reaction; the genetic predisposition must be there as well.

Additional complexities may be added to the foregoing example by considering environmental or genetic alterations that would modify the obtained allergic reaction. For instance, we can choose to change our environment with the use of insect repellents or antihistamines, which can substantially modify the probability of allergic reaction. On the genetic side, we could have an inherited allergic reaction to *antihistamines*, which could considerably complicate the issue. Thus, genetics and environment work together in producing a behavioral outcome. As Anastasi (1958)* has pointed out, it is meaningless to ask *"which one?"* for both are always important. Thus, although we discuss the effects of nature and nurture somewhat separately, they are best considered as the closest of friends, lovers if you will, intertwined in their relationship to behavior. The presence of particular genetic or environmental components merely increases or decreases the probability of specified behavioral results.

Even as we cannot speak of the sole influence of genetics or of environment in the determination of human traits and abilities, nor is it meaningful to speak in terms of the *proportion* of an individual's behavior that is determined by genetics and the *proportion* that is determined by environment. As Anastasi has suggested, such an approach—the *"how much?"* approach—implies that one need only add 20 parts of genetics to 80 parts of environment to come up with a formula for aggression or that one can add 50 parts of heredity to 50 parts of learning to have the formula for nurturance. The question "which one?" is, incidentally, a special case of "how much?" It suggests that zero parts of genetics is added to 100 parts of environment to produce independence or that zero parts of environment is added to 100 parts of genetics to produce passivity. The question "how much?" implies that we have not been dealt a full deck of genetics or that part of our environment is somehow missing.

Anastasi has formulated a third question, the question to which we address ourselves in this book—the question *"how?"* How—in what ways—do genetics and environment work together to produce behavioral outcomes? This question implies that the presence of particular genetic or environmental components merely increases or decreases the probability of specified behavioral results; neither one may in any fundamental sense be considered more or less important, and neither is immune to the influence of the other. Both genetics and environment are always fully present and fully interacting with the other. We bring 100 percent of our genetic endowment into every learning situation, and conversely, 100 percent of our environment is always present and interacting with our heredity.

We can see that Anastasi's three questions are increasingly complex. "Which one?" assumes that either genetics or environment— never both—is responsible for our behaviors. "How much?" assumes

---

*The interested reader who might find Anastasi's analysis somewhat heavy is referred to Lerner (1976), who simplifies some of her more sophisticated concepts. We are, in fact, indebted to his book for the clarification of several points.

that each behavioral outcome is always the result of adding a certain *proportion* of genetics to a certain *proportion* of environment. "How?" assumes that both genetics and environment are fully present for us all at all times and seeks to discover the ways in which they work together to produce our behaviors. Although we are conducting a fruitless search when we try to measure the *relative strength* of environmental factors and genetic factors, there is still much to be gained by examining ways to test how factors such as these might interact to determine sex differences in a myriad of behavioral outcomes.

Heredity: A Continuum of Indirectness. Anastasi stresses that heredity, though always 100 percent present, contributes to behavior indirectly. She envisions the effects of heredity as ordered along a continuum of indirectness from "least indirect" (we will say "most direct" for the sake of simplicity) effect on behavioral outcomes to "most indirect" (or "least direct") influence. To better understand this model in a sex-differences context, let us examine some points along Anastasi's continuum, set into a sex-differences framework. It will help to keep in mind that we are always asking "how?"—how directly does heredity influence the sex-differentiated behavioral outcomes of the inevitable interplay of heredity and environment?

Beginning at the "most direct" end of the continuum, let us examine the possible range of sex-differentiated behavioral outcomes for two hypothetical people: Joan and Bob. The most direct hereditary factor to influence their sex-differentiated behaviors is their karyotype—the composition of their sex chromosomes. Joan, as a function of her XX karyotype, is female; and Bob, as a function of his XY karyotype, is male. At this point in scientific progress, our chromosomes are an immutable fact: Joan will remain XX and Bob XY as long as they live, wherever they live, and whatever they do. They may disguise themselves as members of the other sex; they may take cross-sex hormone treatments at puberty to allow them to develop secondary cross-sex characteristics (e.g., breasts versus a hairy chest); they may even undergo sex change operations to change their genitals; but Joan will forever remain an XX and Bob an XY karyotype. Their environment, the background against which their lives are played, is of course always present; but the directness of hereditary influence is, at this point on the continuum, maximal.

As we move further along the continuum of indirectness, we come to inherited susceptibilities or predispositions. The genes have decreed that Joan is shorter than Bob and has finer bone structure. Although this predisposes her to be lighter and weaker than Bob, she may well be heavier and stronger, as a function of environmental factors that interact with their genetic predispositions. Whereas Joan lifts weights, eats well, and engages in many athletic pursuits, Bob lives on cigarettes and black coffee, never walks when he can ride, and never stands when he can lie down. There is an upper limit to Joan's strength, of course, just as there is a lower limit to Bob's weight, but the environment has interacted with the relatively indirect effect of their heredity and produced quite the opposite of what we would have predicted based upon their predispositions. Heredity is still 100 percent present, of course, but its effect as a determinant of size and strength is much less direct than its effect as a determinant of chromosomal sex.

Biological preparedness is a good example of an inherited susceptibility, as it represents a genetic predisposition to learn certain responses to particular environmental stimuli. As we explore sex differences in aggression in Chapter 9 and sex differences in sexuality in Chapter 12, we discuss the possibility that the two sexes differ in their biological preparedness to learn aggressive and sexual responses. It appears that the human brain differentiates by sex at a certain critical stage of fetal development (see Chapter 3), and it is possible that sex-differentiated biological preparednesses for certain responses are laid down at this time.

Let us continue on to a fourth point on the continuum, to the most indirect influence of heredity: social stereotypes. Although stereotypes are usually considered to be an environmental rather than a genetic factor, Anastasi sees them as genetic insofar as we base them on physical characteristics that are, in themselves, genetically determined. In our analysis, this point on the continuum is of course exemplified by sex-role stereotypes. The physical facts of Bob's maleness and Joan's femaleness are readily obvious to people in their environment who respond differently to them on the basis of the social expectations they have for males and females.

Social stereotypes, including sex-role stereotypes, differ from culture to culture, of course, even from region to region and from person to person. I may expect Joan to be artistic and you may expect her to be nurturant, as a function of our stereotypes of appropriate female behavior. Depending on how well we convey this message and how much Joan is rewarded by our favor, we may influence very different behavioral outcomes.

We see that heredity, though necessarily always present, varies in the directness of its influence on behavioral outcomes. From the most direct influence of chromosomal sex through inherited predispositions to the most indirect influence of social stereotypes, 100 percent of our heredity is with us all at all times.

Environment: Organic Factors. Anastasi's view of environment is a little more complex than many; she views environmental influences as comprising two types—organic and behavioral factors. She calls those factors that directly influence behavioral outcomes *behavioral environmental* factors: a friend's anger, a baby's insistent cry, the culture in which we find ourselves. Behavioral environmental factors are seen as stimuli that directly control behavioral responses. *Organic environmental* factors are influences that produce behavioral outcomes indirectly by contributing directly to the human organism. Broken legs and chicken pox are examples of such influence. By directly assaulting the organism, they may indirectly cause a wide range of behavioral responses such as the failure of an examination (we know that broken legs don't directly cause failed exams).

Let us first examine organic environmental factors. Anastasi orders organic environmental factors along a continuum of indirectness similar to the one she conceptualizes for genetic factors. At the "most direct" end of the continuum—the point at which environmental factors most directly influence the human organism—we would place a sex change operation. At the opposite end, we would employ the same example Anastasi uses: a hair dye job. Both operations make changes in Bob and Joan that would presumably affect the way in which environment would interact with genetics (in this case, their sex—male or female), but the former is obviously a much more direct influence than the latter. Let us assume that Bob and Joan both undergo sex change operations and dye their hair. What differential effects would those factors have on, say, their sexuality? Obviously, the sex change operation would have very direct ramifications for their respective sexualities, whereas the hair color change would have very indirect, yet probably sex-differentiated, implications. There are few organic environmental examples in the study of sex differences, however.

Most of the environmental factors that produce differential effects for males and females in our society tend to be of a more direct type: behavioral environmental factors.

Environment: Behavioral Factors. Behavioral environmental factors are those that serve as direct stimuli and are therefore ordered, not on a continuum of indirectness as are heredity and organic environmental factors, but on a continuum of breadth. Anastasi identifies socioeconomic status as the broadest behavioral factor, because she feels it is one of the major determinants of the range and level of stimulation we receive and a primary factor governing a wide range of interests and motivations. As we move along this continuum, behavioral environmental factors become narrower and narrower: educational level, parents, peers, specific courses we take in university, and specific sports we play. It might be more helpful to think of these factors as ordered in the shape of a funnel with socioeconomic class at the broad base Since many of the factors with relatively narrow influence are determined by factors above them in the funnel (social class, for example, is a strong determinant of educational level; educational level is a strong determinant of those we choose as friends), it is not difficult to see that behavioral effects become less and less pervasive as we move down to the small end of the funnel. Obviously, the broadest factors have the most pervasive influence on a genetic factor such as sex. We would, for instance, expect socioeconomic class to be a very pervasive determinant of sex differences in a wide range of behaviors, and, in fact, it is. Socioeconomic class is a strong determinant of sex differences in sexual behaviors, for instance (Hunt, 1974). On the other hand, it is very unlikely that a narrow factor such as an introductory psychology course would have a very pervasive influence on Joan and Bob's sex-differentiated sexual behaviors.

Anastasi's continuum of breadth of behavioral environmental factors provides us with an especially interesting framework, because superimposed on the socioeconomic class lines of nearly every society of which we are aware is another class distinction: sex. We live in a misogynous society. Obviously, this has a very broad and pervasive influence on a wide range of behavioral outcomes for Joan and Bob. Misogyny is a strong determinant of many choices routinely and predictably made by them: career choices, hobby choices, life-style choices. Much less pervasively influential are the opinions held by one of their mutual friends, Hank. Joan and Bob may modify their behavior to please him in his presence, but he is clearly not as broad an influence on their lives as is misogyny.

As we now see, Anastasi's interactionist model is anything but simplistic. Perhaps you are wondering why we have bothered to present it in such detail. Unfortunately, throughout the course of this book, we are forced—for the sake of brevity and clarity—to present many issues and arguments in a relatively simplistic manner. Although you will often be reminded of this, it is important that you have a good working knowledge of the implications and predictions of the nature, nurture, and interactionist positions, not only to better appreciate the complexities of sex differences in human behavior, but to ensure that you will not be lulled into an uncritical analysis of theoretical ideas.

SUMMARY

Although much of what you read in this book is written from a social psychological perspective, this is not a social psychology text. We could no more ignore the effects of biogenetics in our study of sex differences than could the physiological psychologist ignore the effects of the environment. Thus we try to explore every sex difference or nondifference we address within several frameworks, drawing heavily on the work of our colleagues in many of the subdisciplines of psychology and even treading into sociology.

In the first section of this chapter, we examined problems in the theory and research of the psychology of sex differences. We saw that the area has its roots in an orientation of differences that gives empirical findings of sex differences an edge over findings of similarities between the sexes. This situation, which has many political as well as academic implications, is reinforced by a tendency to confuse statistical significance with social significance—to assume that because research indicates a statistically significant sex difference in nurturance, for instance, our sons must necessarily be less nurturant than our daughters. The patterns of overlap in the traits and abilities of males and females are infinite in number. To remember this and to remember that correlation does not necessarily imply causation will be a big help in critically evaluating sex-differences research and common-sense notions about the differences between males and females.

In our analysis of the problems inherent in sex-differences research, we examined two separate classes of study: animal and human research. We discussed some of the problems that arise in the animal literature: arguing by analogy, arguing for the nonsocialization of animals, and trying to equate the operational definitions of human and nonhuman behavior. In short, nonhumans are not human, animals are socialized, and flea picking does not equal reading.

The human literature is not without fault either. The masculine orientation of psychological research and theory contributes many biases and complexities. Human research is plagued with artifactual sex-differences findings, sex-of-subject-and-experimenter effects, and sex-differentiated responses to demand characteristics.

Next we examined the age-old nature–nurture question: are behavioral differences (for our purposes, sex differences) a function of our biological destiny or of our environment? We concluded, as does Anastasi (1958), that both factors do and must interact to produce every behavioral outcome—that we carry 100 percent of our genetic heritage with us at all times and that our environment—whatever that environment may be—is always 100 percent present. Thus the meaningful question is not "which one?" or "how much?" but "how?"—in what ways do our genetic heritages interact with the worlds in which we live in order to produce the complex packages we know as males and females?

2 Hilary M. Lips

THEORIES ABOUT FEMALE & MALE NATURE

Is "human nature" essentially different for women and men? Many theorists have answered in the affirmative, and the debate about the extent and nature of the differences has been waged hotly over the years.

In the opening chapter of this book, we discussed the fact that much psychological research on sex differences has been influenced (for better or worse) by the unacknowledged assumptions and biases about women and men held by the investigators. Our task in the present chapter is to examine the theories of psychologists who have not only acknowledged their assumptions about the differences between women and men but who also have coded them into more or less comprehensive theories of personality.

A theory of personality is "a set of assumptions relevant to human behavior together with the necessary empirical definitions" (Hall & Lindzey, 1957, p. 15). Such a theory is designed to encompass a wide range of behavior rather than to make predictions only about specific types of behavior. Ideally, it is a theory of the whole person.

Many psychologists now see the accurate construction of such a comprehensive theory as an impossible task and concentrate instead on understanding and predicting particular types of behavior (e.g., aggression, interpersonal attraction). However, personality theory in psychology has had a profound effect on both research directed at and popular conceptions of the differences between men and women. Furthermore, each of us has his or her own private set of assumptions about human nature, which includes notions about the differences and similarities between the sexes. In the light of these facts, an examination of some major personality theories is an important first step toward the understanding of the psychology of sex differences.

PREPSYCHOLOGICAL THEORIES

The early philosophers, often considered to be the forerunners of modern psychology, had rather definite ideas on feminine and masculine natures. One idea that began with the Greek philosophers and stayed to have an impact on personality theory was that of woman as an incomplete man.

The writings of Hippocrates and the early writings of Plato suggest that women and men have equal biological roles in conception. Plato's *Symposium* describes both women and men as whole beings, having the same basic nature and worth, who should receive equal education and treatment before the law. However, Plato's later writings indicate a shift in attitude: women are considered weaker than and inferior to men, and different social roles are considered appropriate for the two sexes (Dickason, 1976). It was not until the writings of Aristotle, however, that a theory of feminine "incompleteness" and inferiority was given detailed explication (Whitbeck, 1976). Aristotle suggested that women, because they had less intrinsic "soul heat" than men, could not process their menstrual blood to the "final stage" of semen. Thus, in the process of conception, the woman contributed nothing to the distinctive character of the embryo, but only the material that formed it. In a sense, Aristotle viewed the female of every species as an infertile male, saying:

> the female in fact is a female on account of an inability of a sort, *viz.*, it lacks the power to concoct semen out of the final state of nourishment

> (this is either blood or its counterpart in bloodless animals) because of
> the coldness of their nature. [Quoted in Whitbeck, p. 56]

and:

> we should look upon the female state as being as it were a deformity
> though one which occurs in the ordinary course of nature. [Quoted in
> Whitbeck, p. 56]

Aristotle believed that there was an even greater difference between the sexes among humans than among other animal species. This notion of woman as a defective man affected theories of human nature for centuries. For example, Thomas Aquinas, who reflected Aristotle's influence in his pronouncement that woman was an "imperfect man" and an "incidental being" (de Beauvoir, 1952), helped set the stage for religious attitudes that relegated women to low status. Juan Huarte, a sixteenth-century Spanish writer who provided the first systematic work on individual intellectual differences, also incorporated the Aristotelian approach to sex differences (Shields, 1975). He stated that the "heat and dryness" characteristic of the male principle were maintained by the testicles. Since "dryness of spirit" was necessary for intelligence, men were more intelligent than women. This theory—one of the first to consider psychological sex differences—had the disadvantage of predicting that male castration was tantamount to severe brain damage!*

The idea of female inferiority that originated with the Greek philosophers has had a strong impact on personality theory, partially through its shaping of the social milieu in which such theories developed. Personality theorists, usually male, tended to encounter women only in subordinate positions. Their theories evolved, therefore, in ways that tended to explain and justify the disadvantaged position of women by postulating differences in nature for women and men. This effect can be seen in the theories of both the functionalist and the psychoanalytic schools of thought. The specific notion of woman as an incomplete man receives strong and elaborate emphasis in the theory of Freud, as discussed later in the chapter.

*This is actually no more bizarre than the notion, long prevalent in medical circles, that the mental "disease" of hysteria was caused by the wandering of the uterus through the female body. The wandering-womb explanation of mental illness, however, received very serious consideration.

FUNCTIONAL PSYCHOLOGY

According to Shields (1975), the rise of functional psychology in the United States during the late nineteenth century served as a major impetus for the academic psychological study of sex differences. This system of psychology was concerned with how an organism's behavior and consciousness were functional for its survival. Men and women, it was thought, had different and complementary functions for the survival of the race and had probably evolved somewhat differently in order to fulfill these functions.

Although the functionalist position did not lend itself to the development of comprehensive personality theories, psychologists within this system came up with generalizations about sex differences in temperament that had implications for a wide range of behavior. Perhaps the most well known of these generalizations is the notion of a "maternal instinct" in women. Many functionalists held that women had evolved with an inborn emotional tendency toward nurturance that was triggered by contact with a helpless infant. Because the biological tasks of pregnancy, childbirth, and lactation were fulfilled by women, these theorists reasoned, the presence of a "maternal instinct" in women but not in men only made evolutionary sense. The behavioral sex differences thought to result from the differential presence of such an instinct, however, went far beyond those directed specifically toward infants. Spencer (1891, cited in Shields, 1975), for example, felt that women devoted most of their energy to preparation for pregnancy and lactation, with the result that there was little left over for the development of other qualities. Edward Thorndike (1914, cited in Shields, 1975), an eminent American psychologist, contended that there were a number of instincts relevant to the female reproductive role. For example, he described a nursing instinct that was manifested in a strong tendency to nurture others. This instinct, he suggested, was the source of women's general moral superiority to men. He also felt that women had an instinctive tendency to submit to mastery by men. Thus Thorndike conceived of women as naturally both more nurturant and more submissive than men—a viewpoint that has gathered little empirical support but that lingers on in many people's assumptions about sex differences (see the discussion of nurturance in Chapter 11 and of power in Chapter 10). The functionalist position, though it has lost much of its formal popularity, is still held informally by the many people who argue that men and women are destined by nature to make different kinds of contributions to humanity and so, necessarily, have different temperaments.

PSYCHOANALYTIC THEORY

At the beginning of the twentieth century, a new theory emerged that included sex differences in its concerns and had sexuality at its very core. This was psychoanalytic theory, developed by Sigmund Freud and refined and modified by his followers and critics until the present day. We cannot possibly do justice to such a comprehensive theory here but will focus on those aspects that are directly relevant to the notion of psychological differences between the sexes.

Sigmund Freud: Castration Anxiety, the Oedipus Complex, and Psychosexual Differentiation

Freud's psychoanalytic theory was predicated on the basic assumption that the human mind could be regarded as analogous to an iceberg, with conscious thoughts and feelings representing only the tip. The rest of the iceberg (the greater part, by far) was represented by the unconscious and preconscious: areas of the mind holding thoughts, feelings, and urges that—although not normally accessible to the individual's awareness—often dictated and controlled behavior. Much of what was stored in the unconscious consisted of sexual and aggressive impulses too unacceptable to be acknowledged. This notion of the unconscious, though considered by many to be far-reaching and brilliant, provides the "catch-22" in attempts to validate Freudian theory. As you read on about psychosexual differentiation, you may find that the theory has little intuitive appeal or that it seems to bear no relation to your own experience. Freud would contend that your failure of recognition is precisely due to the storage of these unacceptable childhood memories in your unconscious!

Freud postulated that the personality consisted of three interrelated systems: id, ego, and superego. The id is the original system, providing the framework for the differentiation of the other two and the reservoir of psychic energy for their operation. It represents the world of subjective experience, contains the instincts, and operates on a principle of discharge of tension and immediate gratification of impulses: the pleasure principle. The ego is the mediator between the id and the world of objective reality. It is "said to be the executive of the personality because it controls the gateways to action, selects the features of the environment to which it will respond, and decides what instincts will be satisfied and in what manner" (Hall & Lindzey, 1957, p. 34). The third system, the superego, represents morality and a tendency to seek perfection. It is the internalized system of values, rules, and ideals of society as taught to the child and enforced through rewards and punishments. As we shall see, the way in which a child moves through the various psychosexual stages is thought to influence the development of and relationship among these systems.

Freudian theory suggests that the child moves through several psychosexual stages before achieving mature "genital" sexuality after puberty. In each stage, strong pleasurable feelings, attributed by Freud to the gratification of sexual instincts, are focused in a different part of the body. In the "oral stage," during the first year of life, the mouth is the focus for pleasurable sensations. The "anal stage," during the second year, is characterized by the association of sexual pleasure with the anus and elimination. During the third stage, the "phallic stage," the sex organs become the leading sources of pleasure. Difficulties encountered at any of these stages result in the "fixation" of a certain amount of id energy at that stage. A serious fixation at one stage could cause difficulties in navigating the rest. By the age of five, the child enters a "latency period," during which sexual impulses tend to be repressed (i.e., relegated to the unconscious), only to reemerge at adolescence in the "genital stage."

Late in his career, Freud put forward the notion that the psychological development of girls and boys diverged during the phallic stage and that the consequences of this divergence were sufficiently profound to produce significant psychological sex differences in adulthood. Always mystified by feminine psychology, Freud thought that perhaps this new theory would provide a key to explaining how and why the sexes differed. Nevertheless, he regarded it as an idea that stood "in urgent need of confirmation before its value or lack of value can be decided" (Freud, 1925/1974, p. 28).*

According to Freud's theory, for both boys and girls, the original love object is the mother because of her association with the infant's sensual pleasure of being suckled and nursed. During the phallic stage, the boy develops a desire to replace his father in his mother's affections. Intense feelings of rivalry toward the father spring from this desire, and this system of feelings is called the Oedipus complex (after the mythical Greek character who unwittingly killed his own father and married his own mother). Unable to handle such strong negative feelings toward his father, whom he also loves, the boy "projects" the feelings onto the father and thus believes that his father sees *him* as a rival. The rivalry with the father leads the boy to the fear that the father will castrate him. This paralyzing fear stems from the combination of a number of factors: the value placed on the penis as a strong source of erotic pleasure, the veiled threats accompanying his parents' attempts to stop him from masturbating, and the realization that some people (i.e., girls) do not have a penis (i.e., have apparently already been castrated). In order to allay the terrible fear of castration, the boy is literally forced to resolve the Oedipus complex. The resolution is achieved by the boy's identifying with the father (i.e., incorporating many features of the father's personality into his own) and destroying his desire for his mother. Freud believed that boys emerged from the Oedipus complex with either a contempt for or a horror of women.

For a girl, Freud suggested, the entire process was quite different. It began when she noticed that boys had something she did not: a penis. The realization was said to produce something that Freud called "penis envy":

> She has seen it and knows she is without it and wants to have it. . . . The
> hope of someday obtaining a penis in spite of everything and so of

*The material on Freud that follows is quoted from Paper 17, "Some Psychical Consequences of the Anatomical Distinction between the Sexes," from *The Standard Edition of the Complete Psychological Works of Sigmund Freud*, Vol. 19, translated and edited by James Strachey, The Hogarth Press Ltd. and The Institute of Psycho-Analysis, London; the material also appears in *The Collected Papers of Sigmund Freud* (entitled "Some Psychological Consequences of the Anatomical Distinction between the Sexes), edited by Ernest Jones, M.D., Volume 5, edited by James Strachey, published by Basic Books, Inc., Publishers, New York by arrangement with The Hogarth Press Ltd. and The Institute of Pscho-Analysis. Revised translation by James Strachey. © Institute of Psycho-Analysis and Angela Richards 1961. Reprinted by permission of the publishers.

becoming like a man may persist to an incredibly late age and may
become a motive for the strangest and otherwise unaccountable actions.
Or again, a process may set in which might be described as a "denial" . . . a girl may refuse to accept the fact of being castrated, may
harden herself in the conviction that she *does* possess a penis and may
subsequently be compelled to behave as though she were a man. [Freud,
1925/1974, pp. 31–32]

In an analysis that contained overtones of Aristotle's "woman as
defective man" notion, Freud went on to explain how the reaction to
the "missing" penis influences the girl's psychological development.
She develops a sense of inferiority and a contempt for her own sex
"which is the lesser in so important a respect" (p. 32). She gradually
displaces her penis envy into a more general attitude of jealousy (with
the ultimate result, Freud believed, that women have a greater tendency toward jealousy than men). She blames her mother for bring-
ing her into the world so "insufficiently equipped" and gradually
withdraws her affection from her. She "discovers" that her clitoris is a
very inferior version of the penis, and since it cannot compete, she
tries to suppress the tendency to masturbate.* Finally, because of her
penis envy, she enters the female version of the Oedipus complex:
"She gives up her wish for a penis and puts in place of it a wish for a
child: and *with this purpose in view* she takes her father as a love-object.
Her mother becomes the object of her jealousy" (p. 34).

Thus, the different ways in which the two sexes approach the
Oedipus complex result in masculine identification and contempt for
women among males and a sense of inferiority, a tendency toward
jealousy, a rejection of clitoral sexuality, and a wish for a child among
females. Momentous changes to be taking place before the age of five!

The way the two sexes moved out of the Oedipus complex was
also thought by Freud to have implications for later sex differences.
He felt that the complex in males, causing as it did the shocking fear
of castration, had to be totally destroyed rather than simply repressed.
The process of its destruction resulted in the formation of a strong
superego in males. Females, on the other hand, did not have the same
strong motivation to destroy the Oedipus complex, and Freud felt

---

*Freud felt that this suppression of "masculine" clitoral activity was necessary for
the emergence of true feminine (vaginal) sexuality. The clitoral orgasm was considered immature and not truly satisfying. Recent research, however, suggests that all
female orgasms originate in the clitoris (see discussion of this issue in Chapter 12).

that in their case it was either slowly abandoned or repressed. Thus, females were not provided with the necessity of developing a superego as strong as that of males.

> I cannot escape the notion (though I hesitate to give it expression) that for women the level of what is ethically normal is different from what it is in men. Their superego is never so inexorable, so impersonal, so independent of its emotional origins as we require it to be in men. Character traits which critics of every epoch have brought up against women—that they show less sense of justice than men, that they are less ready to submit to the great necessities of life, that they are more influenced in their judgements by feelings of affection and hostility—all these would be amply accounted for by the modification in the formation of their superego which we have already inferred. [Freud, 1925/1974, p. 36]

Thus, the resolution of the Oedipus complex led to yet another sex difference: a difference in superego strength for males and females.

Since the pressure to resolve the Oedipus complex is weak for women, it may happen that no resolution is achieved. In this case, the theory suggests that the adult woman will be a neurotic victim of penis envy: she may try to be masculine, reject the feminine fulfillment of pregnancy and childbirth, and become resentful and hostile toward men. It is this suggestion that arouses the anger of many thinking women toward Freud's theory, since it seems to imply that any woman not satisfied with her socially defined feminine role is neurotic and psychosexually immature. Probably for this reason, the concept of penis envy has undergone many reinterpretations, some of which we examine later in this chapter.

Lest this section leave the reader with the notion that Freud thought of females and males as totally and irreconcilably different, we should point out here that this theory included a basic assumption that all human individuals were inherently bisexual. Each person had both masculine *and* feminine characteristics and was capable of being sexually attracted to members of either sex. In the course of "proper" psychosexual development, however, "inappropriate" sexual tendencies were suppressed in favor of the socially acceptable ones. Freud consistently stressed that his notions about the different ways in which the two sexes developed represented the ideal rather than the actual case:

... we shall, of course, willingly agree that the majority of men are also far behind the masculine ideal and that all human individuals, as a result of their bisexual disposition and of cross inheritance, combine in themselves both masculine and feminine characteristics, so that pure masculinity and femininity remain theoretical constructions of uncertain content. [Freud, 1925/1974, p. 36]

Freud's psychoanalytic theory is extremely complex, and we have barely scratched the surface of it here. It has had a profound impact on popular conceptions about human nature in general and sex differences in particular. We turn now to an examination of the way Freudian theory has been criticized, modified, and expanded with reference to its treatment of sex differences.

Karen Horney: An Alternate Perspective

Karen Horney, a member of the early group around Freud and founder of the American Institute for Psychoanalysis, was one of the first psychoanalytic theorists to take issue with the Freudian perspective on psychosexual development. Looking at development from a strictly male point of view, she suggested, led to an overemphasis on the role played by the penis (and anxiety over losing it) in the development of both sexes. Though not denying the existence of penis envy in young girls or castration anxiety in boys, she pointed to a number of other processes that might help to explain psychosexual development. Her own clinical experience had led her to the conclusion, for instance, that males suffered from great envy of the female reproductive role:

... from the biological point of view woman has in motherhood, or in the capacity for motherhood, a quite indisputable and by no means negligible superiority. This is most clearly reflected in the unconscious of the male psyche in the boy's intense envy of motherhood. We are familiar with this envy as such, but it has hardly received due consideration as a dynamic factor. When one begins, as I did, to analyze men only after fairly long experience of analyzing women, one receives a most surprising impression of the intensity of this envy of pregnancy, childbirth, and motherhood, as well as of the breasts and the act of suckling. [1926/1973, p. 10]

Horney suggested that the strength of men's desire to achieve and create was an overcompensation for their unconscious sense of inferiority in the creative process of reproduction. Furthermore, she proposed, the masculine tendency to depreciate women was also an outcome of this unconscious envy, rather than of the male recognition that the female lacked a penis.

Horney also believed that the rejection of the female role in girls was mainly caused, not by envy of the penis, but by an unconscious fear of vaginal injury through penetration, aroused by guilt over masturbation. Thus, she proposed that the girl's psychosexual development centered around her own anatomy rather than that of the male. Furthermore, she noted emphatically, the rejection of the feminine role was reinforced and encouraged by a society that viewed women as inadequate and inferior and that gave them few opportunities for accomplishment and achievements in the professions. Thus, she became one of the first psychoanalysts to draw attention to the possibilities for interaction between cultural and inner dynamic forces in the shaping of personality. Although her work was rejected or ignored in some othodox Freudian circles, its impact on psychoanalytic conceptions of women was considerable.

Clara Thompson: A Cultural Explanation for Penis Envy

During the 1940s, Clara Thompson was instrumental in reorienting the thinking of American psychoanalysis on the subject of women. One of her chief contributions was the notion that the penis envy ascribed by Freud to girls and women was not a literal envy of the male organ but a culturally based envy of men's advantaged position in society.

> The position of underprivilege might be symbolically expressed in the term penis envy using the penis as the symbol of the more privileged sex. Similarly, in a matriarchal culture one can imagine that the symbol for power might be the breast. The type of power would be somewhat different, the breast standing for life-giving capacity rather than force and energy. The essential significance in both cases would be the importance in the cultural setting of the possession of the symbol. [1943/1973, pp. 52–53]

Thompson felt that the restrictions placed on women in a patriarchal culture provided a realistic basis for envy of the male and that this envy was enhanced by the competitiveness of our culture. She also pointed out that women were even more likely to feel inferior as the family and the necessity for a high birthrate assumed diminishing importance. Thus, Clara Thompson issued one of the strongest early calls for an understanding of psychological sex differences in the light of the power differences between women and men.

Current Evaluations of Freudian Theory

Regardless of its accuracy, Freud's theory has had an incalculable effect on our conceptions about women and men. Strong criticisms, however, have been leveled against the theory. Many psychologists claim that it is based on flimsy evidence and is not amenable to empirical investigation, and feminists claim that it demeans women by ascribing so many of their motivations and behaviors to an unconscious envy of the penis.

Psychoanalytic theory was developed through Freud's subjective interpretation of information provided by his patients. These patients represented a rather special group: they were upper-class members of a particular patriarchal culture who were having difficulty coping with their lives. It is quite possible that Freud's generalizations from this group to all people were totally inappropriate. Moreover, it would be surprising if his own particular biases did not, to some extent, influence what he noticed about these people, what he considered important, and the interpretation he placed on his observations. Thus his theory, as well as those of other psychoanalysts, stands in need of empirical validation. Such validation has proven to be elusive, since unconscious processes, if they exist, are notoriously difficult to measure. This difficulty makes aspects of psychoanalytic theory impossible to either prove *or* disprove and accounts in part for its lack of popularity among the current generation of research-oriented psychologists. Sherman (1971) surveyed the relatively small amount of research relating to penis envy and castration anxiety and concluded that no solid evidence for either had been presented. She noted that many studies pointed to the existence of female envy of the male role, but there seems to be no reason to assume that such envy is based on a neurotic desire for the penis.

Feminists have often expressed anger at the fact that a theory that makes such negative statements about women, based on such limited evidence, should be so widely accepted. Particularly disturbing are the notions of penis envy and the necessity for women to reject clitoral sexuality in favor of "mature" vaginal sexuality, since both of these concepts imply a derogation of the female's body and experience. Nonetheless, there are those who suggest that considering the culture in which Freud lived, he was extraordinarily sympathetic to women (Janeway, 1974). Janeway argues that Freud was not trying to put women down through his theory but rather that he saw clearly that women were in a disadvantaged position and tried to rationalize or explain that fact. He was perhaps considerably more sensitive to the position of women in society than were many of his contemporaries. The fact remains, however, that his theory tended to justify the restrictions placed on women rather than to question their necessity.

Mitchell (1974) suggests that Freud's theory presents an invaluable analysis of the oppression of women in a patriarchal society. The family dynamics described by Freud that culminate in the rejection of the mother and the identification with (for boys) or desire for (for girls) the father could only occur in a culture with father-headed families. She argues that as long as our culture is a patriarchal one, its structures will be passed on to our children in the way that Freud describes.

Freud's theory, however complex, elegant, and laboriously derived, does not provide us with the "truth" about sex differences. It may, however, have set us on the right path, if only by spurring its critics to offer alternatives. We now examine two other approaches that, in very different ways, have roots in the psychoanalytic tradition: Lynn's social psychological analysis of sex-role development and Jung's analytic psychology.

A Social Psychological Approach to Sex-Role Development: Reinterpreting Freud

Perhaps the greatest value of psychoanalytic theory lies in its emphasis on the complexity of human nature and in its presentation of ideas that challenge us to formulate alternative perspectives on the developmental process. One of the most compelling alternatives to Freud's theory of psychosexual development is the social psychological viewpoint on the learning of sex roles.

David Lynn (1966) has presented a theory of sex-role identification that seems in some ways to form a bridge between the psychoanalytic and social psychological approaches. Lynn uses the term *identification* (originally a psychoanalytic concept) to refer to an individual's internalization of the characteristics of a person or role and to her/his unconscious reactions characteristic of that person or role. Unlike the psychoanalysts, however, his theoretical formulation emphasizes the learning of behavior through observation, imitation, and reinforcement—the basic concepts of social learning theory.

Lynn's theory makes some of the same predictions about sex differences as does Freud's, although for different reasons. Both theories, for example, suggest that the male will follow the rules of his role more rigidly than the female will follow hers. Both also predict that both males and females will tend to devalue femininity. However, whereas Freud saw these results as virtually inevitable in any society, Lynn suggests that they are a direct result of our child-rearing process and the sex structure of our society.

Lynn suggests, as did Freud, that the first typical human identification of both female and male infants is with the mother and that the male must shift from this early identification if masculine-role identification is to be achieved. In contrast to Freud, however, Lynn (1966) emphasizes the role of the cultural situation in this process:

> Typically in this culture the girl has the same-sex parental model for identification (the mother) with her more hours per day than the boy has his same-sex model (the father) with him. Moreover, even when home, the father does not usually participate in as many intimate activities with the child as does the mother. . . . The boy is seldom if ever with the father as he engages in his daily vocational activities, although both boy and girl are often with the mother as she goes through her household activities. Consequently, the father, as a model for the boy, is analogous to a map showing the major outline but lacking most details, whereas the mother, as a model for the girl, might be thought of as a detailed map. [p. 466]

According to Lynn, the boy attempting to be masculine is helped along not so much by modeling his father, but by following the stereotyped prescriptions of the male role spelled out by his mother and teachers. These socializing agents reward typical masculine be-havior and punish behavioral indications of femininity. Gradually, the boy learns to identify, not with his father, but with the stereotyped masculine role. The girl, on the other hand, maintains an identifica-tion with her mother. In support of his approach, Lynn cites a number of studies that indicate that both males and females are more similar (in personality terms) to their mothers than to their fathers.

The necessity for the boy to learn masculine-role identification in the relative absence of male models and through early and vague demands backed by punishment causes anxiety about sex-role be-havior. Such anxiety causes the boy to adhere very rigidly to the rules of his role—a situation analogous to Freud's notion that males de-velop stronger superegos than do females.

Because boys are so often punished for acting "girl-like," Lynn postulates, they develop a dislike of and contempt for females. Girls, who are not punished so early or so severely for "boyish" behavior, do not develop a similar degree of hostility toward males. Thus, the male contempt for women, which Freud explained as a natural result of women's "inferior" anatomy, Lynn sees as stemming from our cul-ture's process of male socialization. Similarly, Lynn explains any ten-dency for women to feel inferior as due to cultural prejudice against them rather than to their sense of dismay over not possessing a penis.

Lynn's social psychological approach does not make predictions as numerous or as sweeping as those of psychoanalytic theory. It shows us the value, however, of a careful examination of cultural socialization processes in their historical context in our search for an understanding of what Freud called "psychosexual development." It also raises some interesting questions. What if fathers were the ones who did the child care in our society? Would girls have trouble with feminine-role identification? Suppose both parents were able to be equally available to the children. Would the same kind of sex-role anxiety develop? Lynn's approach suggests the possibility that if par-ents were equally available and equally nurturant toward their chil-dren, the male difficulty with sex-role socialization would not arise. Furthermore, if mothers and fathers typically shared childcare on an equal basis, there would be considerably less sex-role differentiation than now exists, and children of both sexes would presumably grow up with less rigid sex roles. In the absence of significant numbers of such "nontraditional" families in our culture, it is difficult to assess the correctness of these speculations. However, the number of couples experimenting with shared child-care arrangements is increasing, and we suspect that the results of their efforts will lend support to Lynn's hypotheses.

Many social learning theorists have gone even further than Lynn has from Freud, dropping the notion of the unconscious from the definition of identification and speaking only in terms of learned sex roles. If sex roles are totally learned, of course, there is no such thing as a female or male personality. As Chapter 5 illustrates, sex roles vary considerably among cultures, and most social scientists have now come to think of learning as a crucial factor in their development. The issue is a complex one, however, as will be seen throughout this book.

Jung's Analytic Psychology

Because of its emphasis on unconscious processes, the personality theory of Carl Jung is often grouped with psychoanalytic theory. Indeed, Jung was closely associated with Freud for many years and was the first president of the International Psychoanalytic Association. Eventually, however, the two men broke with each other, as Jung developed his own theory of personality, which differs greatly from that of Freud. Jungian theory does not rest so totally on sexuality as does Freud's, and his approach paints a somewhat more optimistic picture of human nature—both male and female—than does psychoanalytic theory.

Jung's theory differs from Freud's in many ways, but perhaps the most important distinction is that Freud thought of the person as driven by internal instincts, whereas Jung combined the notion of instincts with that of internally derived human aims and aspirations. Thus, he thought of people as not only *driven by* something but also as *pulled toward* something. His theory places a great emphasis on the notion that human beings are continually striving for growth and wholeness. In order to achieve this wholeness, or self, according to Jung, the person had to bring all the various parts of his/her personality into harmony.

In Jung's system, two important parts of the personality that had to be harmonized were the masculine and feminine principles within the individual. Every man had a part of the personality called the *anima*, which represented the feminine principle. Women, correspondingly, had an *animus*, representing the male principle. Both the anima and the animus were what Jung called "archetypes"—universal ideas containing a large element of psychic energy that were stored in the collective unconscious of the human race and thus passed on from generation to generation. There were many such archetypes, each originating through the repetition of an experience for many generations until it became permanently deposited in the potentialities of the human mind (Jung, 1953). According to Jung, all individuals had much the same collective unconscious—an idea that is unique to his theory. The animus and the anima, therefore, were seen as similar across individuals and also as relatively unchanging.

Jung saw the anima as representing a female principle that emphasized the development of relationships: the ability to make connections. The animus, on the other hand, symbolized a male principle that entailed a tendency toward abstract, analytic thought. These two archetypes, therefore, enshrined the sex-role stereotypes of the day. The negative impact of this was softened, however, by Jung's insistence that both principles are present in every individual as well as by the fact that he, in contrast to Freud, seemed to place a positive value on the feminine principle. A close look at Jung's writings, however, suggests that although he placed a high value on the feminine *principle*, he may still have regarded women as having less potential than men.

> I have called the projection-making factor in women the animus, which means mind or spirit. The animus corresponds to the paternal Logos just as the anima corresponds to the maternal Eros. . . . I use Eros and Logos merely as conceptual aids to describe the fact that woman's consciousness is characterized more by the connective quality of Eros than by the discrimination and cognition associated with Logos. In men, Eros, the function of relationship, is usually less developed than Logos. In women, on the other hand, Eros is an expression of their true nature, while their Logos is often only a regrettable accident. [Jung, 1968; quoted in Goldenberg, 1976, p. 445]

In a feminist critique of Jung's psychology, Goldenberg (1976) argues that Jung's advocacy of a blending of the masculine and feminine principles really applied mainly to males. Jung apparently saw men as gaining wholeness and completeness by developing the feminine side of their personality. On the other hand, as the foregoing quote suggests, he expressed some ambivalence about the development by women of their masculine side. Either they were incapable of such development, or else it violated their "true nature." He even suggested that by taking up a profession or by working and/or studying "like a man," a woman might do some psychic injury to her feminine nature.

Jung's is a multifaceted theory, of course, and we have not begun to do it justice here. Although rooted in a tradition that took female inferiority for granted, the theory did break new ground in psychology by postulating that the integration of the feminine and masculine principles in a single individual was not only possible but desirable. The current rise of interest in the concept of psychological androgyny* (see the discussion in Chapter 6) extends this line of thought.

Newer Perspectives Rooted in Psychoanalytic Theory

Psychoanalytic theory continues to provide some psychologists with the roots from which to develop new ideas on the subject of sex differences. Two such psychologists are Erik Erikson and David Bakan.

Erikson (1968) follows Freud's notion that a person's anatomy can have an impact, via the unconscious, on experience and behavior. Instead of focusing on male anatomy, however, Erikson focuses on the female. He introduced a concept called "inner space," representing the female womb and reproductive system, which, he suggested, acquired an unconscious meaning as a productive, life-giving, safe space in woman's inner body. He believes that the presence of this "inner space" has a profound, although certainly not total, influence on women's psychology.

Erikson supports his notion of inner space through a study of the spatial configurations used by children when they were presented with toys and asked to construct "an exciting scene from an imaginary moving picture" (1968, p. 340). When 300 girls and boys had each completed this task three times over a period of two years, Erikson noted that photographs of the constructed scenes showed sex differences in the ways the children arranged the toys and used space. Typically, he reported, a girl's scene was the interior of a house, with

*Androgyny is the possession of both male and female traits.

no walls or a very simple enclosure. People and animals were generally found within this interior, usually in static positions, and the overall scene was relatively peaceful. Boys, on the other hand, constructed scenes with elaborately walled houses, protrusions such as cannons, and high towers. People and animals were usually outside the enclosures, and there was considerable evidence of movement and even of accidents, collapsing buildings, and ruins. Erikson suggested that the differences in these scenes paralleled the genital and reproductive organ differences between the sexes: the external, erectable, and intrusive male penis versus the internal, protected female womb containing the "statically expectant ova" (p. 343).

It has frequently been argued that the sex differences observed by Erikson are simply the result of the differential socialization of the two sexes. Girls, after all, are rewarded for playing house, whereas boys are encouraged to play more aggressively with toy trucks, guns, and the like. Erikson argues, however, that although social roles may play a part, the two sexes differ widely in their basic experience of "the ground plan of the human body"—a difference that has a profound impact on their respective personality predispositions. Though admitting that his interpretation cannot be proven and that the differences he postulates could conceivably be modified by sociocultural factors, he feels that the different body experiences of women and men tend to predispose them toward different approaches to life. Men show a stronger tendency to be concerned with "outer" space: exploring, conquering, achieving, discovering. Women, on the other hand, tend toward caring, nurturing, and creating a stable environment. Erikson is careful to note that each sex is capable of learning the other's style and that the predispositions he speaks of do not restrict each sex to its own mode but rather provide a preferred orientation. Thus, he says, women can certainly be scientists and engineers, and men can care for children, whenever the culture allows this. He does, however, stand firm in his conviction that the male and female personalities are inevitably different because of the difference in body structure, and he sees some advantages in this difference:

> . . . where the confinements are broken, women may yet be expected to cultivate the implications of what is biologically and anatomically given. She may, in new areas of activity, balance man's indiscriminate endeavor to perfect his dominion over the outer spaces of national and technolog-

ical expansion . . . with the determination to emphasize such varieties of caretaking as would take responsibility for each individual child born in a planned humanity. [pp. 362–363]

Thus, Erikson assumes that women will maintain caring and nurturance as important orientations even if they become scientists, planners, and computer technologists and hopes that they will have a humanizing influence in these areas. In this, he moves a step further toward sex-role liberation than Jung, who assumed that women endangered their feminine nature by developing their masculine side. Erikson is still rooted firmly in the psychoanalytic tradition, however, through his insistence that anatomy has a strong influence on the individual's unconscious processes.

David Bakan (1966), who also suggests that women and men have different behavioral orientations, makes an argument stronger than that of either Erikson or Jung that these two orientations can and should be combined. He postulates two modalities characteristic of all life: agency and communion. Agency refers to the organism's tendency to protect, assert, and expand the self and to separate the self from other organisms. Communion refers to a tendency toward contact and unity with other organisms. Although each modality is present in any individual, Bakan argues that because of the different roles played by men and women in reproduction, agency is naturally the stronger in males, whereas communion is the stronger in females. Recent research (Block, 1973) does seem to indicate that agency is emphasized in the socialization of boys in our culture, whereas communion is stressed for girls. The degree of distinction varies somewhat from culture to culture, however. Bakan's theory holds that it is fundamental to the emotional and spiritual growth of human beings that they achieve an integration of agency and communion. It is the striving for such integration that brings women and men together: the agentic in the male and the communal in the female lead them to seek out each other. Moreover, over time, the contact between the sexes leads to an integration of the agentic and communal within each of the individuals. The latter is an interesting proposition that, to our knowledge, has yet to be put to a formal test. During the recent rise of the women's movement in North America, many women reported finding it necessary to separate themselves temporarily or permanently from men in order to become aware of and to develop their own strengths. Such reports lead to the hypothesis that whereas a true integration of agency and communion might be helped along for *men* in our present cultural situation through a close, loving relationship with another person, women may find their search for integration more fruitful if they begin it alone. Presumably, the optimal conditions for achieving integration would vary from culture to culture.

Bakan's theory is rooted in Freud's to the extent that he accepts the notion of the unconscious and sees biological, reproduction-oriented origins for his postulated sex differences in agency and communion. However, he differs greatly from Freud in his emphasis on the possibilities for growth and wholeness of the human personality. Unique is his notion that it is a fundamental task of the human individual—male or female—to achieve a personal integration of communion and agency. Thus, a mitigation rather than a solidification of sex differences with age would be viewed as normal, natural, and desirable in the context of this theory. Of all the theories that have sprung from the psychoanalytic approach, Bakan's is perhaps the least biologically deterministic (i.e., puts the least causal emphasis on human biology in explaining human behavior). It is a short step from his viewpoint to that of theories that place no emphasis at all on the role of female and male anatomy in the formation of personality.

Abraham Maslow: A Humanistic Theory of Personality

One might well ask at this point whether a theory of personality that stresses *human* rather than male or female nature has ever been developed. A strong attempt in this direction was made by Abraham Maslow (1954), who studied the characteristics of the healthy *person* and believed that these characteristics were essentially the same for women and men. Maslow's theory rests on the assumption that human needs and tendencies are good or neutral. Healthy development of the personality, according to Maslow, consists of actualizing one's basic nature—allowing it to emerge and develop fully as an expression of the individual, undistorted by negative forces in the environment.

Maslow spent years studying people he considered to be "self-actualized"—people who had developed their inner potential to its full expression. These "self-actualized" men and women demonstrated qualities such as self-acceptance, realistic orientation toward the world, empathy, democratic values, spontaneity, openness, creativity, autonomy, and emotional self-sufficiency. The concept of the healthy person that Maslow developed as a result of his investigations is biased toward neither masculinity nor femininity. Within his framework, both women and men are viewed as human beings equally capable of resisting conformity to their culture, transcending societal limitations, and actualizing their own potential.

Maslow was in fact one of the first psychologists to reject the terms *masculinity* and *femininity* as misleading (Maslow, 1939, cited in Klein, 1971). He classified personality types on the basis of "dominance feelings," a psychological state related to a person's self-evaluation. Low-dominance feelings were related to such traits as self-consciousness, inferiority feelings, conventionality, introversion, and suggestibility (traits considered feminine), whereas high dominance feelings were associated with leadership, strength of character and social purpose, lack of fear and shyness, and self-reliance (the so-called manly traits). Maslow noted that dominance feelings were determined by cultural factors such as status, education, and social norms and were linked to sex only indirectly, insofar as cultural factors acted differently on the two sexes. Furthermore, in personality terms, a high-dominance woman was thought by Maslow to be more like a high-dominance man than like a low-dominance woman. Dominance feelings, not biological sex, were considered to be the most important personality factor.

An early study by Maslow (1942) looked specifically at high-dominance women. High-dominance feelings were considered healthy by Maslow for both women and men, and hence these results paint an interesting picture of what a healthy woman would be like, from the standpoint of his theory. These women, who were high in self-esteem, were tolerant of others, assertive, decisive, willing to take initiative, self-reliant, independent, and ambitious. They were not caught up in the sexual double standard but tended to have positive feelings toward their bodies and to allow themselves to enjoy sexual experience. This is a far cry from Freud's healthy woman, who must be passive, resigned to her inferiority, and hopeful of achieving fulfillment by bearing a child.

Maslow's theory of personality does not focus on sex differences as a major issue. We include it here as an example of a theory that sees more similarity than difference between males and females and that focuses on their common humanity. Our own affinity for this type of approach is probably obvious to the reader. However, for those who see vast differences between women and men, Maslow's theory offers little in the way of explanation.

SUMMARY

A number of theorists have developed models of personality with the hope of offering explanations for human behavior. Many of the most influential of these models have treated sex differences as crucial and have used different mechanisms to explain female and male behavior and experience. Just how useful are these personality theories for an understanding of women and men?

The theories are useful in one way as what psychologists call "heuristic devices." Their presence gives rise to questions that can be investigated and to ideas that can be debated. They give us, at least, a place to begin the argument. That is why we have chosen to include theories so early in this book.

The theories lose much of their value, however, when they are treated as the end rather than the beginning of the argument. A theory is something to be tested, not accepted without question because it "seems reasonable." Researcher Naomi Weisstein (1971) has accused psychologists and psychiatrists of just such unquestioning acceptance of theories that stress innate sex differences in personality. She points out that a theory cannot be validated by processes of "insight, sensitivity and intuition" alone, since these processes simply tend to confirm the biases with which one began. For example, she notes, it used to be believed that some people, through a sensitivity to the workings of the devil, could pick out the witches in their midst! She strongly criticizes clinical psychologists for basing so much of their treatment of patients on theory that has not been supported by careful research.

Weisstein also offers a potent critique of the entire personality theory approach to human behavior, particularly to sex differences. Personality theory focuses on variables internal to the individual and tends to ignore the social context in which that individual exists. She points out that the effects of social factors such as expectancy and pressure to conform have been demonstrated in many cases to override personality variables, and she argues that these social forces are the key to an understanding of sex differences.

This, then, is the beginning of a debate. Having examined the personality approach, we turn in subsequent chapters to both the social and physiological theories that attempt to explain sex differences.

In conclusion, it is important to remember that a personality theory involves the outlining of its author's assumptions about human (or male and female) nature. A history of the popularity of these theories, then, tells us much about the assumptions that have guided research on sex differences and influenced the differential treatment accorded to females and males. Since in research, as in life, the answers one gets depend on the questions one asks, it is useful to understand the theoretical ground from which the questions grow.

3 Hilary M. Lips

SEXUAL DIFFERENTIATION & GENDER IDENTITY

At the end of the nineteenth century, a theory was put forward that explained all physical, intellectual, and emotional differences between the sexes on the basis of a primary difference between the metabolisms of women and men. Males, according to this theory, were "catabolic," females, "anabolic" (Geddes & Thompson, cited in Shields, 1975). In other words, males had a relatively quicker, more active metabolism, whereas that of females was slower and more passive. This assumed biological difference between men and women was thought "naturally" to lead to such things as greater agility, creativity, variability, and scientific insight for men and greater patience, open-mindedness, appreciation for subtle details, and intuition for women.

Today we realize that the biological differences between the sexes are somewhat more complex and subtle, and we have ceased looking for a single biological factor that will explain all other sex differences. The notion that a single biological variable, such as the level of a certain hormone, could explain most or all of the observed sex differences in behavior now seems just as absurd as the Freudian idea that the major psychological sex differences are derived from the fact that males have a penis and females do not. Nonetheless, we are aware that the sexes do differ psychologically in a number of ways, and research to determine the relationship between physiological and behavioral differences is still at an early stage.

In this chapter and the next we pay special attention to the physiological aspects of sex differences. This chapter focuses on the process of sexual differentiation: just how does the human organism develop as female or male? The following chapter looks at the behavioral implications of sex-specific processes that have both physiological and social components: menstruation, pregnancy, and the change of life. We will see that biology is certainly a partial determinant of sex differences but not the only, or even necessarily the most important, determinant. We will also see that the extent of biology's role is an issue that is far from settled.

THE BIOLOGICAL PROCESS OF SEXUAL DIFFERENTIATION

The process of sexual differentiation is accomplished in several steps. First, the individual's sex is genetically determined at conception. Then, as the embryo develops, male or female sex glands (gonads) make their appearance and begin to secrete the appropriate male or female sex hormones. These hormones circulate throughout the bloodstream and are responsible for the sexual differentiation of other bodily organs: the internal reproductive tract, the external genitalia, and areas of the brain. We will look in turn at each of these steps.

Genetic Determination of Sex

Every human cell contains forty-six chromosomes, arranged in twenty-three pairs. One chromosome of each pair is contributed by the mother of the individual and one by the father. Twenty-two of the chromosome pairs carry genes that determine hereditary characteristics of the person. The twenty-third pair is called the sex chromosomes and differs for men and women. If the individual is female, the sex chromosomes are represented as XX; if male, the pair is designated as XY. Only males carry a Y chromosome, which is very small and carries little genetic material. Thus, a person's sex is determined by his/her father. If the sperm cell that happens to fertilize the egg at conception carries an X chromosome, the individual will be female; if it carries a Y chromosome, the individual will be male.

Genes carried on the sex chromosomes are called sex-linked genes, and all but one of those that have currently been identified are carried on the X chromosome. The presence of such sex-linked genes on the X chromosome accounts for the greater male than female susceptibility to genetic disorders. For instance, the gene for hemophilia is sex linked. A father carrying this gene cannot transmit it to his son, since he contributes only a Y chromosome to his son, and the gene is carried on the X chromosome. He can, on the other hand, transmit the gene to his daughter, to whom he contributes an X chromosome. His daughter, however, will not express any symptoms of hemophilia unless she has also inherited a hemophilia gene on the X chromosome contributed by her mother. If, as is normally the case, the genetic material on the X chromosome from at least one of the parents is programmed for the development of a healthy blood-clotting mechanism, the daughter will not develop hemophilia. This occurs because the trait of hemophilia is a recessive one and is masked by the presence of a normal blood-clotting gene on the other X chromosome. The daughter continues to carry the gene, of course, and may transmit it to her own sons or daughters. If she does transmit it to her son, the hemophilia will be expressed, because the son has no other X chromosome (only a Y chromosome) carrying a normal gene that would mask the recessive trait. There are about seventy traits that seem to be linked to the X chromosome, and many of these are both recessive and pathological (Hutt, 1972). Thus, males stand in greater danger than females of expressing a variety of genetically transmitted disorders.

Some characteristics are sex limited rather than sex linked. These traits are carried on genes that are not on either of the sex chromosomes but are, nonetheless, generally manifest in only one sex. In this case, the trait requires the presence of male or female sex hormones in order to appear. Baldness, for example, is a trait that is carried genetically but that requires the presence of a certain balance of male sex hormone in order to be expressed.

Occasionally, through errors in cell division, an individual is conceived who has some chromosomal abnormality: extra or missing chromosomes. Such abnormalities are sometimes present in the sex chromosomes. For example, an individual may be born with a single X chromosome (XO), an extra X chromosome (XXX), an extra Y chromosome (XYY), or with patterns such as XXY (Klinefelter's syndrome) or even XXXY. In these rare instances, as long as there is at least one Y chromosome present, the body type will develop as male unless some subsequent factor interferes. If no Y chromosomes are present, bodily development will be female. It is thought that an individual with only a single Y chromosome (OY) cannot survive, since no person with this chromosome pattern has ever been found (Money & Ehrhardt, 1972). Various behavioral, personality, and intellectual difficulties have been ascribed in the presence of chromosomal anomalies, but the rarity of the condition and the fact that in some cases they are noticed only when the individual gets into trouble or seeks help for an emotional problem makes the evidence difficult to evaluate. For example, the XYY male has sometimes been characterized as a "supermale," with stronger than average aggressive impulses and extraordinary physical stature. As discussed in Chapter 9, however, evidence for the XYY syndrome is scant, at best. Persons showing the XXY pattern seem to have an increased vulnerability to a variety of psychopathologies, including mental retardation, but prediction of a specific problem for a given individual may be difficult. Similarly, the XXX condition is sometimes accompanied by mental retardation, but this is not always the case (Money & Ehrhardt, 1972).

Gonadal Development

The influence of the chromosomes on sexual differentiation goes only as far as the formation of the male or female gonads (testes or ovaries). When a Y chromosome is present, cell division seems to occur more rapidly, and during the seventh week after conception, the embryonic gonadal tissue differentiates into a testis. If this does not happen (i.e., if there is no Y chromosome present), the gonadal tissue begins to differentiate into an ovary about a week or more later. There is no possibility of a "neuter" sex, because at this stage, as at every other, if no masculine differentiation occurs, feminine differentiation automatically proceeds. It is as if there is a built-in tendency for the organism to be female, and if nothing interferes, development occurs in that direction.

Hormones

Once the gonads are formed, they begin to secrete the sex hormones. The rest of the process of sexual differentiation is controlled by these hormones—powerful chemical substances secreted into the bloodstream and carried to every cell of the body.

The male sex hormones are called androgens, and the major one of these is testosterone. These hormones cause masculine sex differentiation of the reproductive tract, genitalia, and brain during prenatal development, and at puberty they are responsible for the appearance of male secondary sex characteristics—facial and pubic hair, deepening voice, and so on. They also seem to have a variety of other effects through their influence on enzymes and body metabolism (Hutt, 1972). For example, testosterone encourages the growth and repair of muscle and bone tissue by promoting the synthesis of proteins from fats and amino acids. It is this effect that produces the popularity of "androgen supplements" among athletes and body builders. Another reported effect of the androgens is a speeding up of certain bodily enzyme activity, so that drugs and foreign substances tend to be metabolized more quickly by males than by females.

The ovary secretes two types of female sex hormones: the estrogens and progesterone. The estrogens promote the growth and maturation of the reproductive tract and the development of the mammary glands. Progesterone, sometimes called the gestational hormone, prepares the mature female body for pregnancy by periodically thickening the lining of the uterus and stimulating the secretory cells of the breast. In the mature woman, both hormones have a rhythmic cycle of release that is regulated by other hormones (gonadotrophins) secreted by the pituitary gland, under the influence of the hypothalamus of the brain. This cycle is described in detail later in this chapter.

Estrogens seem to have a variety of nonreproductive effects: they encourage the breakdown of proteins, cause a decrease in fatty substances in the blood (responsible, perhaps, for women's lesser proneness to heart disease), facilitate glucose metabolism, retard the metabolism of certain drugs, and slow down growth (Hutt, 1972).

Males and females each have small amounts of the hormones of the other sex in their bodies. The hormonal difference between the sexes, then, is in the relative *proportion* of androgens, estrogens, and progesterone—all three of which may be produced in the ovaries, testes, or adrenal glands. The balance in males is weighted in favor of testosterone, although estrogen and progesterone are also present. Similarly, in females, estrogen and progesterone dominate, but testosterone is present. An individual's sexual characteristics can be affected by proportions of the sex hormones in his/her body, both pre- and postnatally. For example, if the testes of a male embryo do not produce sufficient androgen, the reproductive tract may fail to differentiate as male and may instead develop as female. Or, if glandular malfunctions or the ingestion of certain drugs produce an inordinately high level of androgen in the body postnatally, a female may experience body masculinization at puberty.

The Reproductive Tract

If testes have been formed in the developing embryo, they will secrete androgen, which under normal conditions will organize the internal ducts into the male reproductive tract: vas deferens, epididymis, urethra, and prostate. At the same time, they secrete another chemical, the mullerian inhibiting substance, which causes the potential feminine part of the internal ducts to atrophy. If ovaries instead of testes have been formed, the testicular hormone and mullerian inhibiting substance will not be secreted, and a female reproductive tract—oviducts, uterus, and vagina—will develop. For female development, it is not necessary for ovarian hormones to be present, merely for testicular hormones to be absent. Anomalies, such as a genetic male with a uterus or a female with a deformed uterus or vagina, can occur in rare instances where the body is unresponsive to the hormonal secretions or the secretions are abnormal for some reason.

The External Genitalia

The external genitals of the male and female differentiate from the same basic structure. Until the eighth week of fetal life, the external genital appearance of both sexes is identical, and the genitals can differentiate in either direction. Under the influence of the male sex hormone, the genitalia develop as male. In the absence of this hormone, they develop as female. Again, we see that in the absence of male differentiation, female differentiation will occur. The same structure—the genital tubercle—either expands to become a penis in the male or shrinks to become a clitoris in the female. Figure 3 illustrates the stages of differentiation.

As in the case at other stages of sexual differentiation, anomalies may occur in rare cases in which androgen insensitivity is present or in which normal secretions are disrupted during development. Thus, for example, a baby may be born with an unfinished phallic organ that could be regarded as either an undersized penis or an oversized clitoris.

The Brain and Central Nervous System

The last stage of sexual differentiation occurs when the vascular system is well developed enough to carry the hormones throughout the fetal body, including the brain. At this stage, if androgen is present, the brain differentiates as male. If androgen is absent, the brain differentiates as female.

Here, we reach a question of some controversy. Ever since the notion that women's inferiority could be explained on the basis of their "smaller" brains was laid to rest (Shields, 1975), we have grown used to thinking of the male and female brain as essentially identical. What, then, is meant by the sexual differentiation of the brain?

The first and most straightforward issue of brain sexual differentiation is that of hormonal cyclicity. In adult females, the gonadotrophins are released from the pituitary gland in rhythmic cycles, which in turn causes the levels of the sex hormones, estrogen and progesterone, to vary cyclically. In adult males, gonadotrophin release does not seem to be cyclic, and hence changes in testosterone production are not as predictable. We examine this issue briefly here. A second, far more complex question involves the degree to which the sexual differentiation of the brain and nervous system affects behavior, personality, and identity, and this will be dealt with in later sections.

The hypothalamus is a small area at the base of the brain that, among other things, is concerned with the regulation of hormonal functions. Below the hypothalamus is the pituitary gland, which se-

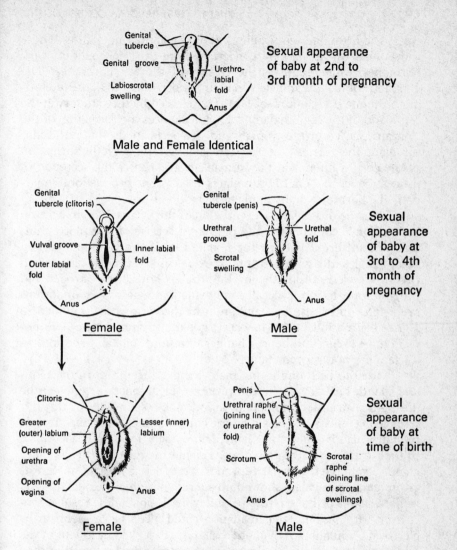

FIGURE 3   Three stages of external genital differentiation in the human fetus. The male and female organs have the same beginnings and are homologous with one another.*

*From *Man and Woman, Boy and Girl* by John Money and Anke A. Ehrhardt (Baltimore: The Johns Hopkins University Press, 1972, p. 44). © 1972 by The Johns Hopkins University Press. All rights reserved. Reprinted by permission of the publisher.

cretes the hormones controlling the other endocrine glands. Those with which we are chiefly concerned here are the gonadotrophic hormones, which regulate the release of the sex hormones. The gonadotrophins (the follicle-stimulating hormone [FSH], the luteinizing hormone [LH], and prolactin) are released by the pituitary at the command of the hypothalamus. FSH influences the formation of the ovarian follicles in the woman and of sperm in the man and also stimulates the ovaries to secrete estrogen. LH, through the formation of the corpus luteum in the woman's ovary, causes the secretion of progesterone. In men, LH stimulates testosterone production. Prolactin is the hormone that stimulates lactation in women.

The issue of sexual differentiation of the brain comes in because hypothalamic control over the pituitary's release of gonadotrophins follows a different pattern for female than for male mammals. In adult females, the gonadotrophins are released from the pituitary in rhythmic cycles, causing the levels of the sex hormones, estrogen and progesterone, to vary cyclically and ovulation to occur at more or less predictable intervals. The operation of the cycle is diagrammed in Figure 4. In adult males, however, gonadotrophin release does not seem to be cyclic, and hence changes in testosterone and sperm production are not as predictable.

It used to be thought that male–female differences in the pituitary gland, brought on by the presence or absence of testosterone during a critical developmental period, was responsible for this difference in cyclicity. However, a series of experiments in which female pituitary glands were transplanted into male rats, and vice versa, showed this idea to be fallacious. Female rats given male pituitary glands maintained normal reproductive cycles. Similarly, male rats given female pituitaries showed no alteration in their normal noncyclic pattern of hormone release (see Levine, 1966). These results, concurrent with findings that ovulation could often be brought on by electrical stimulation of the hypothalamus or blocked by lesions of the hypothalamus, led to the suggestion that it was the brain rather than the pituitary that was sexually differentiated by the action of hormones. An extensive series of experiments on rats, guinea pigs, and monkeys eventually established that in the absence of testosterone during an early critical period, a permanent pattern of cyclic release of FSH and LH by the pituitary was formed. The *presence* of testosterone during this period caused a noncyclic pattern to develop. These results lent support to the view that a mammal's brain will

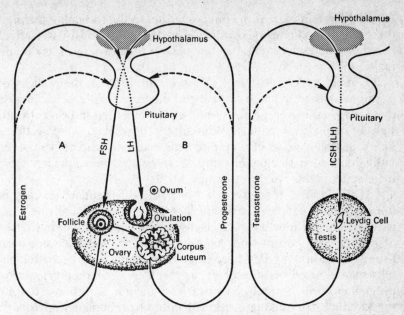

FIGURE 4 Interplay of sex hormones. Interplay of sex hormones differs in the female mammal (left) and the male mammal (right). In the cyclic female system the pituitary initially releases a follicle-stimulating hormone (FSH) that makes the ovary produce estrogen (arrows at A); the estrogen then acts on the hypothalamus of the brain to inhibit the further release of FSH by the pituitary and to stimulate the release of a luteinizing homrone (LH) instead. This hormone both triggers ovulation and makes the ovary produce a second hormone, progesterone (arrows at B). On reaching the hypothalamus the latter hormone inhibits further pituitary release of LH, thereby completing the cycle.

In the noncyclic male system the pituitary continually releases an interstitial-cell-stimulating hormone (ICSH)...(LH) that makes the testes produce testosterone; the latter hormone acts on the hypothalamus to stimulate further release of ICSH by the pituitary. Broken arrows represent the earlier theory that the sex hormones from ovaries and testes stimulated the pituitary directly.*

develop as female unless testosterone is present at a critical developmental stage.

It is always dangerous, of course, to generalize from one animal species to another, and although many people assume that *human* sexual differentiation of the brain operates in the foregoing manner, there are few sources of conclusive evidence. Obviously, we cannot use the same experimental techniques on human fetuses as on animals.

Human males and females do seem to differ in the cyclicity of hormone release. Women ovulate and menstruate in a periodic cycle that lasts, on the average, for twenty-eight days. Men show no obvious signs of such a cyclic pattern, although recent research suggests that a man's testosterone level may fluctuate markedly and that in some individuals such fluctuations appear to be rhythmic. Evidence for male cycles is discussed in Chapter 4.

If the brain is indeed the last organ to differentiate sexually in humans, one might perhaps expect to find an occasional rare individual whose hormonal cyclicity is discordant with all other indicators of his/her sex. To our knowledge, such individuals have not been found. In addition, girls whose external genitalia have been accidentally masculinized because of drugs taken by their mothers during pregnancy show normal cyclic ovarian function at puberty, despite the fact that drug taking continued until birth. Similarly, girls born with the adrenogenital syndrome, in which a malfunction of the adrenal glands causes extra androgens to be poured into the bloodstream from the time of external genital differentiation until the condition is noticed and corrected after birth, show a menstrual cycle after puberty (Money & Ehrhardt, 1972). One wonders, then, precisely when is the critical period in humans during which the presence of male hormones would cause the hypothalamus to differentiate as male.

Synopsis: Sexual Differentiation

To summarize, the process of sexual differentiation follows several steps. The chromosomes provide the initial determination of sex, causing the gonads to differentiate as male if a Y chromosome is present and as female if one is not. The gonads then begin to secrete the sex hormones, which sexually differentiate first the internal reproductive tract, then the external genitalia, then the brain. Every aspect of the process is not completely understood, and the sexual differentiation of the brain in humans remains particularly puzzling. In general, it seems to hold true that male differentiation always occurs more quickly than female differentiation and that in the absence of either a Y chromosome or male sex hormones at certain critical stages, female differentiation occurs. Thus, there is no possibility that an individual will be neutral or asexual. In the absence of maleness, it is femaleness—not neutrality—that develops. It is possible that an individual may differentiate in a male direction at one stage (e.g., inner reproductive organs) and in a female direction at another (e.g., external genitalia). Individuals with a mixture of sexual characteristics are called hermaphrodites and are discussed in the next section. The point remains, however, that *at any given stage* of the sexual differentiation process, the individual will develop in either a masculine *or* a feminine direction, with no possibility of a total failure of sexual development.

It is interesting to note here the way in which biology can lend itself to political rhetoric. Even the rather prosaic process of sexual differentiation can be interpreted to support male or female superiority. Whitbeck (1976), for example, suggests that the literature on human sexual differentiation contains a "woman as partial man" motif in its emphasis on the fact that something (i.e., testosterone) must be *added* to the fetus in order for it to turn out as male. One of our colleagues jokingly referred to femaleness as the "default option" in sexual differentiation. Throwing a slightly different light on the issue. Hoet (cited in Montagu, 1968) has suggested that whereas masculinity is something "additional," the female is the basic surviving human form. Montagu (1968), perhaps not in total seriousness, takes males down a notch further with the following suggestion:

> It is as if in the evolution of sex a fragment at one time broke away from an X-chromosome, carrying with it some rather unfortunate genes, and thereafter in relation to the other chromosomes was helpless to prevent them from expressing themselves in the form of an incomplete female, the creature we call the male! [p. 74]

Speaking with somewhat more bitterness, Solanis (quoted in Cox, 1976) says:

> The male is a biological accident: the Y (male) gene is an incomplete X (female) gene. . . . In other words, the male is an incomplete female, a walking abortion, aborted at the gene stage. To be male is to be deficient, emotionally limited; maleness is a deficiency disease and males are emotional cripples. [p. 29]

It seems an unnecessary and fruitless exercise to try to determine the natural superiority of one sex over the other on the basis of the sexual differentiation process. More to the point, an understanding of the process helps us to understand such issues as why there is no "neutral" third sex, why males are more susceptible than females to genetic disorders, and why sexual differentiation sometimes "goes wrong," producing an individual with external genitalia incongruent with internal reproductive structures or some other inconsistency. This background is necessary for an understanding of the complex issues dealt with in the rest of the chapter: the extent to which physiological differences between the sexes contribute to differences in behavior, personality, and gender identity.

BEHAVIORAL IMPLICATIONS
OF SEX DIFFERENCES IN THE BRAIN

It is the contention of many scientists that brain sexual differentiation implies considerably more than the cyclicity or noncyclicity of hormone release patterns. The suggestion is frequently raised that sex differences in a variety of behaviors can be linked to differences in the brain (e.g., Hutt, 1972). It is hypothesized that there may be differences in the neural pathways of male and female brains or in the sensitivity of various parts of the brain to male and female hormones, which lead the sexes to behave in different ways. Evidence from certain animal studies is consistent with this hypothesis, but that from human beings is equivocal at best.

Animal Studies

The most clear-cut evidence for a link between sex differences in the brain and sex differences in behavior comes from the study of sexual behavior in rats. Male and female rats show very obvious differences in sexual behavior, so there are clear criteria against which to measure abnormal or altered patterns of response. The typical male pattern begins with mounting the female and ends with ejaculation.

The female displays sexual receptivity with what is called a "lordosis response": arching the back and elevating the pelvis. The female's response depends on the presence of the appropriate hormones, so that it is suppressed by the removal of the ovaries and reinstated by replacement injections of estrogen and progesterone. As Levine (1966) reports, however, if testosterone is injected into a newborn female rat, the normal female sexual receptivity behavior seems to be permanently lost. She fails to show the usual response even when later given large replacement injections of female hormones. Moreover, she tends to show extremes of *male* sexual behavior, including the motions connected with ejaculation, when injected with testosterone.

Similarly, if a male rat is castrated immediately after birth (thus eliminating the source of testosterone), small doses of estrogen and progesterone injected into him in adulthood cause him to display normal *female* sexual behavior. Levine concludes that there is a critical period during which the presence or absence of testosterone has a significant and permanent impact on the sensitivity of the rat's brain to sex hormones. If testosterone is present at this critical differentiation stage, it permanently desensitizes the animal (male or female) to female hormones, so that the presence of these hormones will not evoke feminine sexual behavior. If testosterone is absent at the critical period, however, the animal would be left with a sensitivity to female hormones and a tendency to display female behavior patterns. Thus, at least for sexual behavior in the white rat, the sexual differentiation of the brain does seem to have an impact on behavior.

Does this effect generalize to other animal species? Male sexual behavior differentiation in genetic females as a result of testosterone injections at a critical period has been shown with guinea pigs (Phoenix, Goy, Gerall, & Young, 1959) and hamsters (Swanson & Crossley, 1971), and less dramatic but consistent results have been shown with beagle dogs (Beach, cited in Money & Ehrhardt, 1972) and rhesus monkeys (Goy, 1970). Since, in these animals, sexual behavior is usually regulated by the fluctuating levels of female hormones, such evidence lends support to the idea that testosterone injection at a critical period may change behavior by changing the brain's sensitivity to these hormones. One would expect the behavioral changes to be less dramatic in animals higher on the phylogenetic scale, especially primates, since there are indications that these animals are less behaviorally controlled by their hormones than are rats and guinea pigs (Phoenix, 1974). So far, this expectation seems to be supported by the findings, but much research remains to be done.

Do sex differences in the brain also affect nonsexual behavior? Some investigators (e.g., Hamburg & Lunde, 1966; Phoenix, 1974) have suggested that the presence of testosterone at the critical differentiation period "masculinizes" the nervous system by modifying it so that the individual is predisposed or prepared to learn specifically masculine patterns of behavior. This hypothesis has not been proven, but some animal studies do suggest a link between critical period testosterone administration or removal and nonsexual behaviors such as rough-and-tumble play and threat.

Edwards (1969, cited in Money & Ehrhardt, 1972) found that unlike normal female mice, female mice that had been injected with testosterone on the first day of life attacked an intruder to their cage with about the same frequency as did control males. Conner and Levine (1969, cited in Money & Ehrhardt, 1972) found that male rats castrated at birth fought less than normal males in a fighting test. Goy (1970) found that young female rhesus monkeys that had been prenatally androgenized showed more play initiation, rough-and-tumble play, threats, and chasing behavior than did normal females. Such findings offer some support for the notion that testosterone organizes the brain and nervous system during a critical period so that males and females are differentially prepared to learn or perform certain behavioral responses. The extent of the testosterone effect is difficult to assess, however, for two reasons. First, behavioral differences are ascertained through direct observation of the animals by investigators who cannot help but be aware of the animal's condition. Although this procedure probably has no serious effect on the measurement of gross and dramatic behavior shifts, it may possibly have a biasing effect on the interpretation of more subtle changes. Second, animals castrated or treated with testosterone during early development may well differ .in appearance from their normal same-sex peers. Goy's androgenized female monkeys, for example, each had a scrotum and penis. It is possible that their difference in appearance affected their treatment by their cohort—accounting, perhaps, for at least some of their deviation from expected female behavior. It is also possible, as Linton (1971) suggests, that sex-hormone smell is an important social cue for animals. Hermaphrodites may smell different from nonhermaphroditic primates and thus elicit differential treatment by peers.

In summary, the action of testosterone on the developing brain during a critical period has been implicated in the sexual differentiation of behavior, but the implications are strongest for lower animals (rats, guinea pigs) and for specifically sexual behavior. The effect is much more difficult to evaluate with higher animals, whose behavior in general is more subject to learning and the social environment, and less to hormonal action. Nonetheless, there is suggestive evidence that the male-differentiated brain of the primate may be more prepared than the female one to learn certain behavior patterns, particularly aggressive ones. It is important to note, however, that scientists do not know *how* testosterone acts to differentiate the brain, nor do they know the timing of the critical period for specific effects for many species. Thus, research in this area is far from complete.

Human Studies

As a species, humans depend greatly on the learning process in the development of behavior patterns. Our behavior is largely mediated by cognitive factors: our thoughts about the meanings of objects and actions. Also, our social organization tends to be rather complex. These factors make physiological influences on human behavior rather difficult to isolate and interpret. It may well be that sex differences in the human brain provide some of the basis of sex differences in behavior, but the presence of strong social/environmental pressures toward behavioral sex differences is always a confounding factor in the interpretation of physiological effects. Nonetheless, it has been suggested that exposure to androgen at a critical developmental period might affect human behavior in subtle ways. The central nervous system might differentiate in a way that made aggressive behavior patterns easy to learn and that prepared the individual to learn them. Sensitivity to certain stimulus patterns might be affected. Threshold of response to certain stimuli connected with aggression might be lowered, making such stimuli more arousing. Certain response patterns, critical in aggressive encounters, might take on rewarding properties (Hamburg & Lunde, 1966). These are only speculations at present, but they illustrate ways in which brain and central nervous system differentiation by sex *could* affect behavior. This issue is further discussed in Chapter 9, where we consider the evidence for a sex-differentiated preparedness to learn aggressive responses.

Because of the obvious physical dangers and negative social consequences, scientists cannot experiment with the hormone balance of human fetuses. Thus, to the difficulty of interpretation brought about by the heavy dependence of human behavior on learning and cognition is added another drawback: carefully planned experimental studies of the sexual differentiation of the human brain cannot be carried out. How, then, can we acquire information about this question?

Most data on the effects of prenatal hormones on human development and behavior have come from the study of people whose sexual differentiation was disrupted *in utero* by a hormonal imbalance. Such individuals, known as hermaphrodites or intersexuals, form less than 1 percent of our population but have been extensively studied over the past two decades. The hormonal imbalance responsible for the anomaly is thought to be the result of drugs administered to their pregnant mother, stress experienced by her, or of a glandular malfunction of genetic origin. As a result of this prenatal hormonal disruption, they are born with the sexual anatomy incompletely differentiated. For instance, a hermaphroditic baby may be born with ambiguous external genitalia or with genitalia incongruous with internal reproductive structures. By studying the behavioral and personality concomitants of the many varieties of human hermaphroditism, investigators have hoped to discover the connection between specific aspects of physiological sex and behavior.

Studies of hermaphroditic individuals have covered a wide range of disorders, and the interested reader is referred to an important summary work by two pioneers in the field, John Money and Anke Ehrhardt (1972). We focus here on one set of studies, dealing with the effects of a specific hormonal problem: the adrenogenital syndrome (AGS). This syndrome, which is genetically transmitted, causes the adrenal glands of the fetus to malfunction. The malfunction results in a release of excess androgens from the prenatal period onward, thus setting the stage for a variety of masculinizing effects. Girls with AGS are born with masculinized external genitalia, but the internal reproductive organs are female. If the syndrome is diagnosed at birth, these girls receive surgery to feminize their genitals and are placed on lifelong cortisone therapy to compensate for the continuing adrenal malfunction. These individuals, then, are in some respects comparable to the genetically female animals who were experimentally exposed to androgens during the early critical period of central nervous system differentiation. Boys with AGS are born with a normal masculine appearance. However, they too must be treated with cortisone, or the extra output of androgen will cause their puberty to occur years early.

If the presence of significant amounts of androgen during a prenatal critical period causes the brain and central nervous system to differentiate in a masculine direction, children with AGS ought to show evidence of this effect. Two studies have examined children born with this syndrome for signs of masculinization of behavior and personality. In both cases the sample is small and covers an age range of young children to middle adolescence, so the reliability of the findings is difficult to assess. Nonetheless, the results of the two studies are quite consistent, and they provide us with some clues about the effects of prenatal androgenization on humans.

The first study (Ehrhardt & Money, 1967, described in Money & Ehrhardt, 1972) compared twenty-five fetally androgenized girls (fifteen with AGS and ten who had been androgenized by progestin taken by their mothers during pregnancy) with a control group of twenty-five normal girls, matched on the basis of age, IQ, socioeconomic background, and race. Data were collected by interviewing each girl and her mother, using a standard format. On the basis of the interviews, several significant differences were found between the two groups. The fetally androgenized girls were more likely to regard themselves as tomboys, tended to have a higher preference for athletic energy expenditure and for joining boys in energetic play, preferred practical rather than pretty clothes, showed less interest in dolls, and showed relatively more interest in a career and less in marriage than did the control girls. No differences were found on several other dimensions such as aggression, lesbianism, enjoyment of personal adornment such as jewelry and perfume, and observable amount of sexual play or interest. Although these results are interesting, it may be premature to accept them at face value. Data were collected by interview, and the interviewers apparently were not blind to the diagnostic category (androgenized vs. nonandrogenized) of the girls they were questioning. Thus the possibility of unintentional researcher bias cannot be excluded. Furthermore, no observational data were collected, so that the data rest heavily on self-report. Some critics have also pointed out that the social environments of the two groups may have been different: the families of the androgenized girls may have been affected by the birth of an "abnormal" child, and the girls may have received special treatment because of parental guilt over their condition or expectation of a tendency toward masculinity. Finally, the girls themselves, who were aware of their condition, may have felt they had more excuse than their counterparts to behave in a masculine way.

A second study (Ehrhardt & Baker, 1974) was designed to take into account some of the criticisms mentioned. In this investigation, seventeen females and ten males with AGS were compared with their unaffected same-sex siblings and parents. Thus, the possibility of general family differences between androgenized and control children was removed. Also, the inclusion of males in the study allowed for a broader examination of early androgen effects. Data were still based on interviews, however, in a procedure in which interviewers were aware of the diagnostic category of their subjects. This study found several differences between androgenized girls and their unaffected sisters and mothers: the androgenized girls were more often described by themselves and their families as having a high level of intense physical energy expenditure and showed a preference for boys over girls as playmates. Girls with AGS were less likely to show an interest in dolls or infants or to daydream or role play about marriage or motherhood than were their sisters or their mothers during childhood. No differences between groups, however, were found on career interest. Significantly more of the AGS girls identified themselves as having been tomboys during all of their childhood, preferred functional clothing over clothing considered attractive for girls at that time, and showed low interest in jewelry, makeup, and hairdo. Despite these differences from their sisters and mothers, however, the androgenized girls were clearly identified in the female role and were not unhappy about being girls. Their behavior was not considered abnormal by themselves or their families but followed a pattern of tomboyism that is quite acceptable for girls in our culture. This pattern simply occurred somewhat more frequently among the androgenized than the nonandrogenized girls in this sample.

For the males in this study, only one difference between groups was found. Boys with AGS were more often reported as showing a long-term, high energy-expenditure level in sports and rough outdoor activities than were their brothers. Thus, there was little evidence for a "super-masculinizing" behavioral effect of excess prenatal androgen on boys.

In this study, the investigators intensively interviewed parents to determine whether they had any ambivalence or anxiety about their AGS offspring's sexuality that might be manifested in differential treatment. They were able to uncover none. Similarly, their interviews with the girls themselves revealed no significant persistent concern over being "born different." Systematic social-environmental differences between AGS and control groups of children can be ruled out to the extent that accurate information was obtained in these interviews. Once again, such accuracy is difficult to ascertain because of the possibility of unintentional interviewer bias and evaluation apprehension on the part of the subjects.

We are left with two studies with results that are reasonably consistent: girls in the AGS groups more often than control girls showed behavior such as high energy expenditure, tomboyism, preference for functional over attractive clothing, and low interest in and rehearsal for marriage and motherhood roles. Since these are behaviors on which girls and boys are thought to differ under normal conditions, the tentative conclusion has been drawn that prenatal androgenization, through action on the developing brain, masculinizes the girls' behavior. This conclusion *must* remain tentative for the time being until carefully controlled studies on larger samples of children are carried out. Such studies should be structured to avoid the possibility of interviewer bias and to collect long-term observational as well as interview data. The difficulty of this is obvious: AGS is a rare syndrome. Subjects are difficult to find and are identified clinically, so that blind interview procedures are not easily accomplished. Nonetheless, the formation of solid conclusions about behavioral effects of prenatal androgenization in humans will have to wait until such studies are done.

Of course, the most basic difficulty in any attempt to determine physiological influences on sex differences in behavior for humans is that we simply have no clear, agreed-upon criteria about which behaviors are male and which female. We cannot say for people as we can for rats, for instance, that male sexual behavior always follows a certain pattern, beginning with mounting the female! Indeed, the range of male sexual behavior patterns that we would call both "masculine" and "normal" is wide enough that a change brought about by hormonal action would have to be very dramatic to capture our attention. Similarly, the tomboyish behavior of the androgenized females in the foregoing studies would almost certainly have gone unnoticed, had it not been specifically looked for, since it falls well within the range of normal female behavior in our culture. This merely highlights once again the fact that human behavior is complex and multidetermined. If sex hormones, then, through their influence on the fetal brain, do produce the substrata for behavioral sexual differences (an idea that remains intriguing but unproven), these substrata merely provide basic predispositions that interact with environmental forces. Such interactions can produce a variety of behavioral results.

What would be the implications of accepting the position that sex hormones differentiate the brain so that females and males have different behavioral predispositions? Would it mean that our traditional sex roles have made sense all along and that we are flying in the face of biology if we try to change them? Not necessarily, for besides the aforementioned argument that physiology is only one of a complex set of determinants of behavior, there is another very important fact to remember. All males are not hormonally identical, and neither are all females. In fact, there is considerable variation within each sex as to the relative proportions of male and female hormones present in the body at any given developmental stage. This variation is most obvious at puberty, when the release of larger amounts of the appropriate sex hormone in the male or female body results in a more dramatic development of secondary sex characteristics. If hormones influence behavior in any way, then, they may contribute as much to individual differences as to sex differences. As Ehrhardt and Baker (1974) conclude in their report on AGS children:

> If prenatal hormone levels contribute to sex differences in behavior, the effects in human beings are subtle and can in no way be taken as a basis for prescribing social roles. In fact, we rather like to make an argument from the opposite point of view. If it can be documented that prenatal hormone levels are among the factors that account for the wide range of temperamental differences and role aspirations within the female, and possibly also within the male, sex, a great variety of adult roles should be available and can be adequately fulfilled by both women and men, and they should be equally acceptable and respectable for either sex. [p. 50]

GENDER IDENTITY

Money and Ehrhardt (1972) describe a case in which a seven-month-old boy was the victim of a surgical accident that destroyed his penis. The boy had been normal in every respect, but the loss of the penis resulted in a decision by his parents to reassign his sex as female and to rear him as a girl. At the age of seventeen months, the child's name, clothing, and hairstyle were changed to fit feminine norms, and surgery to feminize the genitals was undertaken shortly thereafter. The child had an identical twin brother, and thus it is possible to compare the way in which two children with exactly the same genetic background developed when one was assigned and reared as a boy and the other as a girl.

For this particular case, the records show that the child who was reassigned as a girl quickly developed typical feminine interests and behavior, whereas the boy developed and maintained his masculine patterns. For example, the children's mother reported that the girl had a preference for dresses, took pride in her long hair, was neater and daintier than her brother, copied her mother in her domestic activities, and took a great interest in dolls. The boy, on the other hand, tended to be rougher and dirtier, took no interest in housework, and copied his father's interest in cars and mechanical activities. Moreover, the girl clearly thought of herself as a girl, whereas the boy's self-concept was unambiguously male. Thus, the gender identity of each child was apparently shaped by the sex of assignment and rearing more than by genetic or other physiological determinants.

Gender identity is the individual's private experience of his/her gender: the concept of the self as masculine or feminine. This is such a powerful and important part of a person's self-concept that in most adults it is virtually impossible to change it. (If you don't believe this, try for a moment to think of yourself as still "you," but as the other sex.) Yet research indicates that physiological sexual differentiation notwithstanding, we are not born with a gender identity: it develops after birth.

A number of comparisions have been made between pairs of hermaphrodites with the same physiological indicators of sex, one of whom was assigned and reared as a girl and one as a boy (Money &

Ehrhardt, 1972). Usually, gender identity develops consistent with the sex of assignment and rearing. Two important conditions must be met in order for this to happen, however. First, gender must be decided upon and assigned early in the child's life. Money and Ehrhardt report that great emotional difficulties often accompany sex reassignment that takes place after the age of eighteen months, and they suggest that there may be a critical period for gender identity differentiation, just as there is for other stages of sexual differentiation. Second, there must be no doubt or ambiguity about the child's sex on the part of the parents. Such doubts seem to be transmitted to the child and to result in incomplete gender identity differentiation.

Research also shows that once formed, a person's gender identity is extremely resistant to change. Some of the most dramatic findings on this topic are those reported by Hampson and Hampson (1961), who studied thirty-one females who had been born with the andrenogenital syndrome. In these patients, the syndrome had not been treated at birth, so that they continued to be exposed to excess androgens postnatally. Thus, they had grown from childhood with masculine-appearing genitalia and a tendency to develop male secondary sex characteristics at puberty. They had been raised as girls, however, by parents who had been told they were genetically female. Despite the problems these girls must have had in coping with their paradoxical appearance, however, all but five of them established an unambivalently female gender identity. This identity did not change even when male secondary sex characteristics began to develop at puberty.

It is clear that early postnatal events are crucial in the child's construction of a gender identity. There are several different perspectives on how gender identity is formed, however: psychoanalytic, social learning, and cognitive developmental.

Psychoanalytic theory, it will be remembered, describes a process in which the young child *identifies* with the same-sex parent. S/he internalizes the characteristics and behavior styles of that parent and begins unconsciously to react in similar ways. According to Freud, this identification becomes for the child a way of resolving painful feelings of jealousy and hostility inherent in the Oedipus complex and the discovery of the anatomical differences between the sexes. Thus, motivated by powerful emotions directed at the parents, the child forms a gender identity congruent with his/her biological sex.

Social learning theory suggests that the child develops a gender identity (usually called sex-role identity in this framework) through a learning process that involves modeling, imitation, and reinforcement. (One specific variant of this theory, formulated by David Lynn, was described in Chapter 2.) The theory rests on the assumption that boys learn to be boys and girls to be girls because sex-role-appropriate behavior is rewarded whereas sex-role-inappropriate behavior is more likely to be ignored or punished. Children learn which behaviors are sex-role appropriate by observing and imitating adult and peer models as well as through trial and error in their own behavior. Social learning theory suggests that a child is most likely to imitate or to identify with a model who is readily available and perceived as powerful, nurturant, and similar to the self (Mischel, 1970). According to this viewpoint, parental models, particularly the same-sex parent, would be most effective in influencing the child's behavior. It is suggested that parents map out gender roles for the child, and then the child is differentially reinforced for following the appropriate one. As the child is repeatedly reminded that he is a boy or she is a girl and differentially reinforced for doing boy-things or girl-things, gradually it becomes rewarding for him to think of himself as a boy or for her to think of herself as a girl. Thus, through observation, imitation, and reinforcement, an appropriate role identity is established.

Cognitive developmental theory (Kohlberg, 1966) proposes that gender is a concept that cannot be learned until a child reaches a particular stage of intellectual development. Between the ages of three and five, a child acquires "gender constancy"—an understanding that a person's gender is fixed and cannot be spontaneously altered by a change in hairstyle, dress, or name. Before that age, according to Kohlberg, although a child may have learned that people can be categorized as either male or female, s/he sometimes makes errors in classifying the self or others and thinks that arbitrary changes in classification can occur. The learning of gender constancy is analogous to the learning of other concepts such as the constancy of mass and volume, which some psychologists (e.g., Piaget, 1947) also feel can occur only after the child reaches a certain stage of development.

According to the cognitive developmental approach, once the child has categorized her/himself with some certainty as male or female, s/he will find the performance of sex-role-appropriate behaviors reinforcing. In other words, such behaviors acquire a meaning that makes them self-reinforcing for the child. In a similar vein, behaviors that are perceived as sex-role-inappropriate acquire negative connotations and are avoided. It is as if the child, in the early stages of acquiring a gender identity, tries to solidify this identity by renouncing any form of ambiguity. At a later age, secure in a gender identity, the child becomes less uncomfortable about occasional deviations from the appropriate gender role and therefore less rigid about sex-role behavior.

Thus, the three theories postulate somewhat different mechanisms for the formation of gender identity. Psychoanalysis stresses the powerful emotions generated by the Oedipus complex, social learning emphasizes the role of imitation and reinforcement, and cognitive development pays special attention to the development of the child's ability to learn concepts and to attach self-reinforcing meanings to behaviors. There may well be a degree of truth in each approach. As is seen in the following section, the formation of gender identity is a process that has yet to be completely understood.

THE PUZZLE OF TRANSSEXUALISM

In recent years, several individuals in the public eye have made headlines by going through surgical procedures to change their sex. James Morris, a well-known writer and reporter, chose to become Jan Morris and told the story of the transition from male to female in a best-seller called *Conundrum* (1974). Renée Richards, playing on the female professional tennis circuit, created doubts and protests because she had previously been a man playing on the male circuit. What mysterious process would cause an adult with a settled, stable life to want to change gender identity?

A transsexual is a person—male or female—who firmly believes s/he was born with the body of the wrong sex. This conviction dates from early childhood (usually as far back as the person can remember) and does not seem to be amenable to change through life experiences, rewards for "normal" behavior, or therapy (Green, 1974). To all appearances, the individual has acquired the *wrong* gender identity, and once acquired, this identity seems to be virtually unchangeable. Such individuals may lead lives that are outwardly congruent with their anatomical sex, but their conviction that their body is wrong for them is often strong enough to cause them to seek surgery in order to change it. Thus, a male-to-female transsexual may achieve a body congruent with a feminine self-image by taking regular doses of estrogen and having a vagina surgically constructed from the penile tissue. A female-to-male transsexual, on the other hand, may take male hormone treatments and have surgery to construct a makeshift penis.

The origin of the transsexual's conviction of being born into the wrong sex remains mysterious. Suggestions that it may have a physiological base have received no support, since these individuals appear to be normally sexually differentiated and not hermaphroditic in any sense. Bardwick (1971) has proposed that the prenatal sexual differentiation of the brain in transsexuals may have proceeded in the wrong direction, causing their gender identity to differ from their anatomical sex. This explanation seems inadequate, however, given that transsexuals have generally not been found to differ physiologically from the rest of the population (Green, 1974) and that hermaphrodites usually form a gender identity congruent with their sex of assignment and rearing.

Consistent patterns of socialization and rearing associated with transsexualism have also been hard to find. Green reports that the parents of some of his transsexual patients appear to have wanted a child of the other sex and may have communicated this to the child at a young age, but this pattern is not *always* found. Although psychoanalytic theory might propose that the transsexual identified with the wrong parent at the Oedipal stage, there is little evidence with which to support or reject this notion. Social learning theory, which might suggest that the transsexual's difficulty had been caused by rewards for performing the behaviors of the other sex, does not easily explain why the transsexual often lives a successful life consistent with her/his anatomical sex while remaining firmly convinced that his/her gender identity is different. The cognitive developmental approach might interpret transsexualism as due to a child's initial faulty learning of the male–female concept or a mistaken sexual categorization of the self at a critical period. It does not, however, suggest what forces might bring about such faulty learning.

Thus, transsexualism remains a puzzle—a reminder that we have much to discover about sexual differentiation and gender identity.

SUMMARY

The differentiation of the individual into male or female is seen in this chapter to be both a physiological and a psychological process. The physiological aspect begins at conception with the genetic determination of sex and continues through several stages of fetal development: the development of the gonads; their secretion of sex hormones; and the resulting differentiation of the internal reproductive tract, the external genitalia, and the brain. The initial presence of a Y chromosome orients this process in a masculine direction, whereas its absence points development in a feminine direction. Similarly, at each stage, the presence of the male sex hormones in significant amounts leads to male differentiation; their absence leads to female differentiation.

Under normal circumstances, the differentiation proceeds in the same direction at every stage, producing an individual who is unambiguously either male or female at birth. However, on rare occasions, the process is disrupted, and the individual differentiates as male at some stages and as female at others. Such individuals, called hermaphrodites, provide us with valuable information about the relationship between the physiological and psychological aspects of sex and sex roles.

Many questions have been raised about the biological bases of behavioral sex differences. This chapter dealt with the question of whether sex differences in the brain, resulting from the sexual differentiation process, have an impact on behavior. It was seen that a clear relationship between brain differentiation and behavior seems to exist for lower animals, but evidence for the link becomes more tenuous in moving up the phylogenetic scale toward humans. Studies of girls with the adrenogenital syndrome provide some suggestive support for the notion that human behavior can be masculinized by prenatal exposure to androgens, but much more research is needed before firm conclusions can be drawn about this.

Finally, the question of gender identity focuses on the psychological aspects of sexual differentiation. Studies suggest that people are not born with a gender identity but develop it early in life through interaction with their environment. The identity seems to become virtually irrevocable by the time the child reaches the age of eighteen months but can be changed before that age. Psychologists do not have a complete understanding, however, of how gender identity is formed. Transsexualism—the mysterious phenomenon in which an individual is firmly convinced, despite all indications to the contrary, that s/he was born into the body of the wrong sex—reminds us that we have much to learn.

4 Hilary M. Lips

HORMONES, CYCLES, & THE ADULT EXPERIENCE

One of the most widely recognized differences between the sexes has been that of sex hormones; whereas women's sex hormones show regular monthly fluctuations, men's sex hormone levels do not seem to vary in the same predictable, rhythmic way.* In Chapter 3, it was explained that during the process of sexual differentiation of the fetus, the hypothalamus differentiates in such a way as to cause the pituitary gland to release sex hormones in a cyclic manner in females and in a noncyclic manner in males. The most obvious consequence of this difference is that a woman can become pregnant only during a particular portion of her monthly or menstrual cycle, whereas a man's potential to impregnate a woman is not limited by any such cyclic variation in his physiological processes. The implications of this difference between the sexes, however, have been carried far beyond the area of fertility. For centuries, the existence of the menstrual cycle has been used to characterize women as unstable and therefore unfit for

*Recent evidence suggests that males may in fact have hormonal cycles, but research is only beginning to address this. In any case, their cycles are not obvious, since men do not menstruate. The issue of male cycles is addressed later in the chapter.

certain responsible social positions. This is, of course, in contrast to men, whose physiological state has been thought to be relatively constant. It has been suggested that women should not hold high political office because of possibly dangerous mood shifts that may occur during their menstrual cycle and influence their decision-making capacities. One self-styled expert (Dr. E. F. Berman, speech, July 25, 1970, cited in Cox, 1976) chose a rather poor example to dramatize his point:

> If you had an investment in a bank, you wouldn't want the president of your bank making a loan under those raging hormonal influences at that particular period. Suppose we had a menopausal woman President who had to make the decision of the Bay of Pigs, which was, of course, a bad one, or the Russian contretemps with Cuba at that time? [p. 27]

At the turn of the century, ideas on the restrictions necessary for the menstruating woman were even more extreme. Some educators took strong stands against coeducation in adolescence on the basis that daily association with boys would interfere with the "normalization" of a girl's menstrual period. One theorist even suggested that if girls were forced to exercise their brains at puberty they would use up the blood later needed for menstruation (see Shields, 1975). Obviously, the menstrual cycle has been considered both a very powerful and a very energy-draining process.

In this section, we examine the evidence for the idea that certain emotional and behavioral changes are caused by the changes in hormonal levels that occur during a woman's menstrual cycle. We look at research that touches on the question of whether women actually are incapacitated to any degree during certain times in their monthly cycle. The issue of *male* hormonal cycles is also raised, since it is becoming increasingly clear that the male body is not as completely stable as has long been believed. Finally, we look at the psychological aspects of processes that interrupt the cyclic functioning of the female reproductive system: pregnancy and menopause. We will see that, strangely enough, some psychological effects of pregnancy are felt by men as well as women and that the "change of life" appears to be a complex sociophysiological process, some aspects of which are experienced by both sexes.

THE MENSTRUAL CYCLE

It will be remembered from Chapter 3 that the cyclic pattern of sex hormone levels in women is maintained through a negative feedback system involving the hypothalamus, the pituitary gland, and the ovaries. In this system, the ovaries, which produce the sex hormones, estrogen and progesterone, are regulated by the pituitary gland, which in turn is regulated by the hypothalamus, which responds to the levels of estrogen and progesterone produced by the ovaries (see Figure 5). Levels of estrogen and progesterone are at their lowest during menstruation, at the beginning of the twenty-eight-day cycle.

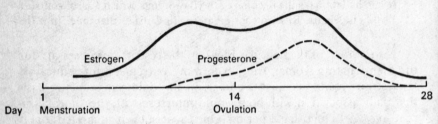

FIGURE 5 Changes in sex hormone levels in women over the menstrual cycle.

The estrogen level then starts to rise and reaches a peak at mid-cycle, when ovulation occurs, declines slightly, then once again rises to a peak and declines sharply before the onset of menstruation. The progesterone level is very low before ovulation, after which it increases rapidly to a peak and sinks swiftly before menstruation.

Given the dramatic shifts in the levels of estrogen and progesterone over the twenty-eight-day cycle, we should not be surprised by the suggestion that the cycle variation affects moods, feelings, and behavior. In fact, many women do report symptoms such as periodic shifts in mood that seem to correlate with their menstrual cycle. Some women report that they become depressed and irritable just before or during their menstrual period. Others report physical symptoms such as headaches at this time of the month. There is a lack of universal agreement on what symptoms occur when, but because a large number of women report *some* symptoms that seem to vary with the phase of their menstrual cycle, it seems worthwhile to pursue the issue of what might cause such symptoms. It must be remembered that the fact that certain symptoms may correlate with (i.e., occur together with) certain phases of the menstrual cycle does not necessarily imply that they are *caused* by the hormonal changes that characterize that part of the cycle. It is very difficult, in fact, to ascertain whether these reported symptoms are due to physiological changes in the woman's body or to her learned expectations of menstrual cycle effects, since research (e.g., Schacter & Singer, 1962; Walster, 1974) indicates that people actually tend to label their moods according to their expectations about how they should feel in certain situations.

Two approaches may be employed to explore the relative importance of physiological versus social learning explanations for the psychological correlates of the menstrual cycle. One possible approach is to critically examine the research evidence that has generally been thought to demonstrate a link between the menstrual cycle and the occurrence of certain psychological symptoms. If the examination reveals that variations in social expectations and cultural bias do not disturb a consistent pattern of response to the menstrual cycle, it can be safely concluded that there is some physiological basis for specific psychological correlates of the cycle. This approach is the one taken by Parlee (1973) in her article on the premenstrual syndrome.

Emotional and Behavioral Correlates of the Menstrual Cycle

According to Parlee (1973), psychologists have for several decades referred to a "premenstrual syndrome" of high tension and irritability that is said to occur during the days immediately preceding the onset of menstruation. In her review article, she identifies four ways in which the syndrome has been studied. The first of these has involved looking for correlations between the phase of the menstrual cycle and the occurrence of specific behaviors. Investigators using this method have reported that abnormal behaviors are most likely to occur in women who are at the premenstrual or menstrual phase rather than at any other phase of their cycle. The alleged link between these behaviors (which include commission of violent crimes, loss of control of an aircraft, suicide, and admission to hospital with acute psychiatric illness) and the onset of menstruation would seem to imply that women are a menace to themselves and others for a few days every month! However, a careful look at the methodology of this research shows this conclusion to be unwarranted. Some of the reports are based on extremely small samples of women, and many have used methods such as retrospective reports of cycle phase, the accuracy of which is highly suspect. Many of these studies, then, cannot be used as strong evidence for the existence of any relationship between the menstrual cycle and behavior. Studies with large samples and careful determination of cycle phase have generally failed to demonstrate such a link. For instance, several studies cited by Parlee that examined school and work performance in relation to menstrual cycle phase showed no evidence for a performance decrement at any stage of the cycle.

Parlee points out that even in cases where a true relationship between the menstrual cycle and behavior has been demonstrated, interpretation is difficult. Most people assume that hormonal changes associated with the cycle cause the behavior change. However, the direction of causality in some cases may be precisely the reverse, as it has long been known that psychological stress can delay menstruation or cause it to begin ahead of schedule. She also cautions that correlational data from special groups of women (e.g., female criminals) should not be used to make general statements about all women or about other special groups of women (e.g., female artists). Even supposing that women disposed to commit violent crime are more likely to commit it premenstrually or menstrually, we cannot assume that women with strong inhibitions about violent behavior will be significantly more likely to commit violent acts at a particular point in the menstrual cycle.

A second set of studies of the menstrual cycle have involved retrospective questionnaires that ask women to report their memory of their experience of certain symptoms and moods at different stages of the cycle. Studies of this type tend to find a variety of negative feelings and symptoms associated with the premenstrual and menstrual phases of the cycle. However, as Parlee notes, the questionnaires used are generally made up of negative responses, and the subjects are questioned mainly about the premenstrual and menstrual period of the cycle, so the research is biased toward finding negative symptoms at these phases. It is also possible that when relying on memory to assess menstrual symptoms, women have their responses shaped somewhat by their learned expectations about various points in the cycle and fail to remember feelings that were not consistent with the "accepted" pattern.

The menstrual cycle has also been studied by means of daily

self-reports by women over a period of several months. This method has the advantage of not relying heavily on memory but still has the disadvantage that subjects may know that effects of the menstrual cycle are being studied. Such knowledge may cause a woman to be more aware of her cycle than she normally would be and thus bias the results. Thus, even a woman who would ordinarily not notice slight painful twinges in her abdominal area (which may be due to any number of causes) might be more likely to notice them during her menstrual period and report them as "cramps" if she were sensitive to the fact that her menstrual cycle was being studied. Nevertheless, this method appears to be superior to the two previously mentioned. According to Parlee, studies using this method generally indicate the presence of a great deal of variability in individual women's patterns of behavior, with individual records showing little evidence of rhythm. However, when the records of many individual women are combined, some studies show regular cyclic changes in such things as fatigue, abdominal pain, headaches, and irritability. However, different studies tend to show cyclic changes in different symptons, and these inconsistencies remain unexplained.

One interesting study using this method was done by Barbara Sommer (1975). Her subjects filled out daily mood adjective checklists for four and one-half weeks. When the results were analyzed, the only statistically significant finding was an increase in positive affect at mid-cycle. Although it is difficult to draw conclusions on the basis of a single study, this one is particularly intriguing, because it used a method that allowed for the measurement of mood changes in both positive *and* negative directions instead of focusing only on changes in such symptoms as depression and irritability. It is interesting to speculate on the changes in attitudes toward the menstrual cycle that might take place if women began to think of the mid-cycle as a high point rather than focusing on the menstrual phase as a time of extraordinary low moods.

A final method of studying psychological changes related to the menstrual cycle involves the analysis of unstructured verbal material. This method also involves assessment of subjects' moods on a day-to-day basis, but instead of asking women to rate themselves on specific symptoms, it simply asks them to talk into a tape recorder for five minutes about life experience. The tape of this material is then analyzed, using a standardized scoring system, to assess levels of hostility and anxiety. Several studies using this method have shown cyclic changes in levels of hostility and anxiety among women. One study (Paige, 1971) suggests that these cyclic changes do not occur among women who are taking oral contraceptives and thus do not have the normal hormonal fluctuations associated with the menstrual cycle. The latter study provides perhaps some of the strongest evidence for the effect of cyclic hormonal fluctuations on psychological states but still does not completely rule out the possibility that women may be responding partially to learned social attitudes surrounding menstruation.

As yet, we do not have sufficient evidence to clearly identify the psychological accompaniments of various phases of the menstrual cycle. It seems clear from Parlee's review, however, that there is little or no evidence to support the claim that women's task performance suffers during the premenstrual or menstrual phases. The evidence on cyclic variations in mood is somewhat more persuasive; however, the tremendous variation among individual women and the lack of consistency from study to study make it impossible at this stage to present an accurate description of a premenstrual or menstrual syndrome.

Social and Cultural Influence on the Menstrual Experience

According to historical and anthropological evidence, menstruation has never been merely a physiological event. The menstruating woman has universally been regarded as unclean and dangerous: a threat to men. In many cultures she was secluded during her period, forbidden to prepare food or to have any contact with men. She could be punished with death if found concealing the fact that she was menstruating, or whipped (for purposes of purification) if her period lasted too long (see Weideger, 1977, for a complete account of the rituals surrounding menstruation). Even today in our culture menstruation is referred to as "the curse," and some people hold a taboo against having sexual relations during the menstrual period.

It would be surprising if the cultural meanings attached to menstruation did not have an influence on how women experience it. Recently, a number of researchers (e.g., Koeske & Koeske, 1975; Paige, 1973; Rodin, 1976) have attempted to demonstrate directly the operation of social–cultural factors.

Paige (1973) explored two issues: the possibility that women use menstruation to explain bodily discomfort and psychological distress that actually have origins in other events, and the existence of differences among the religious–cultural groups in symptoms connected with the menstrual cycle. To a large sample of unmarried university women who identified themselves as Protestants, Jews, or Catholics, Paige administered a questionnaire to assess menstrual symptoms (Moos, 1968), a measure of general psychological stress, a measure of general illness behavior, and a questionnaire tapping three aspects of orientation to the feminine role: family and motherhood versus career orientations, degree of sexual experience, and menstrual social behavior (i.e., the extent to which a woman adheres to conventional taboos and rituals that accompany menstruation). Paige's results seem to demonstrate that learned social attitudes play a significant role in determining women's reactions to the menstrual cycle. They indicate first that women *learn* to attribute various forms of physical discomfort to menstruation and second that groups of women with similar menstrual cycles but different subcultural religious backgrounds differ in the way that social factors relate to their reports of menstrual distress. She found, first of all, that women who reported many symptoms on the Menstrual Distress Questionnaire were significantly more likely than other women to report higher psychological stress, greater use of drugs, and more illnesses in general. Thus the women who report a lot of menstrual distress are the same women to tend to report a lot of general distress. It appears that for some women, menstruation merely represents a specific, socially acceptable explanation for symptoms that actually occur all month long and that at mid-cycle would be attributed to external causes such as overwork, family disputes, and so on. Secondly, Paige found that although there were no overall differences among religious groups in quantity of menstrual symptoms reported, the three groups differed in the ways that various social factors were related to symptom reporting. In particular, the dimensions of menstrual social behavior, family/motherhood orientation, and sexual experience seemed to relate differently to reports of menstrual distress in different religious groups.

For Paige's Jewish subjects, the only dimension that seemed to relate strongly to complaints of menstrual distress was menstrual social behavior. Those women who found sex during menstruation unenjoyable and embarrassing and/or tended to follow certain prescribed social rituals connected with menstruation were the women most likely to report menstrual problems. Among Catholics, on the other hand, the factors that related most strongly to reported menstrual distress were sexual experience and orientation to motherhood and family. Catholic women with more sexual experience were less likely to report menstrual symptoms. Also in this group, the women who indicated most strongly that a woman's place was in the home and who listed no personal career ambitions were those most likely to report menstrual symptoms. For the Protestant group, no especially strong relationship between reported menstrual distress and any of the social factors tested was demonstrated. These results are interesting, since women in all three groups have similar hormonal patterns but different cultural backgrounds. The relationships that Paige demonstrated cannot be used to prove that certain social factors *cause* menstrual distress or vice versa, but her demonstration of intergroup differences provides considerable support for the idea that social and cultural factors have an impact on women's reactions to menstruation. As Paige points out in her article, this should not be particularly surprising, since we are quite aware that cultures label and control other basic biological functions. For example, eating is obviously a response to a basic biological need controlled by physiological processes. Yet, as Paige reminds us, our culture has a tremendous influence on what, when, where, how, and with whom we eat!

The notion that a woman's learned expectations and attributions about the effects of menstruation may have greater influence on her performance than do the actual cyclic changes has recently enjoyed experimental attention and support (Rodin, 1976). Rodin carried out an experiment in which task performance of menstruating women reporting moderate or severe symptoms was compared with that of nonmenstruating women. Half of the women in each group were emotionally aroused by the anticipation of painful electric shock and anxiety about the test. She predicted that menstruating women who normally experience menstrual distress would tend to attribute the emotional arousal they were experiencing in the experiment to the symptoms usually associated with menstruation. Thus, she theorized that this group of women, having a readily available explanation for their discomfort, would perform better, not worse, than similarly aroused nonmenstruating women or menstruating women who do not associate menstruation with distress. This hypothesis is based on a growing body of literature (e.g., Weiner, Frieze, Kukla, Reed, Rest, & Rosenbaum, 1971) that indicates that a person's beliefs about the source of the arousal she is experiencing during an achievement-oriented task can influence her expectations of success and failure and her subsequent performance on the task. If she sees the arousal as stemming from the task itself, she may view the task as more difficult, have stronger expectations of failure, and perform less well. However, if an explanation external to the task is provided for her arousal, the arousal should not have a negative effect on her performance.

The results of her experiment supported her predictions. Although there were no significant differences among low-arousal subjects in the three groups, comparisons among high-arousal subjects showed that menstruating, high-symptom subjects performed significantly better on anagram and digit–symbol-substitution tests than did menstruating low-symptom and mid-cycle subjects. It was also found that highly aroused subjects who were suffering from menstrual symptoms showed greater tolerance for frustration, showed significantly less fear of the anticipated electric shock, and were significantly more willing to be shocked than were mid-cycle subjects. These results have some interesting implications for understanding the psychological correlates of the menstrual cycle. They suggest that if menstruating women explain task-produced arousal and frustration as symptoms of menstruation, they may actually perform better than equally aroused nonmenstruating women and about as well as women who are not distressed at all. They also imply that if a woman *does* experience hormonally based changes in mood and feelings but does not recognize them as related to her menstrual cycle, performance during menstruation may be impaired. Performance impairment might occur because her search for a credible explanation for her arousal could lead her to see the task as especially difficult, herself as incompetent, the atmosphere as hostile, and so on. Rodin concludes that the occurrence of menstrual and premenstrual symptoms in some women should not be used to support the notion that women are less competent than men. Rather, she says, "the regular occurrence of menstruation can serve as an attribution that enhances performance and tolerance for frustration among many women, given that they have correct expectations about how it affects them" (p. 353). Clearly, then, a woman's learned expectations seem to interact with her physiological changes in producing the psychological states that accompany various phases of her menstrual cycle.

Although Rodin's research suggests that it is important for the individual woman to develop correct expectations about the particular symptoms associated with her own menstrual cycle, a study by Koeske and Koeske (1975) indicates that there are general cultural expectations that may make this difficult by predisposing women to react to menstruation in a particular way. Their study used a questionnaire to measure subjects' reactions to a written excerpt from a hypothetical student's interview with a college counselor. They examined the effect of information about the student's menstrual cycle phase, mood, and environment on subjects' formation of attributions about the student. Results showed that subjects displayed a clear-cut attributional pattern in which they linked the negative moods of depression and irritability to the occurrence of the premenstrual phase of the student's cycle. It appears that our culture provides an emotional label of "premenstrual tension" to any negative moods that may occur at this point in a woman's cycle. The researchers note that the acceptance of this attribution pattern presents a number of dangers. It obscures the very wide individual variation among women in menstrual and premenstrual symptoms. It uses women's biology to explain negative, but not positive, moods and may result in the exaggeration of the likelihood or recall of negative moods. It might even have an adverse effect on women's self-esteem by allowing only internal attributions about negative emotional states and might make it less likely that a woman would take action to alter an external situation that was upsetting her.

The research discussed here does not provide a definitive answer to the question of what kinds of psychological symptoms are caused by the hormonal fluctuations of the menstrual cycle. It does indicate that the issue is a complex one and that no simple correlation between hormone level and observed behavior has been demonstrated. Although there are many reasons to believe that the hormonal changes during the menstrual cycle may affect mood and behavior, the research indicates that sociocultural factors also seem to play a major role in determining these effects. On the whole, however, the research has ignored two questions of considerable importance. The first involves individual differences among women. There are wide variations in the degree and kind of menstrual and premenstrual symptoms reported by individual women. An obvious line of research would be to examine the hormonal cycles and cultural backgrounds of individual women to see whether factors correlated with symptom severity can be identified. It might be fruitful to look especially carefully at the kinds of symptoms experienced by women whose menstrual periods are very irregular. Such women can never be sure when they are in the premenstrual phase, and hence their symptoms are less likely to reflect merely learned expectancies about certain phases of the cycle. Dufty (1975) has suggested that individual differences in diet may be an important variable. He contends, albeit on the basis of anecdotal research, that women without sugar in their diet do not experience menstrual distress.

It is important to have information about individual differences, because—in practical terms—it may be more important for a woman to know the magnitude of her particular cyclic mood shift than to know that she and other women experience a mood shift in a particular direction at some point during the menstrual cycle. In general, it is probable that many women do not experience cyclic mood shifts or that these shifts are so small as to be undetectable as part of a regular pattern.

The second question that deserves more attention involves the types of coping mechanisms used by women in order to continue to function normally under conditions of menstrual distress (Maccoby, 1972). Obviously, most women are forced to continue to perform in their jobs and homes despite any menstrual symptoms they may experience. It should be both practical and interesting to study the strategies used by the women who cope most successfully with recurring menstrual symptoms.

Male Cycles

We still have not resolved the question of whether the presence of the menstrual cycle in women has any automatic implications for the presence of sex differences in areas other than fertility. We have seen, however, that social attitudes toward menstruation complicate the interpretation of data bearing on this question and may actually *cause* phenomena that can be interpreted as sex differences. It is interesting, at this point, to look briefly at the issue of *male* cycles—an issue that has been virtually ignored by researchers. Is it possible that men experience physiological cycles that create as much variability and vulnerability as does the female menstrual cycle, but that have been ignored by the culture and hence not magnified in their effects by social expectations? Ramey's (1972) paper on male cycles represents an attempt to gather together the scarce information on this topic. She notes that both men and women experience daily rhythms on a number of physiological dimensions such as body temperature, blood sugar levels, and sleeping–waking and that there is some limited evidence that men show cyclic mood variations ranging in periodicity from four to nine weeks. The few studies that have been done suggest that there may be a great deal of variability among individual men in the cyclic patterns of their moods and physical symptoms, just as there are large individual differences among women. The beginnings of research in this direction acknowledge the possibility that the female menstrual cycle may be only one of a number of human biological cycles that have some impact on our moods and physical symptoms.

Ramey cites one study, carried out in Denmark, in which fluctuations of testosterone levels in male urine were followed (for an unspecified number of subjects) for sixteen years. Reportedly, a thirty-day rhythmic cycle of hormone levels was found. Another study cited by Ramey involved male managers and workers in a factory. The investigator in this case measured, not hormones, but mood and found an emotional cycle of four to six weeks in which low periods were characterized by apathy, indifference, and overreactions to minor problems and high periods by feelings of well-being, energy, lower body weight, and a decreased need for sleep. More recently a study by Doering, Brodie, Kraemer, Becker, and Hamburg (1974) measured both hormonal fluctuations *and* moods in twenty men for two months and found evidence supporting a link between the two. They reported a significant positive correlation between levels of self-perceived depression and concentration of plasma testosterone in the blood. Their data, however, showed only weak evidence for rhythmic changes in testosterone levels.

Much more research remains to be done in this area before the existence of long-term male hormonal cycles can be unequivocally demonstrated. However, it is interesting to speculate on the implications for our present understanding of sex differences of such a demonstration. There would no longer be any weight behind the assertion that because of body chemistry, men are inherently more stable emotionally than women. It might also prove to be the case, following Rodin's (1976) argument, that men—lacking a knowledge of their own cycles—are more incapacitated by them than are women by the menstrual cycle. On the other hand, knowledge of an upcoming "low point" in his emotional cycle might, through a kind of self-fulfilling negative expectation, cause a man to be more depressed or to perform more poorly during this time than he would have, had he not been given this information about his cycle. As researchers begin to attend to the issue of male cycles, we may begin to see whether the menstrual cycle in women is unique among human cycles in the magnitude of its effects and what effects on female and male mood and performance are produced by awareness of and learned expectations about cyclic physiological changes.

PREGNANCY AND CHILDBIRTH

When a woman becomes pregnant, her normal monthly hormonal cycle is interrupted, and she experiences a state in which both estrogen and progesterone levels are more or less constantly high. Hormonally, pregnancy is similar to the phase of the menstrual cycle that occurs just after ovulation and that has been characterized by some researchers (e.g., Bardwick, 1971) as one of generally positive moods. In our culture it is not unusual to hear pregnant women described as happy, content, fulfilled and glowing. Could it be that a sense of well-being associated with pregnancy is produced by the high hormone levels?

In order to answer this question, it is necessary to ascertain, first of all, that pregnancy is indeed a time filled with a sense of well-being. A recent review of the research shows that this notion is subject to considerable doubt (Sherman, 1971). Sherman points out that although some studies describe pregnancy as a time of unusual well-being, others show pregnant women as more depressed, dependent, and anxious than normal. It seems quite possible that the hormonal state may have the effect of predisposing the pregnant woman toward positive moods, at least during some stages of pregnancy. However, even if this tendency exists, the mixed evidence about the types of emotional states actually experienced by pregnant women suggests that it can be overwhelmed by other factors. These factors might include the fatigue and other physical discomforts associated with pregnancy, changes in body image, anxiety about new responsibilities, resentment of an unwanted child, and so on. Even the positive moods associated with pregnancy may not be totally explainable by hormone levels. Many women are pleased and excited at the prospect of having a child, and this could certainly explain a positive mood shift with pregnancy. Furthermore, in a culture that still emphasizes childbearing as the route to fulfillment for women, women are actually socialized to "glow" when they are pregnant, and pregnant women sometimes comment that they feel guilty or inadequate if they display negative emotions.

Besides being a biological state, pregnancy is also part of a social role. Taylor and Langer (1977) recently studied the social stimulus value of pregnancy to see whether pregnant women elicited any special pattern of behavioral response during brief encounters with others. They found that people, particularly men, responded to the pregnant woman with avoidance and staring. Their research suggested to them that the male response was due largely to the fact that the pregnant woman was a novel visual stimulus, whereas the female response was linked to social norms that are disapproving of active or assertive behavior by pregnant women. The authors note that in our society, the pregnant woman is often expected to withdraw from previous social and job-related activities. The result of this societal expectation is that pregnant women are seen in public more rarely than their numbers would predict. Thus, when a pregnant woman does appear in public, she is likely to be responded to with stares, avoidance, and perhaps disapproval. If she notices this response, the woman may become uncomfortable and venture out with decreasing frequency, thus perpetuating the vicious circle. On the basis of their research, the authors suggest that an unacknowledged social rejection of the pregnant woman exists in our culture. If this is indeed the case, the pregnant woman is receiving a double message. On one hand, her role as mother-to-be is being extolled as the glorious fulfillment of her womanhood. On the other hand, she is being socially stigmatized because of her unusual appearance and "delicate" condition. Perhaps it is little wonder that researchers have been unable to sort out the social from the physiological determinants of the psychological experience of pregnancy, when the social ones alone appear to be so complex.

In trying to determine the link between physiological changes and emotion, we should not lose sight of the fact that causality can work in both directions. An example, relevant to this discussion, of an instance where emotional changes apparently have physiological consequences is the case of pseudocyesis or pseudopregnancy. The physiological symptoms that characterize pseudocyesis are much the same as those that characterize pregnancy: menstrual disturbance, abdominal enlargement, swelling and tenderness of the breasts, softening of the cervix, enlargement of the uterus, nausea and vomiting, and weight gain. Pseudocyesis patients have even reported that they can feel fetal movements. According to a recent review of the literature (Barglow & Brown, 1972), the symptoms of pseudocyesis, although not common, are not extremely rare, appear most frequently in women who are sterile, and can appear occasionally even in men. Key causal factors have been thought to be a fear of, or wish for, pregnancy.

Another instance in which emotions appear to lead to the physiological reactions of pregnancy, rather than vice versa, is the "couvade syndrome" (Trethowan, 1972) in which expectant fathers suffer from physical symptoms during their wives' pregnancy or labor. These symptoms are often but not always similar to those experienced by the pregnant woman and include nausea and vomiting, alterations of appetite, toothache, abdominal pain, swelling, and spurious labor pains. These seem to be caused by the father's high anxiety about his wife's pregnancy. Trethowan estimates that this syndrome occurs in about one of four or five expectant fathers and claims that the father is usually not aware of a possible connection between his symptoms and his wife's pregnancy.

When we take pseudocyesis and the couvade syndrome into consideration, we begin to realize the complexity of the interaction that must occur between hormones and social–emotional factors in the production of physical symptoms. Obviously, the current state of the research on this issue does not allow us to say unequivocally which or what percentage of the various physical and emotional symptoms of pregnancy are hormonally based. The fact that nonpregnant women, and even men, sometimes experience symptoms that simulate those of pregnancy lends weight to the notion that our culture teaches us how a pregnant woman is expected to feel and act. If we all acquire this information through a process of social learning, then those of us who find ourselves pregnant may develop the symptoms we (and others) expect ourselves to develop, and it is difficult to determine the extent to which our expectations and/or hormones are responsible for this development.

The issue of postpartum depression is similarly complex. Research suggests that over half of the women who bear children experience considerable emotional upset in the weeks immediately following childbirth (Boston Women's Health Collective, 1971). Medical researchers have theorized that hormonal imbalance combined with the sheer bodily shock of labor may be the cause and/or that the depression is a reaction to the social stress surrounding an event of this magnitude. For example, Hamburg, Moos, and Yalom (1968) report that during labor a woman's progesterone level drops so rapidly as to represent the greatest change in concentration of this hormone she experiences in her lifetime, compressed into a few hours. They suggest that this decrease may be an important factor in postpartum emotional disturbance. Other researchers have investigated the psychological and cultural–environmental correlates of postpartum depression; and their results have suggested that conflict or feelings of inadequacy surrounding the mother role (Melges, 1968); environmental factors that place the burden of responsibility for child care heavily on the new mother (e.g., no relative available for help with baby care); and past experiences of failure, fear, and loss (Gordon, Kapostins, & Gordon, 1965) are all nonbiological factors that may be important in predisposing a woman to postpartum depression. In addition, there are reports of depression in new fathers (Liebenberg, 1967) and in adoptive mothers (Melges, 1968), suggesting that the hormonal changes occurring during labor are not necessary to precipitate these feelings. In general, then, in pregnancy and childbirth as in the menstrual cycle, the relationships that may exist between hormone levels on one hand and feelings and behavior on the other are complicated by the presence of many social and environmental factors, some of which are probably more important determinants of emotions and behavior than are hormone levels.

THE CHANGE OF LIFE

Usually, between the ages of forty-five and fifty-five, women's ovaries cease to function, so that estrogen and progesterone are no longer produced, the breasts and genital tissues atrophy, and the menstrual period is discontinued. The decline of the ovaries is called the *climacteric,* and the cessation of menstruation is known as the *menopause.* Estrogen production in postmenopausal women is continually as low or lower than in the last days of the menstrual period (Sherman, 1971).

Many women going through the climacteric experience physical symptoms, such as hot flashes and headaches, and emotional reactions, such as depression and irritability. The loss of estrogen may be implicated in both the physical and emotional changes, but the mechanism is unclear. The most impressive evidence for the theory that it is a lack of estrogen that produces menopausal symptoms comes from studies of estrogen-replacement therapy (e.g., Wilson, 1966). In general, these studies suggest that providing menopausal women with supplementary estrogen significantly reduces menopausal symptoms. However, in many cases, the studies did not provide adequate control groups.

Although there is little doubt that hormonal changes play a role in the emotional changes that often accompany menopause, it must also be remembered that this change of life usually represents a time of severe stress for women in a sociocultural, as well as physiological, sense. A woman at this stage is losing her ability to bear children—an ability that our culture has tried to define as crucial to her feminine role. At the same time, her children are growing up and moving away and are no longer dependent on her. Therefore, if she has devoted most of her time to motherhood, she is losing a role that has been central in terms of defining her worth and organizing her time. She is also conscious of being less attractive physically in the popular sense and may feel that this jeopardizes her relationship with her husband and/or other men. Given the presence of these types of life changes, it would not be surprising to see a woman become depressed and irritable even if no hormonal changes were present. Pauline Bart's (1971) study of depression in middle-aged women indicated that among her subjects, depression was strongly related to degree of role loss at menopausal age. Also, her investigation of the phenomenon from a cross-cultural perspective suggests that in cultures where a woman is still gaining rather than losing status as she ages, negative emotional reactions at menopause are rare. These findings seem to indicate once more that cultural–environmental factors can strongly modify the person's reaction to physiological changes.

In the male case, there is no sudden change in hormonal level at a particular age. Rather, a man's level of testosterone production decreases very gradually from the age of about thirty onward. However, many men seem to experience a psychological crisis at middle age.

Gutmann (1972) refers to this crisis as a "loss of the future." He claims that at about the age of fifty, many achievement-oriented men begin to feel that they are not going to become any more successful or move any closer to their goals. Gutmann's interviews with men in this age group in several different cultures offer some support for this concept. His research suggests that a man may greet the realization that he cannot improve his future either with a relieved sense of "letting go" and a moving out of the "rat race" or with an inner crisis in which he struggles with the fact that he has not achieved his goals to his own satisfaction. Other research (Braginsky & Braginsky, 1975) suggests that successful, middle-aged men who find themselves suddenly out of work experience depression and dramatically lowered feelings of self-worth. Thus, it seems clear that either sex can experience negative emotional reactions to the important changes in role that occur in later life. Women, however, have been taught to expect these changes and to label them as menopausal. These expectations probably contribute to the strength of the symptoms they experience. Although these symptoms are no doubt somewhat related to the physical aspects of aging, it seems reasonable to suggest that both women and men react negatively when they find themselves no longer able to fulfill the roles that society has defined as central for them: child rearing for women and successful career achievement for men.

SUMMARY

We have seen that although women show cyclic fluctuations of sex hormone levels and men do not, it is nevertheless not the case that male physiology is completely stable. Research seems to indicate that the menstrual cycle and other biological cycles are related to mood and behavior, but it also provides strong evidence that any such physiology–psychology relationships can be and are modified dramatically by factors in the person's environment. Furthermore, although it has been pointed out that women are subject to the special states of pregnancy and menopause that involve both large hormonal changes and recognized sets of physical and emotional symptoms, men are not unaffected by the drastic life changes that go along with having a child and losing an important role. Thus, it seems that even with regard to the particular experiences of pregnancy and menopause, causality of symptoms cannot be attributed simply to hormonal changes but must be considered a blend of biological and social factors. In general, research on these issues seems to have been guided by the assumption that they are "women's problems" and has focused on trying to understand them by reference to hormone levels. Accordingly, research on male reactions to these events has been scanty. Much more research on both women and men is needed before we will be able to talk with any degree of certainty about the relative contributions of hormones and various social factors to the symptoms associated with menstruation, pregnancy, and menopause.

5 Neena L. Chappell

THE
SOCIAL PROCESS
OF LEARNING
SEX ROLES:
A Sociological Viewpoint

The preceding chapters have suggested the importance of sociocultural factors for the development and maintenance of sex differences. Data such as the reactions of women to their menstrual cycles suggest that even in areas of study that could be termed "physiological," sociocultural influences are often working. This chapter provides a theoretical framework within which the student can view the relevance of socialization for sex roles. It presents a social psychological perspective arguing for the greater importance of sociocultural factors over biological factors for determining individual attitudes and behaviors, and indeed for determining one's very definition of reality. Although social psychology is a perspective adopted by both psychologists and sociologists, this chapter presents a sociologist's view.

During the first part of this century, sociology was establishing itself as a separate discipline in an academic milieu that traced social experience to elementary human motives, variously referred to as social forces, interests, and instincts. However, this explanation fell into disfavor, because it lacked scientific precision in a time when science was becoming more and more revered; it was grounded in a particularistic biological determinism that conflicted with basic

sociological assumptions about the importance of the social environment for human nature; and no factual basis existed to establish the
reality and the influence of instincts (Hinkle & Hinkle, 1954). At this
time, Mead developed his symbolic interactionism, arguing that the
development of personality takes place within social groups through
social interaction and the use of language. He endeavored to show
that mind and self are social emergents, thereby incorporating the
relevancy of social groups for individual personality within a
framework acceptable to American individualists (Morris, 1962; Reck,
1964).*

The remainder of this chapter elaborates the general theory of
symbolic interaction (Mead, 1934, 1956, 1964), applying it specifically
to sex roles. The presentation begins by establishing the "fact" of the
social environment and argues for its importance. This section is
devoted primarily to an exposition of the theoretical background
necessary for understanding sex roles from a symbolic interaction
perspective. The next section applies this theoretical framework to a
discussion of childhood and adult socialization into sex roles. Institutions and the larger societal influence are then discussed.

Throughout this chapter it is suggested that at least three factors
contribute to the current structure of sex roles in North American
society: sex-role differentiation at the micro-sociological level (i.e., the
individual interactional level), a reinforcement of this same sex-role
differentiation at the macro-sociological level (i.e., the institutional or
larger societal level), and the individual's tendency to search for and
find continuity that tends to select and interpret consistency in sex-
role behavior. These three factors are discussed in detail in the following pages.

THE SOCIAL ENVIRONMENT

Symbolic interaction begins with the fact that the social process temporally precedes the individual. Every individual is born into a social
environment, which exists prior to the individual and is the context

*Symbolic interaction has since been developed and interpreted by different
schools of thought, not all of which agree with one another. As it is discussed here, it is
derived from the Chicago school (Blumer, 1972; Meltzer & Petras, 1972; Vaughan &
Reynolds, 1968).

within which the individual develops. It is through interaction with this social environment that the biological organism becomes extensively modified.

It is acknowledged that the infant at birth possesses biological impulses, instincts, and emotions. However, these "givens" are considered subject to modification and channeling through interaction with others (Cooley, 1972). From the beginning, the infant is able to interact with others, because it possesses a cooperative attitude. This attitude is a "well-defined tendency" to act under the stimulation of another individual of the same species. That is to say, the human infant is essentially social in character (Homans, 1950) or is essentially a role-taking animal (Morris, 1962). This social nature of the biological infant is assumed insofar as it is obvious that infants do in fact respond to and interact with other people.

Initially, the infant interacts in the form of a conversation of gestures. In this process, one's movements call out a response in another, this response serves as a stimulus for the first and calls out a second response, and so forth (i.e., stimulus–response–stimulus. . . .). Responses that lie inside such a conversation of gestures have meaning. The meaning of a child's crying is that it wants its discomfort removed (perhaps a diaper changed). Any responses that call forth additional responses are therefore meaningful. The infant acts meaningfully. For example, the infant tenses its body and the parent burps the child. The parent holds up a finger and the infant clutches it.

Although the infant acts meaningfully from the start, it is not yet conscious of meaning, because there is nothing in the mechanism of the act that brings this relation to consciousness. At this point the infant experiences its body, its feelings, and its sensations but does not distinguish them from the environment (witness the child who pulls its own hair, cries because it hurts, but continues to pull it). The significance of this characterization of the infant according to Meadian theory is that the infant does not yet have a self. Because it does not have a self, it is initially no different from other lower animal forms. It is not born distinctively human.

Only with the development of self and a mind does the organism gain human status. This development takes place within the social process through the complex development of a number of contributing factors. The formation of images is particularly important in this process. As past experiences accumulate, gestures become identified with the content of the child's emotions, feelings, and attitudes. Images arise of the response that one's gesture will bring out in the other. For example, the child soon associates the parent's gesture of showing the bottle with the meaning that food is forthcoming. The child sees an image of the meaning of the bottle. When images form, the child is said to have consciousness of meaning.

Consciousness of meaning signals the rise of significant symbols in place of mere substitute stimuli. Stimuli now symbolize different things. The bottle symbolizes food, satisfaction from hunger, perhaps even affection. A loud, sharp voice symbolizes "no." The crib symbolizes sleep. The blanket on the floor symbolizes play.

Significant symbols* implicitly arouse in the individual making the gesture the same response that they explicitly arouse (or are supposed to arouse) in the other individual to whom they are addressed. In other words, the gesture has the same meaning for the different individuals involved. When the parent takes coats out of the closet, it has the same meaning for parent and child: going outside. When the child brings a pencil to the parent, it has the same meaning for both individuals: to draw on a piece of paper.

A significant symbol of particular importance in the development of the biological organism is language. Language is the *vocal* gesture that has become a significant symbol. Words have meanings, and these meanings are shared. "No" has the same meaning for parent and child. The critical importance of language lies in the fact that the stimulus can react upon the speaking individual as it reacts upon the person addressed. Language also makes it possible to pick out responses, to summarize them, and to isolate them.

The rise of significant symbols, and with them consciousness of meaning, signals the rise of mind. Consciousness of meaning is the essence of mind. Through mind, or intelligence, the individual can consciously adjust her/himself to the social process and modify the resultant of that process in any given social act. The child hears the parent's angry tone, knows that it means a spanking, and so modifies the resultant of that process by running and hiding. It is through one's mind or thought processes that experiences are interpreted. The individual, therefore, is active as well as passive, an actor as well as a reactor. The individual does not simply respond to the social environment but interacts with and affects that environment. While

---

*The phrase "significant symbol," adopted from Mead, has now become part of sociological terminology.

the individual develops within, learns the meaning of things from, and is shaped by the social environment within which s/he lives, s/he nevertheless is more than a passive receptacle of this environment. Through the use of mind, s/he can respond to, interact with, and affect that environment.

In the development of the child, three stages represent the essential steps in attaining self-consciousness: imitation, play, and game. In the imitation stage, which precedes the other two, the child imitates or mimics those around it. In the play stage, s/he acts the teacher, the pirate, the mother, the firefighter, and then acquires the roles of society. In this stage, s/he is taking the role of the other; continually exciting in her/himself the responses of her/his own social acts. In this way, the child learns the organization of particular individual attitudes. In other words, the child learns roles by playing them.

In the game stage, the child must assume the various roles of all the participants in the game and govern its actions accordingly. The child embeds the organized reactions of others in her/his own playing of different positions. This organized attitude becomes the child's "generalized other": the crystallization of all attitudes from particular others into a single attitude or standpoint. The organization of the self is this organization of attitudes toward the social environment. It is always derived, of course, from the standpoint of the environment.

In the game stage, the child no longer either imitates behavior (without consciousness of meaning) or merely plays at being an incumbent of a single role (with consciousness of meaning). Rather, the child must play the role in relation to other roles. For example, in baseball the pitcher cannot simply "play at being a pitcher" but must take the roles of the other positions into account. The child who plays mother with friends while the other playmates assume the positions of "child," "father," and "neighbor" now adjusts her/his behavior to that of the incumbents of these other positions. During the game stage, the child learns to interact within the family unit as one member whose behavior is integrated with that of the other members of the family.

The organization of the self, then, is an organization of attitudes and experiences derived from the child's interactions with others. It is "molded" by the social environment to the extent that these attitudes come from others in the social environment. However, each individual is unique, because the totality of experiences is different for each individual and is organized into a whole differently for each individual. The core and primary nature of the self is thus cognitive.

Although the self includes the emotional and affective, these features are not considered its essential characteristics.

Although it has become commonplace in sociology to assume that shared values and norms account for cooperation and integration among individuals, within this Meadian view of the self, values and norms are not accorded such a prominent place. Rather, joint action and cooperation are accounted for in terms of the capacity of each individual to take the role of the other. Insofar as two or more individuals interacting with one another can share the other's perspective and define their differences as irrelevant for the task before them, a single perspective is organized for the cooperative activity at hand (Blumer, 1970). Thus, individuals with different values and norms can and do cooperate with one another. I can cooperate with or engage in joint action with another for building a house, even though we have different values on marriage. Similarly, I can cooperate with another in teaching a course on socialization, even though we hold different views of and different values on the socialization process. What is important is that we can each take the role of the other and share in a perspective while considering differences between us as irrelevant for the purpose at hand. Children organizing a game may argue because each wants to play the same position, but in order to proceed with the game, they may eventually agree to take turns playing the desired position.

The symbolic interactionist perspective, then, argues that individuals develop through interaction with others from birth and throughout their lives. Furthermore, this interaction is symbolic and bestows meaning on reality for each individual. Infants and children become what they integrate and organize from their interaction with others. The reality that they perceive and understand is what they absorb through living in a social environment. Action or behavior is constructed by interpreting the situation. From this standpoint, the organization of society is the framework within which social action takes place and is not the determinant of that action. Individual action is not a release; it is a construction by the individual, who notes and interprets features of the situations in which s/he is a participant.

This section has stated some of the arguments within symbolic interaction, as derived from Mead, establishing the relevance of social interaction for individual development. According to this perspective, interaction with others is not only a fact but also crucial for the development of the biological organism into a *human* being who has consciousness of meaning, can interpret the world, and has intelligence or thought processes. This human being, though unique from others, learns the meaning of things from interaction within this social environment. This elaboration of symbolic interaction, which emphasizes interaction between individuals in relatively small groups, is referred to as micro-sociology. The next section discusses this theory of socialization as it applies specifically to sex roles. A discussion of sex roles at the societal level, or within macro-sociology, appears later.

CHILDHOOD AND ADULTHOOD SOCIALIZATION: THE CASE OF SEX ROLES

During childhood, the biological organism develops a mind and a self. That organism becomes distinctively human. S/he develops through symbolic interaction with others. The meaning of things, including sex-role socialization, starts being learned from birth. A newborn baby is classified immediately by sex and treated accordingly. Oakley (1972) informs us that in most maternity hospitals, sex-typed comments on the behavior and appearance of newborns are aired within a few moments of birth. Supporting this contention, she reports studies revealing differential parental expectations for male and female children. Parents expect relatively outward-directed and aggressive behavior for males ("boys will be boys") and relatively passive and inward-directed behavior for females ("girls don't do that"). It is not surprising then, to find personality differences among children. Five-year-olds view the male as more competent, more aggressive, more fear arousing, and less nurturant than the female. Preferences in toys reflect the awareness children have of sex-appropriate behavior. Boys choose toys symbolizing physical and mechanical activity and the world outside the home, whereas girls choose toys symbolizing nurturance and aesthetic adornment (Ambert, 1976; Oakley, 1972).

Given the current structure of North American society–with its small nuclear family—the parents, and in particular the mother, assume particular importance during the early years of the child's life. Chronologically, sex-role socialization begins with the family in both explicit (admonitions, teachings, examples) and implicit ways (subtle attitudes, gestures, and value-laden language). Differential clothing, punishment, toys, and activities as well as the interaction between children and parents and the role models provided by each parent and older siblings all contribute to sex-role socialization within the family (Ambert, 1976; Goffman, 1977). Whereas mothers often tell their sons that they will work "like daddy" when they grow up, they often tell their daughters they will stay at home and be mothers. The importance of role modeling for children has been reported in more than one study: daughters of employed mothers are more likely than daughters of household mothers to see a career as natural for women and to voice desires of being employed later on themselves. Both male and female students stereotype women less when their mothers have been employed than when their mothers have not (Ambert, 1976; Veevers, 1973).

The sex-typed instructions of parents and the effects of maternal employment point to a distinction between two different types of socialization: *explicit* or directive "teaching," and a more subtle, *implicit* learning process of listening, watching, and "being in" a situation. It is being suggested here that within a symbolic interactionist perspective, the latter is a more effective forum for learning. This has been recognized in some of the sex-role literature to date. Specifically, it has been noted that boys experience greater difficulty learning the male sex role than girls experience learning the female sex role because of the greater absence of the father from the home. Girls learn the role of mother through their presence at home with the mother for much of their time. Boys, on the other hand, tend to learn by being taught *not* to act like those they see most often. Since in our society fathers usually work outside the home for a large proportion of their sons' waking hours, boys learn the male sex role by learning not to be like girls and women (Ambert, 1976; David & Brannon, 1976).

Since much learning takes place through association with others in specific roles, directive teaching and in particular verbalization about the appropriateness of different behavior within any given role can be expected to elicit little change in actual role behavior unless such behavior on the part of the role model also changes. In other words, talking about new roles for boys and girls, women and men, is not likely to change the actual behavior of people unless we start behaving differently. This could be a contributing factor to the apparent lack of change currently evidenced in young women today, despite the media coverage given to various women's groups and the recent proliferation of words (both oral and written) about the new roles for women in our society. If young girls are raised primarily by their mothers within traditionally female roles, it is unlikely that talk about new roles for women will be reflected in these children's behaviors. Similarly, it can be suggested that boys are no more likely to enact new roles for themselves, and affect those for girls, if those with whom they associate most often fulfill traditional sex-role models—mothers being the primary homemakers and fathers remaining primarily within the breadwinner role.

Although the educational system is discussed in greater detail in the next section, it is worthy of mention at this point that most of the sex-role socialization begun in the family is reinforced in the school system. Most grade-school teachers are women; textbooks still tend to portray women as wives, mothers, nurses, teachers, or secretaries and men in a greater variety of functions but less often as husbands or fathers. Traditionally, girls are taught sewing, cooking, and typing, whereas boys are taught car repair, woodwork, and welding. In universities, higher up the education ladder where greater prestige and work autonomy are accorded, most of the teachers are male, except in home economics, nursing, and other traditionally female occupations (Ambert, 1976, Vickers, 1976).

Perhaps the strongest support for the influence of the social environment on sex differences comes from cross-cultural studies. Although our culture teaches boys to be aggressive and active and girls to be passive and polite, this is not true of all cultures. Oakley (1972) presents a number of contrary examples. Among the people of Bamenda, women do all the agricultural work. They carry the heavy loads, apparently because they have stronger foreheads than men. (A similar situation was found by Mead [1935] among the Arapesh, who gave the same reason for it.) A researcher among the Bamenda heard a group of men discussing a wifeless neighbor: "He works hard, indeed he works almost as hard as a woman" (cited in Oakley, 1972, p. 55).

Another example of childhood socialization that differs from our own comes from the area of sexuality. In our culture young and adolescent girls are not expected to engage in overt sexual activity, although it is more permissible for boys to do so. Biologically, this has been explained in terms of women's slower sexual arousal and different rate of sexual maturation and men's spontaneous sexuality.

Sociologically, it has been explained in terms of parents' differential expectations of appropriate behavior for boys and girls.

The Arapesh culture, however, devalues sexuality and encourages the development of tenderness and parental responsibility in both females and males. The adolescent girl is not treated as needing protection from male exploitation, and menstruation is not a signal of fear. Rather than regarding the female as the vessel for male satisfaction, she is regarded as an individual whose desirability as a spouse is related to the culture's primary work of child rearing. The sexual feeling between husband and wife is not considered fundamentally different from other feelings or affections that tie siblings or parents and children together. In this culture, adolescence is not a period of fervent mating choice. By the age of nine or ten, girls are already betrothed, and the adolescent male's task is to prepare his own betrothed for the responsibilities of parenthood, a task that both will share. Further, it is interesting to note that although spontaneous sexuality is denied to both sexes, when exceptions happen, it is expected to occur in women rather than in men. Sons are warned by their parents, more than are daughters, against getting into situations in which someone can make love to them (Mead, 1935).

Malinowski's study of the Trobriand Islanders, perhaps a more striking example, is the last illustration to be noted here (1932). Among the Trobrianders, there is no period of childhood during which sexual interests and activities are prohibited. Small children play sexual games together (genital manipulation and oral–genital stimulation). By the age of four or five, children are mimicking intercourse. Girls six to eight have intercourse with penetration, boys by the age of ten or twelve. These activities continue through childhood. At adolescence they become more serious, at which time the women are much more assertive and vigorous in their sexual drive. The conventional invitation of female to male is erotic scratching, which draws blood. The positions during intercourse exclude the dorsal–ventral position (man on top of woman), because the woman is hampered by the weight of the man and cannot be sufficiently active.

These cross-cultural examples illustrate that our own sex roles are not universal. Rather, they are culturally specific. Symbolic interaction, however, claims that individuals do more than simply learn appropriate behavior. It claims that reality itself is defined culturally.

Stuttering serves as a good example of this symbolic interactionist perspective. Boy stutterers outnumber girl stutterers by 5 to 1 (Warme, 1977). Traditionally, it has been assumed that boys are not as fluent as girls and that this unalterable developmental "fact" accounts for the sex difference among stutterers. With this model in mind, let us examine some research on sex differences in stuttering.

Johnson (1961, 1973) studied stutterers through interviews with 300 parents and the tape-recorded speech of 150 matched pairs of stutterers (children whose parents brought them to a clinic specifically because they thought their children had this problem) and a control group of normals. The pairs were matched for age, sex, and socioeconomic status of the family. Johnson found that few parents reported stuttering before the age of two and a half years. The average age was between three and three and a half years. This age range was the time when parents (and in particular the mother) considered their child to have "learned to talk." Before this time, the child was defined as still learning, so that errors in her/his speech patterns were permitted.

Johnson found great overlap between the fluency of stutterers and nonstutterers. No child in either group was perfectly fluent, and some children whose parents regarded them as stutterers actually spoke more fluently than some of the children defined as nonstutterers. Furthermore, there was no significant difference in fluency between boys and girls. In both groups the boys and girls were about equally fluent or disfluent. Some girls spoke more fluently than some boys, but substantial numbers of boys spoke more fluently than a large proportion of girls. Johnson's research supported neither the physiological nor the developmental arguments traditionally assumed to account for sex differences in stuttering.

Johnson explains this sex difference in terms of the social environment, suggesting that we follow different policies and practices in raising boys and in raising girls. Parents may judge the early speech of their girls differently from the way they judge the early speech of their boys. Since the problem of stuttering begins when the child's speech is felt, usually by the mother, to be less smooth or fluent than it should be, it is possible that mothers are more demanding, consciously or otherwise, of their boys than of their girls. Furthermore, the mother may not be sure at first of whether or not her child is stuttering. Having labeled her child a stutterer, however, this crystallizes her feeling and focuses her attention on the hesitations in the speech of the child. The more she listens to her child, the more convinced she becomes that he is indeed a stutterer and that he has a problem.

The parent's feelings are at the same time transmitted to the child. He slowly comes to doubt that he can in fact get the words out soon enough and keep them coming smoothly one after the other. He learns to feel uncomfortable about this. Gradually, over several months, this doubt and lack of ease affects his spontaneity in speaking, and he feels less like talking at all. After a while he no longer talks as much as he used to and eventually becomes hesitant to try to say some things to some people. He holds back so much that he has to force himself, a situation that causes him to speak with effort or strain. To exert this effort, he tenses up the muscles of his lips or tongue or throat. When he does this, he talks more hesitantly, less smoothly, and with more difficulty. While this is happening to the child, the parents and relatives and neighbors worry, and the child senses their concern. The child feels even more uneasy and more hesitant, and those around him worry more. It becomes a vicious circle or what Johnson calls the "sad-go-round."

Johnson's research indicates the importance of a socially determined physiological reaction: the tensing of muscles. It also suggests the overriding importance of culturally derived reality. This last point can be emphasized by imagining a different reality where stutterers were considered gifted prophets from the gods. They would be revered and rewarded for speaking differently. The consequences for their self-images, their confidence, and their interaction with others would doubtless be different from what they currently experience.

The preceding has emphasized the importance of culturally defined meaning, and reality itself, through cross-cultural examples and through the example of stuttering within our own culture. An elaboration of specific agents of childhood socialization (such as the family, school, peer groups, and the media) has not been dealt with at length here, since it has been reported by others (including: Ball, 1967; LaLonde, 1975; Lansky, 1967; Levy, 1975; Lewis, 1972; Weisstein, 1970).

Meanings, then, are socially defined from the start. However, it will be recalled that as the child develops a mind and intelligence, meanings also become interpreted and negotiated. The individual is not simply a passive receptacle but rather acts, initiates, and influences the social environment as that environment affects the individual. This process assures continual change in individuals beyond childhood and throughout their adult years. Change is considered basic to the nature of humans. We are always changing, during both childhood and adulthood. The relevance of this conceptualization of humans as dynamic and constantly changing, however, slowly, gradually, and subtly, is that is argues against the formation of the core or basic personality during childhood. That is to say, this perspective argues that although aspects of sex-role differentiation are established during childhood, they need not therefore remain constant during adulthood. Within symbolic interaction, childhood socialization assumes relatively minor importance during adulthood, not only because we are always changing, but also because we live our reality in the present. This requires some elaboration.

We live in the present, not the past or the future. However, this present is not a piece of chronological time; it is not composed of the past five minutes to the next five minutes, or the last hour to the next hour. Rather, the present consists of socially defined time centering around what Mead calls the *emergent event*. The emergent event is that which is important and puts boundaries on our present. For example, the present for one future bride might include from the time preparations begin for the wedding until after the ceremony is over, the guests have gone, and the married couple are alone. For another, it might consist of from the time preparations begin for the wedding until after the honeymoon is over. For still another, it might consist of only the actual ceremony, from the time the guests start to arrive until after they leave. For the student during exams, the present may consist of the few minutes or hours prior to writing an exam to the time when the actual writing is over.

This socially defined event that locates the present consists of what is disappearing and what is emerging; it consists of both the processes that have led up to it and to what it is leading up to. In other words, we are immediately considering something, but we are already going on to something else. We are continually interpreting our present by assessing our relevant past and by considering what is represented by possible future conduct. For example, as an individual prepares for a date, the events that led up to it are part of that present, and the expectations of the date that is to occur in the future affect that preparation. Past dates can also influence the current preparation and expectation.

Although life is lived in the present, the past—and, therefore, one's childhood socialization experiences—is important to the extent that it has temporally preceded the present. However, the main importance of the past is that we construct our past from the standpoint of the present. We do not construct the present from the standpoint of the past. Furthermore, we reconstruct our past continually as our standpoint changes in the present. How many women have rejected the traditional role of woman and adopted a feminist perspective? In doing so, they reinterpret past experiences. For example, teachings from their parents that used to be accepted as "the way things are done" and explanations of "woman's place" now become examples of an oppressive upbringing. How many men have rejected man's right to superiority and adopted a life-style in which people are judged independent of their sex? In this case, past socialization that they had once accepted as "correct" now becomes reinterpreted as the views of another generation, but now times have changed. So parents who believed in the traditions of femininity and raised their daughter to be a traditional woman may, if she becomes a lawyer, reinterpret her childhood with examples of her intelligence and articulation. Similarly, they may now believe that a woman should have the same right as a man to work outside the home.

We live in the present, then, but the past can nevertheless influence that present as can the future. The past can be used to help interpret the present through memory, association, and generalization. The future provides direction and helps determine our courses of action. How many of us take courses that we do not enjoy because we anticipate their later usefulness for a particular career? Traditionally, women were not as concerned as men about continuing their education, anticipating marriage in which they would be supported by their husbands. Today's high divorce rates, rising life expectancies, and increasing labor force participation rates for women may change young women's preparations for their future.

If the individual lives in the present and is always undergoing change, it may be asked why the sex roles learned in childhood are currently perpetuated in adulthood. The answer is twofold, referring to both the types of situations likely to lead to change in adulthood and the individual's search for continuity.

Within Meadian theory, only a portion of the self is changed at a time, and it is that part that is involved in problematic situations. In unproblematic situations, we draw on our past through generalization and through association. Certain stimuli call out certain responses, and inhibitions are built up through experience, so that certain responses tend not to be called out. However, the mind enables self-conscious selection and purposive conduct. When we self-consciously direct our attention, that to which attention is not directed comes in memory images as the familiar and is assumed insofar as it is valid. This unquestioned portion comes from the past unchanged. Specifically, if sex-role prescriptions and expectations in adulthood are consistent with those experienced in childhood, it is unlikely that behavior will change from the latter to the former. Only when that role or parts of it become problematic will it become questioned and open to change. For example, a girl who is raised to be a traditional wife, who finishes high school and goes to university, who then meets and marries a man who expects and reinforces the traditional wife role, is unlikely to question that role. Similarly, a boy who is raised to be a traditional husband, who marries a woman who expects and reinforces that role, is unlikely to change his behavior within that role. However, a boy who is raised to be a traditional husband but who marries a successful career woman unwilling to accept the traditional role of housewife is likely to find himself in a problematic situation that will lead him to question expected behavior within the role and that will consequently lead to change.

It can be suggested that sex-role behavior is similar in adulthood to that in childhood and that this contributes to its perpetuation beyond our early years. This suggestion is explored further in the next section on institutions. Many of the explanations of the continuity of sex roles involve the idea that the very structure of society reinforces the current sex role differentiation. Before discussing this, however, the individual's tendency to seek continuity is discussed.

Within Meadian theory, actual continuity becomes irrelevant and is replaced by the individual's tendency to search for and construct continuity from the past and into the future. As Gerth and Mills (1953) note, the influence of the past can be seen here as due to the simple fact that the adult develops temporally after childhood (see also Lindesmith & Strauss, 1968). This is no less true of sex roles than of other areas of our lives. Within our sex roles, we seek and find a continuity within our ever-changing environments and selves. We construct sex-role continuity throughout our lives, irrespective of the changing nature of our experiences (Becker & Strauss, 1956). The relevance of this point is that we tend to see continuity and consistency from childhood to adulthood, although we may in fact have changed greatly. The working woman who never trained for an occupation and never thought she would work finds that at age thirty-five she needs money to help maintain the household. Others may see various changes in her behavior (she is more organized, more efficient with the housework, talks extensively about topics she never used to talk about, is less dependent on her husband for certain tasks), but she may describe herself as "the same person I've always been." The husband whose friends tell him he has been "tamed" by his wife protests, "No, I'm still the same, I just have responsibilities now."

To summarize, this section has discussed sex roles within a symbolic interactionist perspective. Unlike many other writings, this discussion has not centered on a detailed account of specific agents of socialization within our society. These useful and informative works have provided us with an elaboration of one of the basic premises of symbolic interaction—that meanings are culturally defined and learned. In a different vein, this discussion has identified additional premises of symbolic interaction to illustrate their relevance for the study of sex roles. It began with the importance of interaction and illustrated that the learning of sex roles starts at birth. Two types of socialization or learning processes were distinguished: directive teaching, in particular verbalization; and a more subtle process of learning through association or living in the situation. The latter was suggested as a more effective method of socialization. Cross-cultural examples were used to underline the fact that both the attitudinal and overt behavioral components of sex roles are culturally defined. Stuttering was used as an example of the profound and differential consequences that cultural definitions have for males and females.

In addition to positing culturally defined meanings, symbolic interaction also argues that individuals develop the capacity to interpret and negotiate meanings, to direct attention and to act, to affect the social environment as that environment affects them. The significance of this formulation for sex roles lies in the fact that this perspective argues against simply learning appropriate sex roles in childhood that are enacted during adulthood. Rather, change is an inherent characteristic of both persons and social environments. In addition, although we draw on our past to help interpret the present, although we build up inhibitions from past experiences and generalize from the past and associate the old with the new, the past does not have a deterministic influence on the present. Instead, we live from the perspective of the present and continually reinterpret our pasts in light of the present. That is to say, from a symbolic interactionist perspective, it is insufficient to account for the continuity of sex roles from childhood to adulthood simply in terms of learning or internalization in the early years that maintains relatively stable behavioral patterns thereafter.

To understand the continuity, it is necessary to comprehend how situations lead to change and how others maintain past interactional patterns. Mead's explanation is in terms of problematic situations that lead to a questioning of past behaviors and past learned responses. However, if current sex-role behavior is consistent with or reinforces that learned earlier, then it is unlikely the individual's behavior will change. Furthermore, he posits the individual's tendency to seek continuity through selective memory and reinterpretation of the past in light of the present.

It is being suggested here, of course, that our experiences during adulthood tend to reinforce the sex-role behavior we learned in childhood, so that few situations cause us to question what we learned in our early years. To explore this further, we turn to the next section on institutions where it is argued that the very structure of society reinforces our current sex-role differentiation.

INSTITUTIONS AND THE LARGER SOCIETY

A sociological perspective often includes two complementary aspects or approaches. Thus far, primary emphasis has focused on the micro approach—the study of how individuals affect individuals, the learning of attitudes, values, and behaviors through interaction with others. A second approach is referred to as macro-sociology and directs attention to the wider social structure and its organization (Connelly & Christiansen–Ruffman, 1977). Micro-sociology focuses on the reality within which members of society live as largely of their own construction, as a negotiated reality emerging from the interaction of individuals (Scheff, 1973). Macro-sociology focuses on the influence of institutions, of culture, implying a larger societal force than simply reciprocal influence between interacting individuals.

What is meant by an institution? An institution is simply a common response or set of responses in the community in which we live. Or the institution represents a common response on the part of all members of the community to a common situation. Thus institutions are organized forms of group or social activity—forms so organized that individuals can act adequately and.socially. Furthermore, the individual is always a member of a larger social community, a more extensive social group than that in which s/he immediately and directly finds her/himself.

Although institutions are common responses, they can take varied forms. One such institution is education. Common responses include the student and teacher roles. Varied forms within these common responses are evident. Some students memorize, others criticize, others integrate the two. Some teachers lecture, some discuss, some talk theoretically, some use examples. However, there is a common response referred to as education.

The relevance of the educational institution for sex roles is aptly described by Vickers (1976). The university educational system favors men and disfavors women. It reinforces the sex-role differentiation experienced during childhood. Female undergraduates still tend to be restricted or to restrict themselves to a relatively small number of disciplines and fields that are traditionally female preserves and to others that do not give access to the higher professions or to occupations with high status and high levels of remuneration. As Vickers states, young women entering university have already absorbed notions of appropriate careers for women, and every institution in our society from the family onward reinforces these stereotypes. Young girls seldom see women performing anything other than auxiliary or helper roles. High school teachers do not encourage young women to enter mathematics and science. In university, women must contend both with the attitudes of their male counterparts and instructors and with their own attitudes. There is also an absence of female role models. Female undergraduates encounter only slightly more difficulty in finding summer employment than their male counterparts, but the salaries earned are significantly less, and seldom do the jobs lead to permanent careers after graduation. Furthermore, male undergraduates do not drop out because of pregnancy and rarely because of marriage. Women are more likely to be part-time students than are men, and part-time students usually do not qualify for loans or bursaries. Although the situation is changing, there are still few day-care services on campuses. That is, the game is played according to a set of rules that have been made to suit the male life cycle (see Chapter 8 for a further discussion of this issue).

Another institution in our society that reinforces sex differentiation is religion. As Gorham (1976) informs us, Christianity from its
beginnings has offered women a double message: women are free
and equal in God's eyes, and women are to obey their husbands and to
remain silent in the church. The patriarchal structure of the church,
however, has tended to reinforce the negative part of the message.
God is, after all, a man, neither a woman nor a person. Furthermore,
the central figures of the church have been male and its ritual controlled almost exclusively by men. Wallace (1976) notes that this
Christian view of the inferiority of women is a reinterpretation by
Greek philosophers and Judeo-Christian theologians of a so-called
pagan antiquity. The older tradition has seen women's ability to give
birth as awe inspiring and powerful. The creative power of God included both male and female forces, and both male and female gods
were worshiped.

Men also dominate in the economic institution. Ownership over
two important resources, the means of production and access to the
occupational structure (and therefore control of policymaking in the
major areas of social life), is mainly in the hands of a few men. These
few men have power over almost all women as well as other men
(Connelly & Christiansen–Ruffman, 1977; Porter, 1965). The *Report
of the Royal Commission on the Status of Women in Canada* (1970) informs
us that in 1967 women received approximately 20 percent of the total
Canadian income. Men received the remainder. The report goes on
to document women's virtual absence from the boardroom and the
executive suite. Of 5,889 directorships and 1,469 corporate offices
selected for study, 41 directorships and 8 offices respectively were
held by women. That is, women held less than 1 percent of the top
corporate positions in the country. Similarly, women's absence from
the political arena is clear. In Canada in the 1967 and 1968 leadership
conventions of the Progressive Conservative and Liberal parties, 16.5
percent and 15.3 percent (respectively) of the delegates were women.
Finally, of all candidates in the fifteen federal elections since 1921,
only 2.4 percent were women (*Report of the Royal Commission on the
Status of Women in Canada*, 1970). These figures are not unlike those
for the United States.

The very institutions of our society are structured to reinforce
the sex roles we learn in childhood and at the micro or interactional
levels. The structure of society is consistent with the sex-role differentiation found among interacting individuals. Sex roles at both the

micro and macro levels of study reinforce one another. This consistency of sex-role differentiation in virtually all spheres of our lives is no doubt a contributing factor in their perpetuation.

SUMMARY

The symbolic interactionist perspective accords primacy to interaction between individuals for the development of the biological infant into a human being capable of intelligent thought. From such interaction, individuals learn attitudes, behavior, and meaning. However, within this view, the individual is more than a passive receiver in the learning process. With the development of mind and self, the individual actively participates in the construction of meaning and so affects the social environment. In addition, change is considered basic to the nature of humans, so that continuity of behavior from childhood to adulthood cannot be assumed. Rather, the explanation for the current continuity of sex roles is found in the lack of situations that lead us to question our roles and consequently to potential change in sex roles. It was suggested that sex roles continue relatively unchanged, from childhood to adulthood, due to a reinforcement of those roles during both the earlier and later years and at the micro and macro levels of interaction during both our childhood and adulthood experiences.*

The sociological theory of sex roles discussed in this chapter uses the concept of differential socialization to explain differences between women and men. We must be careful, however, not to use the notion of socialization to perpetuate mistaken beliefs about what sex differences actually do exist. The fact that females and males are socialized differently in many respects does *not* necessarily imply that their behavior will differ in every situation. Indeed, current evidence suggests

*Although this chapter has illustrated the applicability of a general sociological theory to the area of sex roles, it has not focused in detail on any specific studies in that area. Detailed studies in different areas of sex roles are, however, growing: histories and analyses of the women's movement (Teather, 1976); the male sex role (David & Brannon, 1976); the division of labor between husbands and unemployed wives and husbands and employed wives (Meissner, 1977); the effect of the wife's decision-making powers on both the wife and the husband (Henshel, 1975; Matthews, 1977); sex role differentiation in old age (Watson & Kivett, 1976), to name but a few.

(and many of the chapters in this book indicate) that countless beliefs about male–female differences are simply false. For example, the chapter exploring sexuality indicates similarities rather than differences between women and men. Similarly, a recent study of commitment to work among women (Chappell, 1978) suggests grounds to question the belief in women's lower commitment to work relative to that of men. Data collected for that study indicate women may exhibit similar levels of commitment when their conditions of work are comparable to those of men. Not until the social conditions under which women and men live are equal will the impact on behavior of such antecedent conditions as socialization and physiology be truly assessable.

Mead's symbolic interaction theory is, of course, only one approach to socialization. Other approaches such as social learning theory and classical and operant conditioning are treated elsewhere in this book. Regardless of the theory used to understand it, socialization is clearly an important variable in the emergence of sex roles and figures in virtually every question of sex differences raised in this book.

6

Nina Lee Colwill
& Hilary M. Lips

MASCULINITY, FEMININITY, & ANDROGYNY:

What Have You Done for Us Lately?

The frequent use of the phrase "opposite sexes" is indicative of a host of cultural assumptions surrounding femininity and masculinity. Indeed, most of us have been taught that masculinity and femininity *are* opposing concepts: it is no more possible for a person to incorporate both of them simultaneously than it is to experience day and night at the same time.

This notion runs so deep in the thinking of our culture that it seems almost absurd to question it. Yet in order to study the nature of sex differences, it is imperative that we examine the assumption that masculinity and femininity are opposite (or, at best, complementary) poles of existence, experience, and behavior.

It seems obvious that a large part of the idea that masculinity and femininity were nonoverlapping concepts stemmed from the observation that an individual could be either female or male as defined by genital structure, but never both.* Still, one wonders why the fact that both men and women possessed arms, legs, heads, hearts, and digestive systems did not influence people to think that the similarities between men and women were just as important, if not more impor-

*Except, of course, in the rare cases of hermaphroditism discussed in Chapter 3.

tant, than the differences! Certainly the anatomical similarities far outnumber the differences. However, femininity and masculinity evolved as concepts that stressed the differences between the sexes and created new ones in the process. The dichotomy that these concepts represent has shaped not only our commonsense thinking but also psychology's approach to the study of women and men.

MASCULINITY–FEMININITY: A HISTORICAL OVERVIEW

The history of human thought suggests that whenever two apparently opposing principles were observed, they were linked to maleness and femaleness. Thus the sun came to represent the male principle whereas the moon represented the female; rationality and logic became associated with men and intuition with women; light and clarity were termed masculine, darkness and mystery feminine. De Beauvoir (1952) claims that these dualities were not originally associated with sex but that the association grew up through the attempts of men to rationalize their advantaged position by defining themselves as the One and women as the Other. Others (e.g., Stern, 1965) suggest that it is woman's connection to what men have considered the mysterious processes of menstruation, birth, and lactation that led to her association with darkness, irrationality, moon, and magic. It is interesting to note that both explanations depend on the notion that these associations were created by men. Women have probably never thought of themselves as particularly mysterious, although they too have been awed by the processes of conception and birth.

However the notion arose, the idea of masculinity and femininity as opposite poles of experience is found in the history and mythology of many cultures. Interestingly, however, many philosophies view each of the two concepts as one-half of a whole, neither of which can ever be complete in itself. According to this viewpoint, not only do women and men need each other but also each individual must develop both the masculine and feminine side of his/her nature in order to be a whole person. Bazin and Freeman (1974) discuss the way this belief serves as a basic principle of Taoism, the ancient Chinese philosophy:

In Taoist philosophy, Yang, the male principle, and Yin, the female principle, signify the two archetypal poles of nature. The Tao—the middle way, the undivided unity which lies behind all earthly phenomena—gives rise to the Yin and the Yang. Yin represents death, darkness, secretiveness, evil, demons, earth, and the invisible world. Yang represents life, light, righteousness, gods, heaven, and the visible world. The two principles, although they appear to be conflicting opposites, define their existence through a creative relationship with each other. . . . As opposite poles of a single process, death defines life, and life, death; light gives rise to darkness, and darkness to light. . . . According to Chinese thought, the complementary interaction of Yin (female) and Yang (male) in the universe and in humanity brings prosperity to the world, for the underlying harmony of the two principles resolves all the conflicts of nature. Only when we completely perceive the implicit interdependence of the two principles within ourselves and within the universe, when we transcend the duality and opposition and perceive the underlying unity of the two—only then can we find wholeness and peace. Having thus transcended the opposites, we also transcend the sexual duality, for the whole or complete human being is androgynous; he or she is at once male and female. [pp. 190–91]*

Most myths of the origin of the sexes tell of the division of a whole individual into two incomplete halves: the Biblical myth of the creation of Eve from the rib of Adam, the Hindu story of the separation of the Supreme Self into male and female, Plato's *Symposium* account of how Zeus decided to cut all beings in two. The division results in a striving to reunite in order to regain a sense of wholeness. For many writers, this wholeness is viewed as an androgynous state—a psychological merging of the masculine and feminine (see Heilbrun, 1973, for an overview of the presence of the androgyny concept in mythology and literature). It has even been suggested that the moment of ecstasy and wholeness experienced by mystics is related to a fleeting integration and reconciliation of the masculine and feminine principles in an individual's consciousness (Bazin, 1974).

On the whole, there is considerable evidence for the existence of two traditions: that masculinity and femininity are opposing principles, and that they must be joined in an individual and in a society in

*From "The Androgynous Vision," in *Women's Studies* by N. T. Bazin & A. Freeman, 1974, *2* (2), pp. 190–91. © 1974 by Gordon & Breach Science Publishers Inc. Reprinted by permission of the publisher.

order for the experience of wholeness to occur. Let us turn now to an examination of the way that psychology has been influenced by these traditions.

THE PSYCHOLOGICAL MEASUREMENT OF MASCULINITY–FEMININITY

Psychology has made much use of the concept of masculinity–femininity (M–F) in its "opposing principles" tradition but until very recently has ignored the tradition of wholeness through the union of these opposing principles. This section examines psychology's approach to the measurement of M–F.

Psychologists have utilized the concept of masculinity–femininity to devise tests that they feel can *measure* a person's "masculinity" or "femininity." The scores on such tests have carried weight in many different realms of psychology. There has been a value judgment attached to M–F scores: it has been considered "better" for females to score on the "feminine" end of the M–F continuum and even more important for males to score on the "masculine" end. "Deviant" M–F test scores have been interpreted as evidence for poor sex-role identity and even homosexuality. Needless to say, these interpretations make some very large assumptions about the meaning of M–F. To better understand these assumptions, implications, and interpretations, let us now examine some of the problems in the psychological measurement of masculinity–femininity.

The Validity of M–F Tests

The validity of an instrument refers to the extent to which it measures what it purports to measure. How well do our various psychological tests measure masculinity–femininity? To even begin to answer this question, we must obviously define what we "purport to measure." To what do psychologists refer when they use the term *masculinity–femininity?*

Although the terms have been used for many years in psychological contexts, the concepts have never really been defined. After searching the literature in vain for adequate definitions, Constantinople (1973) concludes that the terms were simply adopted by psychologists and used by them with the same imprecision characteristic of their colloquial use:

> The most generalized definitions of the terms as they are used by those developing tests of M–F would seem to be that they are relatively enduring traits which are more or less rooted in anatomy, physiology, and early experience, and which generally serve to dinstinguish males from females in appearance, attitude and behavior. [p. 390]

According to this approach, any characteristic that reliably distinguishes women from men can be defined as an element of femininity or masculinity. Thus, if men are found to behave more aggressively than women, aggressive behavior is labeled masculine. If women prefer baths and men prefer showers, bathing becomes feminine and showering, masculine.

Constantinople points out that most psychological tests of masculinity–femininity were developed using this strictly empirical approach. A large pool of items was generated, including many that were not related to even an intuitive definition of masculinity or femininity. These items were administered to large numbers of persons, and those items on which males and females tended most often to respond differently (i.e., items that discriminated between male and female respondents) were kept as test items. The content of such items was not thought to be particularly important. For instance, on one recently developed test of masculinity–femininity (Sechrest & Fay, 1973), one of the items that discriminates between men and women is: "I become quite irritated when I see someone spit on the sidewalk" (men tended not to). This is hardly the stuff of which distinctions between darkness and light, or intuition and logic, are made.

There are a number of psychological tests, consisting of items that differentiate between males and females, that attempt to measure masculinity and femininity: e.g., Terman–Miles M–F test (1936); Strong MF Scale of the Strong Vocational Interest Blank (SVIB) (1936); MF scale of the Minnesota Multiphasic Personality Inventory (MMPI) (Hathaway & McKinley, 1943); Gough Femininity Scale (1952); Guilford Masculinity Scale (1956). Given the way in which such tests are constructed, we must question the exact meaning of a high masculinity or femininity score. Generally, the higher an individual's masculinity score, the more closely s/he approximates the norm for the particular group of men whose responses were used to develop the scale. Similarly, a highly "féminine" response pattern would simply indicate that the person was responding in very much the same way as the normative sample of women for that particular test. Thus M–F tests do not measure any "essence" of masculinity or femininity. They simply assess how much the individual conforms in her/his written attitudes to certain cultural norms that happen to be different for men and women in the particular population sampled at the particular time and place at which the test was developed.

To illustrate this point, let us consider what would happen if a masculinity–femininity test had been developed in Margaret Mead's (1935) famous Tachambuli culture of New Guinea and was used to assess North Americans. Mead tells us that the Tchambuli women were dominant, impersonal, and managing, whereas men were less responsible and tended to be emotionally dependent. In such a culture, then, it would be considered "feminine" to be dominant and "masculine" to be dependent. When judged against the norms of this group, the North American woman socialized to conform to our traditional sex roles would be regarded as masculine and the typical North American man as feminine. What meaning is left to the concept of M–F if men are less masculine than women and women less feminine than men?

Unfortunately, we will not overcome our validity problem by barring Tchambuli M–F tests from North America. As Constantinople (1973) has pointed out, a version of the same problem occurs each time we use M–F tests that were developed on normative groups of decades past. The constant against which respondents are compared is usually the normative response pattern of males and females of their parents' or even grandparents' generations. Add to this problem the multiple definitions of acceptable male and female attitudes across various age, social class, educational and geographical groups, and we are faced with a mammoth validity problem.

For the most part, it is unclear how well an individual's score on a traditional M–F test relates to sex-role behavior, let alone sex-role identity or sexual preference. Psychology has failed to define masculinity and femininity in any terms except "that which differentiates males from females." Since that varies dramatically as a function of time and place, the whole concept of M–F is very fuzzy. Obviously, we cannot measure what we cannot adequately define. If psychologists have had this much difficulty measuring masculinity–femininity, the implications that they have drawn from M–F scores begin to seem rather presumptuous. In this light, the assumption that sex-role deviance or sexual preference can be inferred from those scores seems ludicrous.

One obvious conclusion is that the entire concept of masculinity–femininity is meaningless. Another is that there are major flaws in the psychological interpretation, perhaps rooted in our historical definition of the concept. Let us now examine some of these flaws.

Masculinity–Femininity as a Bipolar Concept

Clearly, psychology has been strongly influenced by the tradition that masculinity and femininity are opposing principles. All the traditional psychological tests that attempt to measure these concepts express them as a single construct: as opposite ends of a continuum ranging from high masculinity to high femininity, presumably with a neutral midpoint.

The assumption of bipolarity, which is built into traditional M–F tests, means that a person attains only one M–F score: high masculine, low feminine, or whatever. Thus we have no information about a person's masculinity *and* femininity, only about his/her composite M–F score. For instance, two people could receive low masculinity scores on a twenty-item M–F test in two very different ways: by agreeing with ten masculine and nine feminine items, or by agreeing with one feminine and two masculine items. Clearly, the similar scores obtained by two such people cannot reflect equal amounts of some "essence" of masculinity–femininity.

There is some evidence that the entire bipolarity assumption of masculinity–femininity is invalid—that "femininity" and "masculinity" are two completely different concepts and can thus coexist independently in the same individual. For example, Vroegh's (1971) research has shown a high positive correlation between peer-rated masculinity and femininity in children from grades one to six. In other words, the more masculine a child was rated, the more feminine s/he was rated. It is very unlikely that peers would have rated these high masculine/high feminine children as "neutral"; yet if traditional M–F scoring had been used, their masculinity and femininity scores would have canceled each other.

Further evidence for the invalidity of M–F as a bipolar construct was provided by Colwill's research (see Anderson, 1974). Her results suggest that our conception of sex-role appropriateness includes two important factors: the acceptance of sex-role-appropriate attitudes and behaviors and the rejection of that which is sex-role inappropriate. Obviously such a complex sytem is inadequately represented when M–F is conceptualized as one bipolar construct.

In acknowledging the "opposite-concepts" tradition, the common psychological approach to masculinity–femininity has ruled out any possible validation of the other historical tradition—that the individual personality has both a masculine *and* feminine side that must be integrated and developed if wholeness and health are to be achieved. Sandra Bem (1974) has developed an instrument—the Bem Sex Role Inventory (BSRI)—that attempts to address the second tradition. It treats masculinity and femininity as two separate and independent concepts, thereby tapping respondents' scores on both.

The BSRI was developed by having judges rate 200 adjectives on a 7-point scale for their desirability for an American man or woman: e.g., "In American society, how desirable is it for a woman to be shy?" Items rated by both male and female judges as significantly more desirable for a man than for a woman were placed in the masculine pool, and those rated more desirable for a woman were placed in the feminine pool. Twenty masculine and twenty feminine items* were then selected for the Masculine and Feminine Scales. BSRI respondents are asked to indicate on a 7-point scale how well each of the BSRI adjectives describes them. Respondents of each sex fall into four categories as a function of their scores: Masculine (those who score high on masculinity and low on femininity), Feminine (those who score high on femininity and low on masculinity), Androgynous (those who score high masculine and high feminine), and Undifferentiated (those who score low masculine and low feminine). In keeping with the tradition of wholeness through androgyny, there is a strong positive value attached to fitting into the Androgynous category. This is discussed in more detail later in the chapter.

The BSRI has obviously made an important contribution to the study of masculinity and feminity. There are some who feel that Bem's conceptualization still falls short of the ideal, however—that

*The BSRI also contains a Social Desirability Scale consisting of twenty nondifferentiating items.

both masculinity and femininity are multidimensional concepts that cannot be adequately represented by four classifications on a test that treats masculinity and femininity as unidimensional constructs.

Unidimensionality

Another difficulty with traditional M–F tests has been their treatment of masculinity and/or femininity as unidimensional concepts: as single dimensions rather than combinations of many factors. To reject this assumption of unidimensionality is, in effect, to reject the entire notion of masculinity and/or femininity as a single underlying concept. It may be more meaningful to concern ourselves with the constellation of attitudes and behaviors that make up traditional M–F scores.

To help clarify this issue, let us return for a moment to the traditional myths. Suppose we say that the truly feminine person is dark, intuitive, and evil. The unidimensional approach would attempt to subsume these three concepts into a single dimension called femininity and to give each person a single femininity score based on his/her darkness, intuitiveness, and evilness. To look at a hypothetical example, two individuals might obtain a "femininity score" of 24 points out of a possible 36 in highly different ways. Person A scores 12 points each for darkness and intuition, but nothing for evil. Person B scores 8 points each on darkness, intuition, and evil. According to their total scores, each person would be equally feminine, yet these scores would not reflect individual differences that might be very important. A psychological test that provides a profile of subscores rather than a single masculinity and/or feminity score might contribute more to an understanding of the concepts than one that takes a unindimensional approach.

Such a test, developed by Sechrest and Fay (Fay & Sechrest, 1973; Sechrest & Fay, 1973), features twelve masculininity–femininity subscales. Although this test does attack the unidimensionality problem, it does not address the bipolarity problem and is therefore a multidimensional bipolar M–F test. We have yet to see a psychological instrument that combines the multidimensionality of the Sechrest and Fay approach with Bem's use of masculinity and femininity as independent concepts.

Scaling

In the broad area of psychological testing, one very technical issue continues to surface: what are the scaling properties of a given instrument? M–F tests are no exception. This section examines how this technical aspect of M–F tests may have implications for some of our stereotypic views of males, females, masculinity, and femininity.

The ideal test would yield scores that could be considered as *ratio* data. This means that scores could be meaningfully multiplied and divided, enabling us to say that a score of 20 was worth twice as much as a score of 10. Psychology can boast few, if any, such instruments. We cannot meaningfully say, for instance, that a person with an IQ of 100 is twice as intelligent as a person whose IQ is 50.

Usually, psychologists are more than happy to be able to interpret psychological test scores as *interval* data—to be able to say that every interval or item in the test is "worth" the same as every other item. In an M–F test with interval scaling properties, then, we would be justified in giving 1 point to each item in the test. We would be secure in the knowledge that irritation with sidewalk spitters is worth the same amount in the calculation of one's total femininity score as is the preference for a bath over a shower.

Are there attitudes and behaviors that, though counting only one unit in an M–F test, have a disproportionately large influence on our real-world evaluation of a person's masculinity or femininity? Is the enjoyment of crocheting worth the same as the enjoyment of babies, for example, in our day-to-day perceptions of a person's femininity? Does the knowledge that a person enjoys driving a racing car influence our evaluation of his/her masculinity to the same extent as the knowledge that a person enjoys watching hockey? Probably not.

The interval problem becomes more complex when we compare items across people. Are some items worth more for some people than for others? Let us assume that we have prejudged one man to be very masculine and another to be very unmasculine by whatever method we use to make such judgments. Would the knowledge that they are both mathematically inclined change our evaluation of the masculine man in the same amount as it would change our evaluation of the unmasculine man? Similarly, does the knowledge that they both love to bake add the same increment of change to our evaluations of the feminine and the unfeminine woman? It is difficult to believe that our

135

stereotypes and attributions of masculinity and femininity subscribe to the clean interval pattern that M–F tests must assume.

To this point we have been considering the issue of scaling with respect to masculinity *and* femininity. Tests that assume the bipolarity of masculinity–femininity take on an even more difficult task with the assumption of interval scaling. They must assume that adding one unit of femininity to the score of a masculine man is equivalent to adding one unit of femininity to the score of a feminine man. But would our perceptions of these two people not be differentially affected by the information that they were both afraid of thunder? Unless every unit of femininity and masculinity is equal to every other unit of femininity and masculinity, the interval assumption is, of course, untenable.

Why is the issue of interval scaling so important? Unless we can assume equal intervals in the psychological testing of masculinity and femininity, we are unable to calculate meaningful test scores. If we do not believe every item to be worth the same amount, we cannot add and subtract them to form a composite score, and M–F test scores become virtually meaningless.

To this point in our analysis of M–F tests, we have been largely considering people rather than males versus females. The issues of validity, bipolarity, unidimensionality, and scaling could apply equally to the evaluation of men and women. Now let us turn to the most obvious, yet in some ways, the most complex of all the M–F test issues: the sex specificity of M–F test scores.

Sex Specificity

If you were to see a woman busily crocheting an afghan, how much would that sight add to your estimate of her femininity? On the other hand, suppose that the individual crocheting were a man; how much would the sight of him crocheting add to your impression of *his* femininity? For most people, the judgment of femininity in this case would be more strongly influenced if the individual were a man rather than a woman. Social psychologists have known for years that a behavior that appears "out-of-role" seems to weigh more heavily in our judgments of people than behavior that is expected, or "in-role" (Jones & Davis, 1965). Thus, the way we use behavioral information to make judgments about the masculinity or femininity of an individual will depend on whether the individual performing the behavior is male or female.

Whether or not masculinity and femininity are conceptualized as two independent constructs, it is difficult to view them independent of the sex of the incumbent. Perhaps, as Fay and Sechrest (1973) have suggested, they should be conceptualized differently for males and females. This is the issue we call the sex specificity of M–F.*

Do we equate a woman who scores on the feminine end of the M–F continuum with a man who attains the same score? We would suggest that this is not the case—that stronger negative valence is attached to the feminine man. The word *effeminate*, which is not considered to be particularly complimentary, is reserved only for males who tend toward femininity.

Colwill's research (see Anderson, 1974) investigated the stereotypes surrounding hypothetical males and females who agreed or disagreed with statements previously rated as obviously and stereotypically "masculine" or "feminine." On the basis of this information, subjects were to rate these hypothetical males and females on three continua: masculinity–femininity, homosexuality–heterosexuality, and high to low sex drive. Both male and female subjects rated feminine males as homosexual with high sex drive and masculine males as heterosexual with low sex drive, but females were not viewed differently as a function of M–F. Obviously, sex of the incumbent is a very important variable in our evaluation of masculinity and femininity.

Can we equate the high masculinity of a man with the high masculinity of a woman, or is one seen as more masculine than the other? And what of the androgynous? Do we view them differently as a function of their sex? As we asked at the beginning of this section: are the implications for a man crocheting the same as for a woman crocheting? Do we attach the same stereotypes to the male as to the female mechanic? All the problems we discussed in the section on scaling are compounded, because we are measuring two different groups of people: males and females. By their very definition, our ideas of masculinity and femininity are inseparable from the biological fact of males and females.

*Although we have never seen this term in print, the present authors cannot lay claim to it. Dr. Todd Fay was discussing the concept of sex specificity in his sex differences classes at University of Western Ontario in the early 1970s.

In general, the psychological testing approach to the concepts of masculinity and femininity leaves much to be desired. The approach reflects the historical and mythological tradition of masculinity and femininity as opposite poles of existence, but neither questions the tradition nor incorporates its many complexities. Masculinity and femininity have been defined only in terms of what differentiates men from women. Thus, the more different from women a person is, the more masculine is that individual. Conversely, a person becomes more feminine as s/he becomes increasingly different from men, whatever that difference entails.

The problems of validity, bipolarity, unidimensionality, scaling, and sex specificity are only beginning to be addressed by those who create and administer psychological measures of masculinity and femininity. Meanwhile, the psychological approach to masculinity and femininity continues to shape our concepts of what is mentally healthy for women and men.

MASCULINITY, FEMININITY, AND MENTAL HEALTH

The development of scales to measure masculinity and femininity as part of the MMPI and other tests of psychological functioning was an implicit acknowledgment of a relationship between sex-role identification and mental health. Since Freud's era, psychologists have been arguing that the unfeminine woman and the unmasculine man were victims of underlying emotional problems. Obviously, the woman or man who is not "appropriately" sex typed is abnormal by definition, since, as we have seen, the norms for masculinity and femininity are determined by dominant cultural standards. If one believes, as some mental health professionals do, that good mental health entails an acceptance of, adjustment to, and ability to cope with one's situation in life, then an individual who does not wholeheartedly embrace her/his sex role is considered maladjusted. A man (but not a woman) who is masculine is considered healthy, as is a woman (but not a man) who is feminine. There appears to be a double standard of mental health.

The existence of different standards of mental health for women and men stems not just from the psychological tests of femininity and masculinity but also from the sexual stereotypes held by clinical psychologists, psychiatrists, counselors, and members of other helping professions. As members of our culture, these professionals are not immune to the biases that pervade it. In a landmark study, Broverman, Broverman, Clarkson, Rosenkrantz, and Vogel (1970) showed that clinicians actually held different ideals for a healthy, fully functioning adult male than for a healthy, fully functioning adult female. The ideal healthy woman was described as being:

> ... more submissive, less independent, less adventurous, more easily influenced, less aggressive, less competitive, more easily excitable in minor crises, more easily hurt, more emotional, more conceited about [her] appearance, less objective, and less interested in math and science. [p. 6]

Also, the clinicians' ideal of the healthy man was similar to that of a healthy mature adult, but their idea of a healthy woman was quite different from both. Thus, it appears that women are caught in something of a double bind. If they meet the mental health standards for their own sex, they automatically fall short of those for the general adult population. If they meet the standards for a healthy adult, they are defined as unfeminine. In fact, Belote (1976) has shown that the concept of the healthy female obtained from Broverman's clinicians closely parallels both that of the "hysterical personality" and that of masochism! She argues that when females in our culture exhibit aspects of hysteria or masochism, these signs often go unnoticed because of their similarity to stereotyped feminine behavior. On the other hand, as Tennov (1976) has noted, a woman who refuses to show the passivity and dependency that characterize the so-called healthy feminine personality may be quickly labeled as sick. There seems to be some truth to Simone De Beauvoir's (1952) famous dictum that "Man is defined as a human being and woman as a female, whenever she behaves as a human being she is said to imitate the male" (p. 47).*

There is another way in which our culture's definition of femininity leads to the labeling of women as mentally ill. Studies show that women report more emotional problems, are more likely to seek psychiatric help, and are more frequently hospitalized for mental

*From *The Second Sex* by Simone De Beauvoir, translated and edited by H. M. Parshley. © 1952 by Alfred A. Knopf, Inc. Reprinted by permission of the publisher.

health reasons than are men (Chesler, 1971; Gove & Tudor, 1973). It is clear that our culture's stereotype of femininity, allowing as it does for considerable weakness, emotionality, and dependency, makes it more permissible for a woman than for a man to acknowledge and seek help for emotional problems. Indeed, the feminine role may even encourage women to treat seriously problems that they might otherwise ignore and to enter into dependent relationships with male therapists (Chesler, 1971). Thus, our cultural concepts of masculinity and femininity may artificially be making women as a group appear less healthy and men more healthy than they actually are.

One might well ask at this point: Just what is the evidence that people who are appropriately sex typed *are* emotionally healthier than people who are not? For the sake of discussion, we may conceptualize an emotionally healthy person as one who functions well in a variety of situations, relates satisfactorily to others, and is reasonably happy and content.

Such evidence as there is offers little support for a link between appropriate sex typing and positive mental health. Bem (1976) cites a number of studies that show positive correlations between femininity in females and high anxiety, low self-esteem, and low social acceptance. Sherman (1976) notes that a number of researchers have found the passivity and dependency characterizing the ideal feminine role to be associated with inadequate functioning even in the traditional female arenas of wifehood and motherhood. Femininity, as defined by psychologists, does not seem to be correlated with good mental health in women. Although a woman may be labeled as sick if she strays too far from society's ideal of femininity, she may actually make herself sick if she adheres too closely to it.

For masculinity, the evidence is somewhat more mixed. Mussen (1961) reports that among adolescent boys, masculinity is positively correlated with psychological adjustment. Heilbrun (1965, 1968, cited in Sherman, 1976) concludes after reviewing the literature that masculinity is associated with positive mental health in males. On the other hand, Bem (in press) cites two studies that show high masculinity among adult males to be correlated with high anxiety, high neuroticism, and low self-acceptance. Of course these problems might be due to problems with the measurement of masculinity. We might also speculate that high masculinity is associated with high social acceptance by peers for the adolescent boy as he tries to carve out an identity for himself. One of the signs that a degree of comfort with his own identity has been achieved might be a relaxation of the need to constantly reaffirm his masculinity. Thus one might expect the well-adjusted adult male to be less stereotypically masculine than the man who is unsure of himself. Such an explanation is consistent with Hartley's (1959) analysis of male socialization. She notes that the male role tends to be defined as an avoidance of anything feminine rather than as a positive set of desired behaviors and that the harsh enforcement of the demands of this role at a young age can create emotional problems:

> . . . a great many boys do give evidence of anxiety centered in the whole area of sex-connected role behaviors, an anxiety which frequently expresses itself in overstraining to be masculine, in virtual panic at being caught doing anything traditionally feminine, and in hostility toward anything even hinting at "femininity," including females themselves. [p. 8]

An adult male who has never come to terms with the anxiety described by Hartley might well show high extremes of masculine behavior and test scores. There seems no reason to suppose, however, that moderately high masculinity is associated with emotional ill health. In general, it appears that extremes of either femininity or masculinity can be dysfunctional.

The most interesting recent developments in this area involve Bem's (1974) measure of sex typing and androgyny. She theorized that the individual who possesses both masculine and feminine positive traits (i.e., who is androgynous) is more behaviorally flexible and hence more fully functional than one who is strongly sex typed. Using her scale, the BSRI, to measure sex typing, she has now shown in a number of studies (Bem, 1975; Bem & Lenney, 1976; Bem, Martyna, & Watson, 1976) that strong sex typing in the direction of either masculinity or femininity is associated with restricted behavior in certain settings. For example, she demonstrated that in a situation that required the "feminine" behavior of nurturing a small baby, subjects of both sexes who were classified as either feminine or androgynous performed significantly better than masculine men and women (Bem, Martyna, & Watson, 1976). In this case, then, rigid masculine sex typing was associated with an inability or unwillingness to be nurturant. Subjects whose BSRI scores indicated that they saw themselves as androgynous, however, performed this "feminine" task as well as did the female subjects. In another study, Bem (1975) demonstrated that masculine and androgynous subjects of both sexes performed better than feminine subjects at a task that required the stereotypically "masculine" behavior of independence in the face of social pressure. A third study (Bem & Lenney, 1976) demonstrated that masculine men and feminine women were more likely than androgynous women or men to choose activities that were "appropriate" for their own sex and to reject out-of-role activities. After performing cross-sex activities, masculine men and feminine women also reported experiencing more discomfort and feeling worse about themselves than did androgynous subjects of either sex. Other researchers (e.g., Myers & Lips, 1978; Turner, 1977) have also reported positive relationships between androgyny and participation in out-of-sex-role behavior. Thus there seems to be some evidence that "appropriate" sex typing, as measured by the BSRI, is related to behavioral inflexibility and a tendency not to adopt one's role to the requirements of unfamiliar situations. In contrast, androgyny seems to be associated with behavioral flexibility.* On this dimension at least, androgynous people seem more mentally healthy than do masculine men or feminine women.

Given the problems associated with tests of masculinity and femininity, some of which are shared by the BSRI, what conclusions about sex typing and mental health can be drawn from the foregoing findings? We would suggest that rigid socialization into *any* role (not just sex roles) would lead to behavioral inflexibility and poor functioning in unfamiliar situations. One possibility that has not been explored is that BSRI scores may be reflecting an overall orientation that is somewhat broader than sex typing: a general ability and willingness to deal with complexity and to transcend narrow definitions of what is appropriate behavior for certain categories of people. Someone who, in our sex-role-conscious society, is capable of giving a self-description that includes a significant number of both female and male traits would seem to be capable of seeing a variety of issues in other than oversimplified black-and-white terms. This idea represents speculation on our part, however, and has yet to receive empirical support.

We can conclude, at least, that the available evidence tends to discredit the notion that an individual must be strongly sex typed in

---

*The evidence on this point, although convincing, is not totally consistent. Female subjects do not always follow the predicted pattern (see Bem, in press). Some of this inconsistency may be traceable to the problem of sex specificity in the measurement of femininity and masculinity, as discussed earlier in the chapter.

order to be healthy. Studies based on traditional M–F measures do not offer significant support for the idea that "proper" sex typing is associated with good mental health, and the more recent ones using the BSRI suggest that persons scoring as androgynous have some advantages over masculine men and feminine women. The traits that psychologists have labeled as masculinity and femininity do not seem to confer any special benefits when they are rigidly adhered to and mutually exclusive.

SUMMARY

Early in this chapter we examined the two historical and philosophical traditions of masculinity and femininity: the notion of masculinity–femininity as a bipolar concept, and the notion of wholeness through the merging of these two opposites. Except for the work of Jung and Bakan, discussed in Chapter 2, psychology has virtually ignored the latter tradition. A revival of the concept of androgyny appears to be occurring, however. Indeed, the preceding section offered evidence for the attainment of mental health and flexibility through the merging of seemingly incongruous traits and attitudes. However, we question whether the reconciliation of two opposite poles for the attainment of wholeness need encompass the concept of masculinity–femininity.

As we researched for and wrote this chapter, we came more and more to question the utility of the notion of masculinity and femininity. Is it not more informative to know that John is nurturant, emotional, expressive, and intuitive than to know that he is "feminine"? What new information does his femininity add? What *is* femininity beyond that which differentiates females from males, and what meaning does *that* hold if John is more feminine than Mary?

As discussed in the previous section, it is possible to view Bem's research in terms of cognitive complexity rather than androgyny. Other authors have managed to convey this complexity–flexibility pattern without resorting to the concepts of femininity and masculinity. Brown (1973), for instance, has suggested a model wherein one's intellectual and emotional forces must work together for sound decision making. Since intellectualism is considered masculine in our society and emotionalism feminine, one might be tempted to use M–F terms. Brown was not so tempted and thus conveyed maximum information with his model. Setting his message in a framework of masculinity–femininity would have added nothing.

Rebecca, Hefner, and Oleshansky (1976) have recently presented a model that they call sex-role transcendence. For them, the ideal is not that everyone should be unisexual or androgynous but that our society should evolve into a pluralistic one in which individuals could experience the full range of behavioral and emotional choices. Such a society would not necessarily laud the sex-role stereotype of androgyny, which is nearly as binding as the sex-role stereotypes of masculinity and femininity. Instead, we would be free of all sex-role norms, even that of androgyny.

Obviously, we are far from such a utopian day. But perhaps we can speed its coming with reconceptualization of sex roles. We must constantly remind ourselves that masculinity and femininity are nothing more than the many attitudes and behaviors that differentiate the average male from the average female at this particular time and place.

7 Hilary M. Lips, Anita Myers, & Nina Lee Colwill

SEX DIFFERENCES IN ABILITY:
Do Men & Women Have Different Strengths & Weaknesses?

Are women really the weaker sex? Are men more logical than women? Are women more sensitive than men? These and a host of related questions have become the subject of furious debate in recent years as the two sexes have demanded access to each other's vocational territories. Chapter 5 showed that females and males tend to be channeled into different social and occupational roles. Much of this channeling has been based on assumptions of men's "natural" superiority in some areas and women's "natural" superiority in others. Some of these assumptions are beginning to fade, however, as women have proved themselves capable of being excellent lawyers, accountants, airline pilots, and racing-car drivers and men have demonstrated their competence as nurses, child-care workers, secretaries, and figure skaters.

This chapter examines sex differences in three broad areas of ability: physical ability, social skills, and cognitive ability. Some evidence exists for sex differences in all three of these areas. However, the origins of the differences are certainly not clear. The extent to which these sex differences are the inevitable results of human physiology, the products of socialization, or the outcome of interactions between the two is an issue that is explored in some depth.

PHYSICAL ABILITY:
WHICH IS THE STRONGER SEX?

Women have long been regarded as members of the weaker sex. As a group, they are shorter, lighter, and less muscular than men and are regarded in our society as generally unable to perform heavy manual work or to compete in certain stressful or potentially violent athletic events. These differences have been used as justification for keeping women out of certain jobs, such as construction, and such sports as weight lifting, football, and hockey. Recent research, however, has demonstrated that young women (college students without special training) are able to do strenuous work, expending 2,369 kilocalories for eight and a half hours. This expenditure of energy is approximately equal to that required in unmechanized coal mining—usually considered one of the most physically demanding occupations (Wardle, 1976). Therefore, although women may be relatively weaker than men in muscular terms, there seems to be little reason for excluding them from "heavy" work on this basis. We might also note here that women's traditional role of housewife involves considerable strenuous physical effort, including lifting and carrying, scrubbing floors, painting, wallpapering, and weeding the garden. Women are not strangers to physical effort.

Males, although enjoying the status of being muscularly the stronger sex, appear to be constitutionally weaker than females (Montagu, 1968). They are more likely to suffer injury or death prenatally or during the birth process and to be victims of childhood diseases. The illness rate is higher among females than males in most parts of the world, but females are more likely to recover from illnesses than are males, and women's life expectancies are almost universally higher than those of men. Montagu asserts that women's endurance of such conditions as starvation, exposure, fatigue, and shock is better than men's. It thus appears that the so-called weaker sex actually has some physical advantages.

Men's advantage in size and muscular strength is amply demonstrated by their performance in athletic competition. In Olympic events in which both sexes participate, men consistently obtain better performance records. Interestingly enough, however, the differences between men's and women's records in certain events are decreasing rapidly, and observers (e.g., Dyer, 1977; Luce, 1976) are now suggesting that women may someday run and swim as fast as men. In at least one event, this is already the case: women hold the speed record for swimming the English channel in both directions.

The areas in which women's performance is improving most rapidly are long-distance swimming and running (Dyer, 1977). It is only recently that women have ceased to be actively excluded from these events. The following table (Luce, 1976) shows world record comparisons for women and men in 1934 and 1974.* It can be seen that in almost every event, the gap is closing; the percentage difference between the men's and women's records has decreased.

Event	Women's Record		Men's Record		Differences (%)	
	1934	1974	1934	1974	1934	1974
100-m Run	11.9	10.8	10.3	9.9	16	9
200-m Run	24.1	22.1	20.6	19.5	17	13
800-m Run	2:16.8	1:58.3	1:49.8	1:43.7	24	14
400-m Relay Run	46.9	42.8	40.0	38.2	17	12
800-m Relay Run	1:45.8	1:33.8	1:25.2	1:21.5	23	15
High Jump	1.65m	1.94m	2.04m	2.30m	19	15
Long Jump	5.98m	6.28m	7.98m	8.90m	25	23
Shot Put	13.70m	21.03m	15.43m	21.82m	11	4
Discus	42.43m	67.44m	51.73m	70.04m	18	4
Javelin	44.64m	62.40m	74.02m	94.08m	40	34
100-m Freestyle	1:06.6	57.54	57.4	51.22	16	12
200-m Freestyle	2:43.6	2:03.56	2:08.8	1:52.78	21	10
400-m Freestyle	5:28.5	4:18.07	4:47.0	3:58.18	14	8
800-m Freestyle	12:18.6	8:52.97	10:15.6	8:17.60	20	7
1,500-m Freestyle	23:17.2	16:54.14	19:07.2	15:31.85	22	9
100-m Breaststroke	1:26.0	1:13.58	1:13.6	1:04.02	17	15
200-m Breaststroke	3:03.4	2:38.50	2:44.6	2:19.28	11	14

It seems to be the case, then, at least in terms of maximum possible performance, that the athletic potential of females is closer to that of males than has previously been realized. This impression is enhanced as one observes the incredible strength and endurance of the Russian female gymnasts or watches Jan Todd, the Nova Scotia

*From "Women's Athletic Potential" by Sally R. Luce, in *Atlantis*, **2** (1) autumn 1976, p. 13. Reprinted by permission of the publisher and the author.

woman who challenges her limitations by lifting weights in excess of four hundred pounds. Clearly, women do not have to be weaklings!

Some may argue, however, that it is only the very rare woman who has the physical potential to become strong and athletic. This is a very difficult assumption to evaluate, however, given the social context in which athletic training takes place. Dyer (1977) notes, for instance, that preconceptions about women's biological inferiority have kept certain events closed to women until recently, and Luce (1976) reminds us that adequate encouragement and training is still not available to most aspiring female athletes. Meaningful comparisons between men and women as groups must wait until true equality of opportunity has been achieved in this area.

Such equality, however, is likely to be slow in arriving. The concepts of male strength and female weakness are central to the stereotypes on which our sex roles are based. A number of researchers have demonstrated that female athletes are regarded somewhat negatively as being "unfeminine" (e.g., Griffin, 1973; Kennicke, 1972) and that they tend to experience dissonance between their "athletic" and "female" roles (Tyler, 1973). Obviously, physical strength is not seen as congruent with femininity—a fact many women acknowledge when they develop an "inability" to lift heavy parcels or open jars in the presence of a man. Furthermore, the competitiveness that is necessary to gain recognition in many sports is also seen as unfeminine (Horner, 1970). Such attitudes will have to be overcome in the course of providing equal opportunities for female and male athletes.

It is difficult to imagine a world in which physical strength is unrelated to sex. We tend to assume that women have always been weaker than men and that this sex difference is basic to our species. This assumption can be challenged, however. Friedl (1975) suggests that the sex difference in physical strength evolved in primitive societies as a result of the necessary division of labor implied by women's role in reproduction and child care. If her argument is correct, men gradually developed their superior strength over the generations in response to the demands of the environment. Given that the division of labor by sex seems to be slowly breaking down, perhaps we can anticipate that evolution will eventually eliminate sex differences in physical strength.

At present, however, it is clear that males have the advantage over females in physical strength. It is likely that this difference will decrease as females begin to receive the same encouragement and training for physical strength that males have traditionally received. Still unresolved is the question of the extent to which the differences will diminish.

SOCIAL SKILLS: WHICH SEX IS MORE SENSITIVE?

Many people credit women with a superior ability to relate to others and to manage interpersonal situations. It has been suggested that women are better at establishing friendly interpersonal relations, are more sensitive to the needs and feelings of others, and are more effective nurturers than are men. The issue of nurturance is dealt with at length in Chapter 11. The present chapter examines sex differences in several other interpersonal skills.

Are females better than males at establishing friendships with their peers? Research suggests that at least among children, this is not clearly the case. A review of the research on children's social interaction (Maccoby & Jacklin, 1974) suggests that boys are in fact more gregarious than girls. Among school-age children, boys tend to play in large groups, whereas girls focus their interaction on one or two close friends. This sex difference in friendship patterns, which appears to continue throughout childhood and adolescence, could be interpreted as evidence of greater social skills for either sex. One might argue that boys show a greater ability to relate well to a variety of other individuals and that girls demonstrate a stronger capacity for intimacy and "deep" relationships. Evidence for the depth of the girls' more exclusive relationships is difficult to find, however. There is some research that suggests that girls are more likely than boys to like those with whom they interact and that girls are more likely than boys to disclose secrets to friends (Maccoby & Jacklin, 1974). Although it is probably a premature conclusion, these findings do suggest that girls may form more intimate friendships.

Among adults, there are indications that the sexes behave differently in interpersonal contexts. Such differences may relate to success rates in social relationships. Women, for example, are consistently reported as smiling more than men in virtually every social context (Weitz, 1976). Similarly, eye contact appears to be higher among women than men (Exline, Gray, & Schuette, 1965). Both of these are behaviors that are likely to initiate, prolong, or render more pleasant many types of social interaction.

Patterns of self-disclosure, the act of revealing personal information about oneself to another individual, also appear to differ by sex. Women usually report themselves as more likely to self-disclose than do men (e.g., Cozby, 1973; Jourard, 1971), and they also seem to volunteer more intimate information about themselves and ask and answer more intimate questions (Sermat & Smyth, 1973). Since self-disclosure (at least under appropriate circumstances) seems to be related to liking and to reciprocal self-disclosure (e.g., Rubin, 1973), there is some suggestion that women's self-disclosure patterns may sometimes give them an advantage over men in the initiation and development of interpersonal relationships. There are, however, some unresolved issues. Although women generally report higher self-disclosure than men, laboratory studies of actual self-disclosure often show no sex differences or a greater male tendency toward this behavior. Colwill and Perlman (1977) have suggested that since it is consistent with sex-role stereotypes for women to report higher self-disclosure, males may underreport and/or females overreport their disclosures. Also, they note that the artificiality of the lab situation makes it difficult to generalize experimental results to spontaneous interpersonal situations. It appears, then, that findings of sex differences in self-disclosure are at least partly a function of the way self-disclosure is measured.

Women are often considered superior to men in social sensitivity and empathy. Strangely enough, although this stereotype has earned them countless positions as receptionists, social directors, official hostesses, and welfare workers, it has not won for them a significant number of appointments as international ambassadors or politicians. Perhaps this situation is due to the presence of the notion that someone who is too responsive to the feelings of others cannot make decisions in a rational, principled manner. Kohlberg (cited in Wrightsman, 1977), for example, believes that women are less likely than men to achieve higher stages of moral development because their strong relationship to their children interferes with the development of abstract moral principles!

A number of studies have found women to be more sensitive than men to nonverbal cues (Henley, 1977). The most ambitious of these studies (Rosenthal, Archer, DiMatteo, Kowumaki, & Rogers, 1974) exposed subjects of a large number of different ages and cultures to a film of a woman expressing various emotions. When subjects were asked to identify the emotions being expressed, females were consistently more accurate than males. This difference also held up when the stimulus was an audiotape on which the speaker was a man.

More recent research (Weitz, 1976) has investigated the behavioral responses of men and women to nonverbal communication. Male and female subjects were filmed as they interacted with another person of the same or other sex. Raters made judgments of what was communicated by each subject's face and body, without knowing the sex of the interaction partner. The most striking finding was that the nonverbal behaviors of women in interaction with men were significantly related to the male partner's scores of dominance and affiliation. Nonverbally, women are more submissive with dominant male partners and more dominant with submissive male partners. Weitz suggests that such accommodation on the part of the woman creates an equilibrium in the interaction that results in maximum interpersonal comfort. Interestingly enough, men showed no evidence of making such adjustments, nor did women when interacting with other women. Thus, there is a suggestion of a "female monitoring mechanism" specifically attuned to male characteristics. Such results seem to support the notion that women's greater attentiveness and sensitivity can be traced to her subordinate status relative to men. This same notion is further reinforced by reports that blacks in the United States are more nonverbally sensitive than whites (Gitter, Black, & Mostofsky, 1972).

There are, of course, other possible reasons for women's apparently superior social sensitivity. Rosenthal et al. (1974) suggest, for example, that women may have acquired this ability in the course of evolution because of the necessity that mothers be able to interpret a variety of nonverbal cues. Alternatively, a person's sensitivity may be increased by practice if s/he is engaged in an occupation that requires this type of skill: child care, acting, teaching, or counseling, for example. Rosenthal's research suggested that men in this type of profession are as good as women at decoding nonverbally expressed emotions. As he points out, however, we do not know whether such work increases a person's social sensitivity or whether these professions simply draw men who are especially sensitive.

The observed tendencies for women to be more sensitive to nonverbal social cues, to smile more, to maintain more eye contact, to self-disclose more in certain situations, and possibly to form more intimate friendships than men may all be reflections of the way females are socialized. Hoffman (1972) makes a powerful argument for the notion that girls are brought up to be more dependent on social relationships than boys are. One might argue as well that the many women who find themselves economically dependent on a man find relationship skills to be crucial to their very survival. Also, since the main occupation of many women in our culture involves the running of a home and family—a task that requires considerable adeptness at relating to others—it would not be surprising to find that women are strongly oriented toward social skills. This orientation seems to be reflected in their self-concepts. Maccoby and Jacklin (1974) report that women consider themselves socially more competent, less shy, and more attractive or acceptable to others than men do.

Although the evidence suggests that women may have an advantage over men in social sensitivity and in some other aspects of interpersonal skills, it would be wrong to conclude that women are generally superior to men in terms of social skills. For example, as is discussed further in Chapter 10, women often do not do well in situations that require direct, assertive interactions with other people. Perhaps this fact is due in part to the very sensitivity that serves them so well in other situations. On the whole, it is likely that women and men excel in different types of social skills and that many of the sex differences that have been observed in this area will be modified as the sex roles and structure of our society are changed.

COGNITIVE STYLE: DO MEN AND WOMEN THINK DIFFERENTLY?

Many of the popular stereotypes of women and men are based on the assumption that the two sexes approach the task of thinking in very different ways. It is widely held, for instance, that men are logical and women are intuitive, that it is a rare woman who has "a head for figures," and that men are more quickly frustrated and bored when performing simple, repetitive tasks. Is there any basis to the idea that males are better suited to the task of calculating formulas or that females are better at spelling and typing? If such differences truly exist, the implications are profound. There is a sad seriousness underlying Baxendale's (1975) witty comment: "Women menstruate, give birth, scrub tubs, and type letters. Men found empires, fly airplanes, fight wars and make money. Women, typing letters, become nimble-fingered and attentive to detail. Men, making money, become rich" (p. 49).*

According to Maccoby and Jacklin's (1974) recent review of studies on this topic, there seems to be some evidence for the existence of sex differences in three types of cognitive ability: verbal skills, mathematical or quantitative ability, and some forms of spatial ability. In general, females are reported to be superior to males in verbal skills, whereas males are found to excel over females in mathematical and visual–spatial ability. We look briefly at the evidence that these sex differences exist and then turn to the question of the possible reasons for such differences. As with previous issues, we use a number of different perspectives based in physiology, evolution, and socialization.

Verbal Skills

It has been consistently reported in the psychological literature that females perform better than males on verbal tasks (Maccoby & Jacklin, 1974). This finding continues to receive general support, although specific aspects of it are now open to question. It used to be thought that sex differences began at the babbling stage, with female infants verbalizing more than males. However, Maccoby and Jacklin's review suggests that there are distinct developmental phases in verbal ability for both sexes throughout the growth cycle. They report that evidence of a female advantage before the age of two is not particularly strong, that at the age of three boys tend to catch up and perform similarly to girls, and that it is actually not until the age of ten or eleven that girls begin to outscore boys consistently on a variety of verbal tasks. Some recent evidence, however, indicates that female superiority on some verbal tasks appears among children younger than ten (e.g., Bayne & Phye, 1977; Koenigsknecht & Friedman, 1976). In any case, once the advantage appears, it is maintained right through the high school and college years.

---

*Excerpt from *Are Children Neglecting Their Mothers?* by Hadley V. Baxendale, 1974, courtesy of Doubleday & Company, Inc., New York.

One problem in discussing sex differences in verbal skills is the indiscriminate labeling of a wide variety of tasks as verbal. For instance, vocabulary recognition, word naming, and pointing out and naming objects are all called verbal tasks. It is likely that there are large differences among verbal tasks in the level of reasoning or concept formation they may require. To our knowledge, no one has examined the development of sex differences in verbal skills with a view to discovering whether there are particular types of verbal tasks on which the sex difference is larger or develops at a different rate.

Another issue that remains to be resolved is the importance of the mode of presentation of verbal material. There is some evidence that boys and girls respond differently to material presented visually and orally. For example, May and Hutt (1974) presented lists of nouns to nine-year-old children. They found that boys learned the list better when it was presented visually, but girls did better with oral presentation.

In summary, research evidence in general favors female superiority on verbal tasks. However, there is some work to be done in sorting out the developmental course of this sex difference and the specific conditions under which it exists.

Quantitative Ability

Both sex and developmental stage seem to be related to quantitative ability. Until early adolescence, the majority of studies show no sex differences in quantitative skills, but males move ahead after this point and show consistently superior performance. Though the sex difference is consistent, however, its magnitude seems to vary widely across populations (Maccoby & Jacklin, 1974).

It has been suggested that adolescent boys are superior in mathematics performance because in response to societal expectations, they take more math courses than girls do. However, even when grade twelve students are matched on the number of math courses taken, males show higher average math scores (Flanagan, 1961, cited in Maccoby & Jacklin, 1974). This finding suggests that the tendency for males to outscore females in tests of quantitative ability is not solely the result of a higher level of training.

Spatial Abilities

Spatial abilities are those that enable a person to locate an object in space, mentally rearrange objects, recognize shapes, and so on. This broad class of abilities is tested using tasks such as block design, jigsaw puzzles, mazes, and matching forms. Sex differences favoring males have been found quite consistently in this area, so perhaps there is a grain of truth to the old stereotype that women tend to have severe difficulties deciphering road maps! Maccoby and Jacklin (1974) report that on the whole, studies of spatial abilities tend to show no sex differences until adolescence, when boys begin to excel. Male superiority in this area then increases through high school and lasts into adulthood.

One of the major difficulties in analyzing the findings in this area is the general lack of agreement about what abilities can properly be called "spatial" and what factors are responsible for the sex differences that are observed in performance. There has, for instance, been considerable controversy over the interpretation of sex-difference findings on tasks that require disembedding: the ability to respond to a stimulus object without being distracted by its context. A task that requires disembedding is the Embedded Figures Test (EFT), in which a subject is asked to identify a simple design embedded, or hidden, in a more complex design. The more quickly a person can do this, the more field independent s/he is said to be. A field-dependent person is one who has relatively more trouble ignoring the background figure in order to find the embedded one. Sex differences on the EFT appear to follow the same developmental pattern as those on other spatial tasks: male superiority is first observed in adolescence and is maintained in adulthood. However, Witkin (1950), who developed the test, argued that the sex difference found in performance on the EFT did not reflect only a difference in spatial ability but was also an instance of a more general sex difference in a form of analytic ability. Field independence, it was asserted, was a general ability to ignore a task-irrelevant context, whether or not the task in question was a spatial one. Witkin's interpretation was disputed by Sherman (1967), who proposed that it was the visual–spatial component of the EFT that accounted for males' superior performance. Sherman's argument has received support from two sources. First, in 1968, a small sample of congenitally blind subjects were tested on tactual versions of a block design test and an embedded figures test (Witkin, Birnbaum,

Lomonaco, Lehr, & Herman, 1968). No sex differences were found—a result that sheds doubt on the notion that sex differences in performance on a visual–spatial disembedding task can even be generalized beyond the visual mode, let alone to nonspatial tasks. Second, Maccoby and Jacklin's (1974) review of the literature indicates that in nonspatial tasks that require ignoring an irrelevant context (such as selective listening) or restructuring the elements of a problem (such as anagrams), women often perform as well as or better than men. Thus, the evidence appears to favor the interpretation of sex differences in EFT scores as being due to differences in spatial rather than analytic ability. However, Witkin and Goodenough (1976) have recently rekindled the controversy by asserting that field dependence–independence should not be equated with spatial ability, saying that although the two abilities do share some common properties, they differ on others.* Field dependence–independence is discussed more fully later in the chapter, since a great deal of research has accumulated regarding sex differences in this particular aspect of cognitive style.

Other Cognitive Abilities

Claims regarding sex differences in other abilities such as creativity, analytic ability, and reasoning have appeared in the psychological literature. It appears, however, that sex differences in these abilities are grounded in verbal, quantitative, or visual–spatial ability differences. Sex differences on tests of creativity, for example, tend to appear in favor of females when the responses depend on verbal skills. However, on nonverbal measures, no trend toward superiority of either sex emerges (Maccoby & Jacklin, 1974). Similarly, attempts to demonstrate the existence of sex differences in general analytic ability have been unsuccessful. When the analytic task is a verbal one, such as solving anagrams or finding camouflaged words, those studies that find sex differences report a superiority for females. On the other hand, when the analytic task requires visual–spatial disembedding, as in the Embedded Figures Test, males generally outperform

*For an extended discussion of this issue, interested readers are referred to H. Witkin & D. R. Goodenough, *Field Dependence Revisited* (research bulletin, Princeton, N.J.: Educational Testing Service, 1976.)

females (Maccoby & Jacklin, 1974). Therefore, there seems to be no solid evidence that males are generally more analytical than females.

A similar argument can be made in the realm of reasoning. Sherman (1967) cites evidence to show that sex differences in mathematical reasoning can often be accounted for by differences in spatial visualization, since many mathematical problems require geometric thinking. In general, there is no evidence to support the notion that men are more logical than women.

On the whole, then, it appears that few general sex differences in cognitive ability have been demonstrated. We have seen that where sex differences do exist—in the areas of verbal, quantitative, and visual–spatial and disembedding skills—they seem to be developmentally based, with verbal sex differences appearing very early and the other two appearing just before or at the age of puberty.

We have also seen that field dependence–independence is a problematic issue. The debate continues over whether this ability is simply a perceptual–spatial one, an analytical one, a combination of the two, or a completely separate ability. We have grouped it with spatial ability here but acknowledge that it may deserve a certain amount of special consideration. Thus, in the sections that follow, field dependence–independence is considered separately to some extent.

EXPLAINING THE DIFFERENCES
IN COGNITIVE ABILITY

What accounts for sex differences in cognitive ability? The answer to this question has some rather impressive practical implications. For example, if women's physiology is responsible for their relatively poorer performance in math, perhaps it would be counterproductive to encourage our daughters to go to engineering school! On the other hand, if the key to the performance difference is differential reinforcement and encouragement for mathematical problem solving, we should be reexamining the way children are taught and developing programs to counteract the negative social messages that girls and women receive about mathematics.

As is the case with other issues in the psychology of sex differences, however, neither a strictly biological nor a strictly cultural viewpoint appears to tell the whole story. An examination of several theories demonstrates that these sex differences, like most others, derive from an interaction of physiological and cultural factors.

Biological Factors

Researchers have attempted to link sex differences in cognitive abilities with human physiology in the areas of genetics, hormones, and brain development. The research results are rather complex, but we look briefly at the major findings in each of these areas and attempt to draw conclusions.

Genetics. The research on genes and cognitive ability has focused specifically on spatial ability. Several studies have shown a pattern of cross-sex correlations in spatial abilities between parents and children. That is, boys' scores are correlated with their mothers' scores but not with the fathers', whereas the reverse is true for girls (Maccoby & Jacklin, 1974).

This pattern of correlations could be interpreted to mean that at least one component of spatial ability is sex linked (i.e., a recessive gene carried on the X chromosome, as discussed in Chapter 3). If this interpretation is correct, males inherit the recessive trait through the mother, who may carry it without its being expressed. There is no reason, then, why a boy should resemble his father in spatial ability.

A girl must inherit the gene for spatial ability from both parents in order for it to be manifest. Girls tend to resemble their fathers in spatial ability, because though their mothers may carry the gene without expressing the trait, their fathers cannot. Thus, high-spatial girls will have high-spatial fathers, and low-spatial girls will have low-spatial fathers. Such a theory suggests, of course, that females will show a high degree of spatial ability only in the event that they possess two of the recessive genes for this trait. The proportion of persons with the given genetic potential for spatial ability should therefore be different for the two sexes, with approximately 50 percent of males and 25 percent of females expressing the trait. Bock (1973) has in fact shown that approximately 25 percent of women score above the male mean on standard tests of spatial ability.

The sex-linkage explanation, put forward by Stafford (1961), is carried a step further by Bock and Kolakowski (1973). These authors propose that spatial ability has two major components, one of which is sex linked and one of which is sex limited (i.e., is carried on one of the chromosomes but is expressed only in the presence of a certain sex hormone). They argue that the sex-limited component of spatial ability depends for its expression on the presence of testosterone and suggest that for females to express this trait, their bodies must produce testosterone above some threshold level. Evidence regarding the latter claim is still being gathered, and that which is available contains many apparent contradictions.

It must be remembered, of course, that everyone has some degree of spatial ability; thus, the presence of the appropriate recessive genes on the X chromosome cannot be the total determiner of the possession and expression of this trait. Maccoby and Jacklin (1974) suggest that although there probably *is* a sex-linked genetic component to spatial ability, there must be other determinants, both genetic and cultural. Obviously, we cannot overlook the role of experience and training in actualizing any genetic potential. The realm of genetics provides only a partial answer to questions about the origins of sex differences in spatial ability and little or no information about male–female differences in verbal or mathematical abilities.

Hormones. One theory that achieved some temporary popularity used sex hormones to explain sex differences in cognitive abilities. Broverman, Klaiber, Kobayashi, and Vogel (1968) postulated that male and female sex hormones affect intellectual performance by interacting differently with transmitter substances in the brain. They suggested that this differential interaction resulted in a higher level of skill on either "Type A" or "Type B" tasks, depending on the individual's sex. They described Type A tasks as those requiring overlearned, repetitive behaviors (for example, typing, naming colors, and rote learning), whose performance depended on an *activation* of the central nervous sytem. In contrast, Type B tasks were said to involve the *inhibition* of the nervous sytem's initial response tendencies in order to facilitate the reorganization of the elements of a problem (as, for example, in anagram problems or the EFT). These authors hypothesized that excess amounts of either estrogens *or* androgens (the female and male sex hormones) tended to predispose the nervous system toward activation (and skill at Type A tasks) rather than inhibition (and skill at Type B tasks). However, they believed estrogens to be more powerful than androgens in this respect; so the predisposition toward activation and Type A skills was thought to be greater in females than in males (leaving males with a superiority on Type B tasks).

This theory has received very little empirical support. As Maccoby and Jacklin (1974) point out, the classification of tasks into Types A and B does not prove useful for making sense of the observed sex differences in cognitive style. There are no consistent sex differences in tasks requiring inhibition of learned responses or in those requiring overlearning and repetition. Parlee (1972) has written an extensive critique of the Broverman hypothesis, and the reader who wishes more detail on this issue is referred to her paper.

Despite the lack of support for the Broverman hypothesis, its investigation has led to some interesting findings suggesting that sex hormone levels may be related to spatial ability. Several studies link highly "masculine" physical characteristics among males (presumably an indication of androgen level) with *low* spatial scores (Maccoby & Jacklin, 1974). This pattern of results is very difficult to interpret, given that male superiority in spatial skills becomes apparent only at puberty—the time when androgens are being poured into the bloodstream at a higher rate than ever before!

In summary, there is some evidence suggesting that sex hormone levels in the bloodstream may relate to spatial but not to other cognitive abilities. Even the results for spatial abilities, however, tend to leave one somewhat puzzled. Obviously, we must look further for an understanding of sex differences in cognitive abilities.

Brain Development. One direction in which the search has recently turned is toward an investigation of possible effects of sex hormones on the development of the brain. The human brain has two hemispheres, one of which (usually the left) is the center for language and speech and one of which seems to control spatial perception and perception of nonverbal sounds. The degree of specialization of specific abilities to one or the other of the two hemispheres varies among abilities, individuals, and stages of development. The cerebral hemisphere in which the language center is localized becomes dominant during childhood. Some theories about sex differences in cognitive abilities are based on male–female differences in the timing of the onset of cerebral dominance or in hemispheric specialization.

Attempts to relate cerebral dominance and hemispheric specialization to sex differences in cognitive abilities have been rather inconclusive. Some investigators have noted that girls often develop left-hemisphere dominance at an earlier age than boys and have suggested that this earlier development accounts for females' superior verbal performance. Though this may sound like a plausible argument, it is weakened by the fact that in addition to verbal skills, the left hemisphere seems to be the location for some analytic and sequential skills in which the sexes do not differ. If female superiority in verbal performance is due to earlier or stronger left-hemisphere dominance, it seems reasonable to expect that females should also excel in other left-hemisphere skills, unless these skills can be shown to be independent of one another in their development.

Concerning spatial skills, there are two contradictory hypotheses that involve brain lateralization. One, developed by Buffery and Gray (1972), suggests that spatial skills are stronger when they are bilaterally represented to some extent (i.e., are located in both hemispheres). Thus, males' later and weaker hemispheric specialization facilitates their development of spatial skills. The other hypothesis, proposed by Levy (1972), makes precisely the opposite prediction: strong cerebral dominance enhances performance on spatial tasks. These authors report that there is a tendency for left-handed men (whose cerebral specialization is weak) to obtain low spatial scores. According to Maccoby and Jacklin (1974), there is some evidence to support each position, and the issue is as yet unresolved.

One recent study (Waber, 1977), though not exactly resolving the issue, provides some backing for the second hypothesis. This study attempted to show a relationship among verbal and spatial abilities, degree of hemispheric specialization, and rate of physical growth at adolescence. Girls and boys aged ten to sixteen years were classified by a medical examination as early or late physical maturers and were tested for verbal ability, spatial ability, and lateralization of speech perception. The results were striking, because they indicated that the relationship between sex and spatial ability was overshadowed by the relationship between maturation rate and spatial ability. Late-maturing adolescents, regardless of sex, performed better on tests of spatial ability than did early-maturing adolescents. No significant relationship between verbal performance and rate of maturation was found. However, the older an individual subject was at the onset of puberty, the better was his or her performance on spatial relative to verbal tests. These data fit with the general observations that boys usually mature physically later than girls and also tend to be better than girls at spatial tasks.

How does hemispheric specialization fit into these results? Waber found, among the older children only, that late maturers showed greater hemispheric specialization for speech perception than did early maturers of the same age and sex. Admitting that certain aspects remain to be investigated, she postulates the following mechanism to explain her findings: maturational rate has certain physiological correlates that are probably present from a very early age. Some of these correlates (probably those having to do with hormone levels) influence the development of the organization of brain functions and thereby help to determine the level of spatial ability. She suggests that late maturers show more hemispheric specialization of abilities than early maturers and that it is this difference in specialization that mediates the effect of maturation rate on spatial ability. Her data do provide partial support for this suggestion (which is in line with the Levy hypothesis mentioned earlier), but further examination of the links between maturation rate and brain function organization and between brain function organization and cognitive abilities is necessary before it can be accepted uncritically.

Since our present understanding of how the brain processes spatial and verbal information is still quite limited, it is probably premature to draw conclusions about the degree to which brain lateralization may contribute to sex differences in cognitive abilities. The issue is extremely complicated, particularly if we add a consideration of the suggestion, made by Buffery and Gray (1972), that learning and practice of certain tasks may influence the lateralization process. Until now, we have been considering the possibility of a one-way causal relationship in which the degree of specialization influences the ability to learn certain cognitive skills. Obviously, the relationship may be a two-way one, or both factors (specialization and cognitive skills) may be influenced by other factors. We do not know whether the relationship observed between hemispheric specialization and cognitive performance implies that one influences the other. The difficulties in finding a clear-cut, unidirectional relationship between hemispheric specialization and sex differences in cognitive abilities point once again to the conclusion that these differences are multidetermined.

Learning and Cultural Factors

Training. The fact that an ability is determined to some extent by physiological factors such as genes or hormones does not mean that it is not susceptible to training. It is quite clear, in fact, that verbal, mathematical, and spatial skills do improve with proper practice. Direct training has been shown to increase performance on the EFT and other measures of visual–spatial performance. Moreover, there is some evidence that extended practice on the EFT benefits college women more than it does men and thus reduces or eliminates the sex difference in performance (Goldstein & Chance, 1965, cited in Maccoby & Jacklin, 1974). Research suggests that training in one specific task often does not seem to generalize in its effect to other tasks requiring similar abilities. Any teacher will argue, however, that this does not imply that such training is useless!

Recently, some very interesting developments have occurred in the area of mathematical education. Educators have become aware of an attitude they have labeled math anxiety or "mathophobia," which they believe is considerably more prevalent among women than men and which leads people to avoid courses, jobs, and other situations that require any type of quantitative skill (Tobias, 1976). A study of the entering class at Berkeley in 1973 (Sells, cited in Tobias, 1976) indicated that 57 percent of the freshmen males but only 8 percent of the females had had the four years of high school math necessary for eligibility to study calculus or intermediate statistics. Since all but five of the twenty possible majors at the university required calculus or statistics, 92 percent of the first-year women were left with a choice among five areas of study: the humanities, music, social work, elementary education, and guidance and counseling. Such a restriction of choice is in itself a handicap. Furthermore, the restriction is likely to become greater as the use of computers spreads and as more fields begin to emphasize research that is at least partly dependent on quantitative skills.

Both Tobias (1976) and Fennema and Sherman (1976) have suggested that the greater female avoidance of math is at least partly due to socialization. Women, they suggest, are taught to believe that math is a male domain, that females who excel in math are strange and different, and that girls are not expected to have "mathematical minds." Such attitudes are reinforced by peers, parents, and even by teachers. Ernest (1974) reports that both female and male teachers

hypothesized that for problems on which males typically show superior performance to females, more "masculine" men would do better than "feminine" men and "masculine" women would excel over "feminine" women. He used the Terman–Miles M–F (masculinity–femininity) test to measure sex typing and tested college students on problems that had shown sex differences favoring males on pretest trials. His results confirmed his hypothesis: problem-solving skill in both sexes was significantly related to sex typing, as measured by the Terman–Miles test, with masculinity being positively linked to problem-solving performance. Moreover, scores on the Terman–Miles test accounted for so much of the variance in problem-solving performance that the sex difference was no longer statistically significant. On the average, then, a man and a woman equated on their sex-typing score did not perform significantly differently on Milton's problems. Milton concluded that some aspect of the masculine sex role favored the development of problem-solving skills. Perhaps, he suggested, some types of problem solving are simply not viewed as appropriate to the feminine role, so that the girl who develops a strong feminine-role identification never engages in such behavior and hence never develops those particular skills.

Milton's results form an interesting contrast to other findings that suggest that males who are physically "highly masculinized" tend to have *low* scores on at least spatial problems (e.g., Peterson, 1973, cited in Maccoby & Jacklin, 1974). One would expect that a very masculine appearance would tend to correlate with a strong masculine-role identification. The problems Milton used were not spatial, however, so it is difficult to know what to make of this apparent inconsistency.

In dealing with either physical or psychological measures of masculinity–femininity, results are difficult to interpret because of the bipolar framework intó which they are cast. In looking at Peterson's finding that physically masculinized females have high spatial scores, for instance, we do not know whether the good performance is properly related to higher than normal levels of androgens, lower than normal levels of estrogens, or both (if, indeed, the performance is related to hormone levels at all rather than simply to the way in which the girl's physical appearance affects her socialization). Similarly, Milton's demonstration of a link between women's masculinity scores on the Terman–Miles test and their problem-solving performance does not tell us whether problem solving is related to high masculinity, low femininity, or both, since this test assumes that masculinity and femininity are opposite ends of the same dimension. Some recent research using the Bem Sex Role Inventory (BSRI), described in detail in Chapter 6, has begun to address this problem. This inventory, it will be remembered, is based on the idea that masculinity and femininity are separate, independent dimensions. Myers (1977a) examined the relationship between field independence as measured by the EFT and sex typing as measured by the BSRI. Using a small sample, she found that the most field-dependent subjects were those who were traditionally sex typed (i.e., masculine males and feminine females), whereas field-independent subjects tended to be androgynous (i.e., attributed both masculine and feminine characteristics to themselves). Such a finding is quite congruent with Witkin et al.'s (1962) hypothesis that rigid sex-role specialization is associated with field dependence.

Cognitive Style and Personality

It can be argued that the way a person thinks is inextricably related to her/his personality and interpersonal orientation. The findings relating sex-role socialization to cognitive style, discussed in the previous section, lend some suggestive support to this idea. For example, it is entirely possible that the BSRI is incidentally measuring a level of human information processing and that the androgynous subjects are what Schroder, Driver, and Streufert (1967) refer to as complex (as opposed to simple) people. The level of information processing that a person attains is thought by these authors to exert a profound influence upon the individual personality as well as the ability to integrate and differentiate in problem solving. For example, a very simple person (one who rates low on Schroder et al.'s 7-point scale) tends to think categorically and carry this black–white reasoning process into all facets of his/her existence, including, one would assume, adherence to his or her sex role. The simple person must exclude from consideration all conflicting stimuli, as s/he possesses no conceptual apparatus that can generate alternatives. A simple person should score sex-role appropriately (high masculine or high feminine) on the BSRI, therefore, because the traits would be congruent with each other and with her/his sex. Almost by definition, also, the simple person should have a simple cognitive style, including field dependence and/or low abstract reasoning ability.

The complex person, on the other hand, operates on a more

empirical plane. Thought processes are characterized by a higher degree of diversity, greater ability to discriminate between stimuli in the many dimensions s/he can observe, and an ability to integrate information into complex organizations. Because s/he is not as dependent on the external environment for making rules and decisions, one would suppose that the complex person would be more likely to incorporate traits and behaviors traditionally seen as incongruent—to act "like a man" and "like a woman," as the situation decreed—in short, to be androgynous. To our knowledge, this hypothesis has never been tested.

Witkin and Goodenough (1976) have also argued for a connection between cognitive style and interpersonal orientation, but the implications of their argument for sex typing are somewhat different. They suggest that the most important difference between field-dependent and field-independent persons is their level of self–nonself-segregation—a factor in both the cognitive and social domains. In the cognitive domain, high self–nonself-segregation refers to the tendency to rely on internal cues, whereas low self–nonself-segregation implies a reliance on external frames of reference, such as the surrounding background in the EFT. In the social domain, high self–nonself-segregation means self-reliance and autonomy in interpersonal relationships, whereas low self–nonself-segregation refers to sociability and affiliation tendencies. Thus, they argue that a field-dependent person possesses such stereotypically feminine traits as a high need for social approval and sensitivity to the needs of others and that a field-independent person is stereotypically masculine: independent, assertive, and analytical. This argument obviously makes different predictions about the relationship between field independence and sex typing than does the one just presented, and Myers's (1977a) results would seem to support the first of the two arguments. There is considerable work to be done in this area, however, and it is probably too early to draw conclusions. Myers (1977b) has suggested that the tendency to rely on internal cues in the cognitive domain (high self–nonself-segregation) and the tendency toward affiliation and sociability in the social domain (low self–nonself-segregation) are not mutually exclusive, as Witkin has proposed. Rather, she argues, the two tendencies are independent dimensions that should be measured separately. The interested reader is referred to Witkin and Goodenough (1976) and Myers (1977b) for the beginnings of an analysis of this issue.

It is still possible that an individual's performance on the EFT is simply not indicative of a general personality orientation at all but simply reflects an aptitude for visual–spatial disembedding. Attempts to link cognitive style with personality differences have been very controversial, particularly since Witkin's descriptions of the field-dependent and field-independent "personalities" are so closely matched with stereotyped female and male sex roles. At this point, it is safe to say only that men and women perform differently on the EFT. If there are broader implications of this difference, they are not yet understood.

SUMMARY

Men and women do have different strengths and weaknesses, but the number and size of such differences is smaller than sex-role stereotypes would have us believe. Men are physically larger and more muscular than women. Women seem to be constitutionally stronger than men. Women have a tendency to be more socially sensitive than men and perhaps to form more intimate relationships. Men perform better on cognitive tasks that are mathematical or visual–spatial, whereas women do better when the task is a verbal one. In examining these differences, we have seen that all of them can be viewed as multidetermined—produced by various combinations of social and biological factors. Certain differences, such as the one in visual–spatial ability, have been more clearly linked to biological sex differences than others. However, even a difference that is based on a genetic predisposition can be magnified or reduced by cultural–environmental influences. At this point in the history of our culture, differences between the sexes in the abilities that we have listed do exist. If the social structure shifts in the direction of sexual equality, however, some of these differences may well diminish or disappear.

Several points about sex differences in abilities should be kept in mind here. First of all, none of the abilities we have discussed here is an all–or–nothing thing. Women, though showing lower levels of spatial skills than men, are not so inept that they cannot keep from bumping into things as they walk down the street. Men, though less sensitive to nonverbal social cues than women, are highly unlikely to be totally impervious to their social surroundings. Thus, to say that one sex shows a higher level of a particular ability than the other is not to say that the other sex does not possess that ability.

A second point to remember is that we are discussing men and women as two groups with average levels of performance on certain tests. Within each group, a certain number of individuals deviate from the average. Thus, certain women can lift heavier weights than certain men, and particular men can outscore particular women on verbal tests.

Finally, it must be noted that for the most part, these sex differences in ability, though consistent, are not particularly large. Thus, none of the facts we have mentioned in this chapter presents any justification for the segregation of certain jobs according to sex. Individual differences rather than sex differences are the ones to be kept in mind when deciding who is the best person for the job. As a favorite women's-movement slogan so aptly puts it: "The best man for the job is often a woman," and we might add, "The best woman for the job is often a man."

8

Hilary M. Lips

THE LADDER
OF SUCCESS:
Sex Differences
in Achievement

Why are there no great women . . . ? Perhaps, we are tempted to suggest, because women have no wives. (Remember . . . "Behind every successful man . . ."). Obviously, the answer is not quite that simple. Still, one is forced to acknowledge that rarely have women achieved eminence in fields such as science, philosophy, or politics. Linda Nochlin (1973) could find no female equivalents for Michelangelo or Rembrandt, and others have looked in vain for female Beethovens.

Why this shortage of "great" women in so many areas? Are there sex differences in the drive to achieve? Is "genius" more common among men than women? Do the two sexes have a natural tendency to pour their energies into difference enterprises—women into child rearing and men into achieving mastery, success, and recognition in the world outside of home and family?

This chapter examines some of the complexities of what appears to be one of the most salient sex differences: sex differences in achievement. We take a close look at the motive to achieve: how it is aroused in women and men and how factors such as the parent–child relationship and sex-role socialization can influence its development and expression. We also investigate the aspects of the social structure that may influence achievement behavior in adult men and women. Finally, we examine the values surrounding different types of achievement in our society and ways in which these values may shape our perceptions of "typical" male and female achievements.

ACHIEVEMENT MOTIVATION

When psychologists discuss achievement motivation, they are usually referring to the concept as defined by McClelland, Atkinson, Clark, and Lowell (1953): a stable, general personality disposition to strive for success in any situation where standards of excellence are applied (in short, a disposition to seek success). The strength of a person's motive to achieve (n Ach) is measured using the Thematic Apperception Test (TAT), a projective test in which the subject is asked to tell stories about a series of pictures. The stories are then scored for the presence of themes indicating an orientation toward or concern with achievement.

McClelland and his colleagues found that achievement motivation, as measured by the TAT, could be shown to relate to performance in competitive situations in the lab as well as to later career performance for subjects tested in many different parts of the world. They also found that achievement motivation scores tended to rise, often dramatically, when subjects were given "achievement-involving" task instructions: instructions that stressed that their task performance would reflect their intelligence, organizational ability, or leadership capacity. There was only one catch: these clear, sensible, well-replicated findings applied only to male subjects. Data from female subjects appeared much more troublesome to explain. McClelland and his colleagues (1953) summarized their findings on sex differences in achievement motivation as follows: "1) Women get higher n Ach scores than men under neutral conditions (2 studies). 2) Women do not show an increase in n Ach scores as a result of achievement-involving instructions (3 studies). 3) Women's n Ach scores seem as valid as men's in that they relate to performance in the same way" (p. 178).

The fact that women's achievement motivation did not seem to be easily aroused by the instructions that McClelland had found to be achievement involving for men was interpreted by many people to mean that women simply had less need for achievement than did men. This interpretation, combined with the observation that women did indeed appear to be achieving less than men in many fields of endeavor, led to the conclusion that sex differences in achievement orientation were immense and obvious. Since achievement appeared to be mainly a male preserve, researchers in the area focused on males. Atkinson's (1958) classic work on achievement motivation mentioned women in only a single footnote, and McClelland's (1961) book, *The achieving society*, omits any mention of women. It has been only in the context of the recent interest generated by the women's movement that researchers have again turned their attention to achievement orientation in females.

The research now emerging indicates that the achievement motive is more complex than had originally been thought. For example, Crandall, Katkovsky, and Preston (1960) suggest that achievement motivation is not stable or global but may vary dramatically from one achievement area to another; Atkinson (1964) hypothesizes that a motive to avoid failure is an important determinant of achievement behavior; and Veroff (1977) proposes that there may be as many as six types of achievement motivation. Some of the recent approaches to achievement have shed new light on the problem of sex differences in achievement orientation. In the next section we examine some of the attempts to explain, from a personality perspective, the different reactions of women and men to some achievement situations.

ACHIEVEMENT AND
THE MALE AND FEMALE PERSONALITY

One of the first suggestions put forward to explain the apparent discrepancies between the sexes in achievement arousal was that perhaps women and men had the same amount of achievement motivation but that this motivation required different forms of arousal for men and women. Perhaps women's achievement motivation could be more easily aroused in areas that were stereotypically feminine. We have seen that men, but not women, responded to the achievement-involving instructions stressing leadership ability. Researchers reasoned that leadership was often thought of as a masculine prerogative. What would happen if a "feminine" set of skills (e.g., "social" skills) were stressed in the instructions? One study (Field, reported in McClelland et al., 1953) focused on convincing subjects to try to "achieve" social acceptance in a group. The arousal instructions in this case stressed the idea that social acceptance by a group was the most important determinant of life satisfaction and claimed that acceptance in the present situation was a good predictor of acceptance in a wide range of social situations. In response to these arousal instructions, women's achievement motivation scores rose sharply and significantly, whereas the men's scores showed a smaller (and statistically nonsignificant) increase.

It seems, then, that women and men may differ in the conditions required to arouse their achievement motive. A little reflection shows that some of the possible interpretations and implications of this idea are quite staggering. Most of them boil down to the basic notion that for some reason, females are caught up in an affiliation motive (a need to be liked, loved, accepted) that interferes with or takes precedence over the achievement motive, whereas for males the achievement motive predominates. This notion implies that the best way to arouse a woman's achievement motive is to link it with her need for affiliation. It also implies that for women, a conflict between the two motives will tend to be resolved in favor of affiliation, whereas the reverse will hold for men. Finally, it suggests that men will be more easily threatened by failure than will women.

Female affiliation and male achievement needs have been used as the basis of more than one psychological model of sex differences in achievement. It has been suggested, for example, that men get more satisfaction from the "intrinsic rewards" of task achievement than do women, that women more than men tend to develop a "fear of success," that men are psychologically threatened at the prospect of female competence, and that men and women differ in the extent to which they relate to the "process" and "impact" aspects of achievement. Once we have examined these viewpoints on male–female personality differences with regard to achievement, we return in the following section to the question of the possible origins of such differences.

Task versus Person Orientation
in the Motive to Achieve

It has been suggested that males are task oriented and females are person oriented: that males tend to be intrinsically interested in the task at hand whereas females tend to focus on the praise and approval for doing well that they obtain from others. Such a hypothesis would explain the apparent male–female discrepancies in achievement motivation and behavior by saying that females simply find ways to gain approval and praise that do not necessitate engaging in achievement-oriented behavior.

Straightforward and compelling though the foregoing explanation may appear to some, the evidence regarding it is somewhat mixed. Maccoby and Jacklin's (1974) extensive review of the literature showed no evidence to indicate that boys were more intrinsically interested in task performance than were girls, with the exception that preschool-aged boys showed more exploratory behavior than did their female counterparts. In terms of person orientation, Maccoby and Jacklin's review suggests that task performance of males is more likely to be affected by the presence of peers than is task performance of females—a finding that argues for person orientation in males rather than females. These authors also note that a comparison across many studies of the effectiveness of social versus nonsocial reinforcement for task performance provides no evidence for the notion that girls are more responsive than boys to social (as compared with nonsocial) reinforcement. They conclude that the task-orientation versus person-orientation distinction is not particularly useful in understanding achievement motivation in the two sexes. In fact, they point out, the greater responsiveness of males to McClelland's original "leadership" achievement-arousal instructions reflects a competitive set that, in its own way, is just as person oriented as is the female response to the "social acceptance" instructions. The implication is that males and females are both oriented toward social approval to some extent but that each sex has learned to view a different achievement strategy as effective in getting that approval.

A recent review of studies on the socialization of the achievement motive in females (Stein & Bailey, 1973) casts a new light on the issue of affiliation versus achievement. These authors point out that females, not surprisingly, attach higher value to performing well in sex-role-appropriate than in sex-role-inappropriate areas of achievement.

They argue that in contrast to intellectual, artistic, mechanical, and athletic skills, social skills are somewhat unique in being viewed as appropriately feminine in our culture and suggest that this fact, rather than the presence of an overpowering affiliation motive, is the factor that underlies women's responsiveness to achievement-arousal instructions emphasizing social skills. Their argument is supported by experimental findings that show that arousal treatments stressing social skills tend to result in increased achievement imagery (rather than affiliation imagery) for women.

Thus, although Stein and Bailey agree that achievement striving and social activity appear to be more closely related for females than for males, they take issue with the interpretation of this relationship that states that females' achievement behavior is motivated by a desire to be liked, accepted, or praised rather than by an internal desire to meet some standard of excellence. Instead, they suggest that the attainment of excellence is often a goal of both males' and females' achievement efforts but that the particular areas in which these efforts are directed are determined to some extent by cultural sex roles. For women, one of the most important areas of achievement is social skill.

Fear of Success

If we assume that women do tend to inhibit their achievement strivings in sex-inappropriate areas, we are still left with the task of explaining this phenomenon. One recent hypothesis (Horner, 1970) tries to explain the phenomenon by focusing on the anticipated consequence of success. It should perhaps be pointed out here that men may also shy away from achievement in sex-inappropriate areas. However, as is discussed later in the chapter, most areas that are considered "achievement" areas in our culture seem to be defined as appropriately masculine. Men, therefore, are less likely than women to find themselves in a situation where high achievement is sex inappropriate.

According to a widely accepted analysis of achievement motivation (Atkinson & Feather, 1966), the motivation to achieve that is aroused in a given situation depends on three things: the strength of the person's achievement motive (a personality disposition that, according to Atkinson and Feather, is comprised of both "hope of success" and "fear of failure"), the probability of success, and the incentive or reward value of success in that situation. Using this approach, it can be seen that even if a person has a very strong motive to achieve, s/he may not be motivated to achieve in a particular situation if, for example, s/he perceives that the consequences of such success would be negative (i.e., if the incentive value of success is low).

Horner (1968) hypothesized that since achievement in many areas is considered sex inappropriate for women, a woman achieving in one of these areas might feel she was losing some aspect of her femininity. Thus, success for a woman would be an ambivalent experience, having both the positive consequences of self-respect and external recognition and the negative consequences of feeling untrue to one's "womanly" nature and smarting under the real or imagined disapproval of others for being "unfeminine." If the negative consequences appeared to outweigh the positive ones, motivation to achieve in a given situation would be low. It should be noted that here again is a theory that, to some extent, pits a woman's desire for love and approval against her need to achieve excellence.

Horner's theory arose from her own observations that successful career women often seemed to feel a need to demonstrate that besides being successful in their vocational sphere, they were also successful as "real" women—that they were loving mothers, devoted wives, marvelous cooks, and impeccable housekeepers. It seemed, somehow, that society in general and even women themselves found it unacceptable for a woman to be outstandingly successful at her career if that led to the slightest suspicion that she was giving short shrift to her "proper" feminine role. These observations led Horner to postulate that for women, the negative consequences of success in terms of loss of femininity would often outweigh the positive consequences, leading to a situation where the woman developed a motive to *avoid* success. (This does not imply that the woman would be motivated to fail, just that she would avoid being outstandingly successful.) Since success for a man rarely implies any loss of maculinity, Horner predicted that a motive to avoid success would appear much less frequently in men than in women (although in certain situations, men too may anticipate negative consequences of success and therefore avoid succeeding.)

Horner (1968) began testing her predictions on a group of University of Michigan students by giving them a projective test that she hoped would measure "fear of success" (the anticipation of negative consequences for success). In the projective test, female students were asked to complete the story beginning with the following sentence: "After first-term finals, Anne finds herself at the top of her medical school class" (Horner, 1970, p. 59). Males completed a similar story about a male medical student named John. As Horner had predicted, many of the women (65 percent) told stories that incorporated either negative consequences of Anne's success (social rejection, anxiety over her normality or femininity) or denied the possibility of that success by attributing it to an error in marking, cheating, and so on. A common theme in the stories told by these women was that Anne's success threatened her relationship with the men in her life or with men in general. In contrast, fewer than 10 percent of the men told stories in which any negative consequences came to John because of his success. These results, then, supported Horner's predictions.

People who told stories in which Anne or John was shown to receive negative consequences for success were said to have shown a fear of success. The results of this and subsequent studies of "fear of success" were interpreted as supporting the same general theory of conflict between women's achievement and affiliation motives that has been referred to throughout this chapter. It appeared that many more women than men were threatened by the prospect of highly successful outcomes. The model suggested that women were actually motivated to avoid winning in order to protect their relationships with men.

This interpretation can be questioned on two counts. In the first place, it has not been shown conclusively that Horner's projective test actually taps a stable internal motive. Perhaps the negative consequences described in the stories represent not a personal fear of success but simply an awareness that negative consequences can result from success, particularly, in our society, for women. This argument gains support from the fact that male subjects, given the opportunity to tell a story about Anne instead of John, also tend to include many negative consequences for her success. Similarly, women as well as men tend more often to complete the story about John without negative consequences (Monahan, Kuhn, & Shaver, 1974). Thus the results of this type of test may be reflecting a cultural stereotype that success is often aversive for women instead of (or as well as) an actual motive to avoid success.

In the second place, it can be argued that the sex difference in "fear of success" is more apparent than real. A recent study suggests that what Horner calls fear of success may vary according to the situation. Cherry and Deaux (1975) found that men indicated more fear of success when writing about John in nursing school than in medical school, whereas the reverse was true for women writing about Anne. They concluded that although both men and women have an awareness and perhaps a fear of the negative consequences of succeeding in a "sex-role-inappropriate" situation, there is little reason to believe that women fear success in general more than men do. One can argue, of course, that the situations in which it is role inappropriate to achieve are simply more numerous for women than for men in our culture. Such an argument would explain the sex differences that often appear on this measure.

Despite the arguments about the extent to which Horner's test merely reflects subjects' appreciation of cultural stereotypes of sex roles rather than any underlying motive, there are many who believe that individuals do differ in terms of a motive to avoid success. One way of evaluating this concept is to look at how a person's score on the fear-of-success test relates to achievement behavior. Horner (1968) obtained results that suggested that women who scored high in fear of success performed more poorly in competitive than in noncompetitive situations, whereas those who were low in fear of success did better under competitive conditions. Her procedures have been severely criticized (Tresmer, 1976), but other studies appear to have shown a situationally mediated relationship between measured fear of success and achievement behavior. Makosky (1976), for example, found that women who were low in fear of success performed best when they thought they were competing with a man or when the task had been labeled as masculine. On the other hand, women who were high in fear of success did better when in competition with another woman and when performing a task labeled as feminine. It appears that if there is a motive to avoid success, it is most likely to be aroused in situations where the person has some reason to fear that negative sanctions will result from success, and such sanctions are often attached to behavior that is outside culturally approved sex roles. It must be remembered that by being outstandingly successful in a sex-role-inappropriate situation, a person is calling dramatic attention not only to unusually good performance but also to the fact that s/he has chosen to pursue a task or career that is deviant. Deviance is often punished. It has been shown, however (Jellison, 1974, cited in Deaux, 1976), that when there is a clear indication that good performance will be highly valued, both sexes tend to perform well, regardless of their scores on a fear-of-success measure.

Thus, fear of success, if it exists, appears to affect achievement behavior only in situations where there is reason to believe that negative consequences will attend success (or, at least, where there is ambiguity about the perceived consequences of success). Where there exists a clear message that success will be rewarded, both men and women, both high and low scorers on fear of success, will probably perform well.

As a final perspective on this issue, it should be noted that a successful person is not necessarily free from anxiety about the consequences of his/her success. Shaver (1976) points out that many people may be successful despite their anxiety and pay a high price in strained interpersonal relations and psychosomatic ailments. Were we to develop a foolproof measure of fear of success, we might find that its most frequent correlates were various symptoms of stress rather than behavioral measures of achievement. Following this line of argument, one could speculate that in our society, the male who fears success is much worse off than his female counterpart, since he is under greater pressure to ignore his feelings and pursue the thing he fears.

Male Threat from Female Competence

Recently, a small amount of research has been aimed at uncovering a male personality disposition that may interlock with female fear of success. Pleck (1976) calls this disposition "male threat from female competence" (MTFC) and claims that males who score high on a sentence-completion task designed to measure it experience competence in females as psychologically threatening. The results of Pleck's (1976) research showed that when in competition with their dating partners, college males high in MTFC showed an elevation in performance and a greater desire to avoid future task interaction with their partners than did other males.

If one adopts the perspective that males are seldom socially rewarded for failure or mediocrity* whereas females more frequently

*This may well be a valid assumption. Take, for instance, the case of the housewife who, after taking paid employment, finds herself unable to cope with the extra pressure this entails and retreats back to the house. The rewards are high. Pressure is removed, and she can structure the situation to emphasize her concern for her children—a concern that typically generates social approval. Few men would receive as favorable a reaction for the same behavior.

are, it is reasonable to assume that men can be more easily threatened by the competence of a competitor than can women. Pleck, however, has hypothesized a threat that is specifically relevant to the competence of a female competitor. Although one may accept the logic that competent females are more threatening because they are not *supposed* to be competent, Pleck has unfortunately not demonstrated that high-MTFC males are not also highly threatened by male competence. Nonetheless, it is interesting to speculate on the possible relationship between male MTFC and female achievement behavior. It may be, perhaps, that female partners of high-MTFC males tend to have a high fear of success. However, much research remains to be done on this concept. The possible origins of individual differences in this disposition have not been explored. A comparison between the prevalence of high threat from female competence among males and threat from male competence among females has not been made. Ultimately, however, this type of research may lead social psychologists to the place where they can investigate ways in which personality dispositions of a man–woman pair (husband and wife, working partners, or employer and employee) may interact to influence the achievement behavior of each.

Cognitive Definitions of Achievement: Process versus Impact

Veroff (1977) suggests that another personality-type variable that may help to explain sex-differentiated patterns of achievement is the individual's cognitive definition of achievement. His work in factor analyzing the responses of large numbers of adults to questions about achievement and success led him to conclude that people differ widely in the ways they cognitively define and experience a successful accomplishment. One dimension he believes to be useful for explaining sex differences in achievement behavior is that of "process" versus "impact": in considering an accomplishment, does a person emphasize the process and effort of achieving or the resulting impact of the achievement? Veroff claims that females in our culture are taught to emphasize "process," whereas males are taught the importance of "impact."

As Veroff points out, the implications of such a sex difference might be quite profound. If a creative or productive task were defined as a complex step-by-step task, perhaps women would be more motivated than men to perform well, whereas if only the end product were seen as important, men would be more motivated to succeed. Unfortunately, the examples he uses to illustrate his point are rather value laden, making those who emphasize process sound rather plodding and dull and those who are interested in impact appear insightful and quick (Alper, 1977), making his hypothesis rather difficult to swallow. Interestingly enough, if Veroff's hypothesis receives support, it will do nothing to boost the credibility of the notion that women achieve only when social factors are favorable whereas men, oblivious to social factors, take pleasure in the act of achieving. If women really do appreciate the achievement process and men focus mainly on the impact they make, it seems likely that men are more conscious of the social ramifications of achievement than are women! No conclusions are warranted at this point, because a considerable amount of research is required to test the validity of his claims. We feel that the evidence will not allow women's and men's achievement orientations to be so conveniently polarized. Nevertheless, the issue Veroff raises is potentially one of the utmost importance to our understanding of achievement patterns in women and men: how do individuals differ in their conceptions of achievement and success?

This section of the chapter has focused on some of the personality factors that psychologists have sought to use in explaining sex differences in achievement behavior. At best, the evidence for stable sex differences on the four dimensions discussed here (task versus personal orientation, fear of success, threat from opposite-sex competence, and process versus impact orientation) is weak or contradictory. On occasions (such as in the fear-of-success research) where sex differences on one of these dimensions do appear, they can often be explained as an outcome of the situational context (e.g., trying to succeed at a job that is unusual for a woman but not for a man) rather than by an underlying personality disposition. In the final analysis, we cannot be sure that there is a tendency for the two sexes to develop differing personality orientations toward achievement and success in general. It appears more likely that women and men direct their achievement efforts into different specific areas and that those who deviate from these expected patterns so often find their efforts thwarted by situational and social pressures that they are rarely able to produce highly visible accomplishments. The following section deals with the ways in which males and females become oriented toward differing achievement goals and styles.

DIFFERING PATTERNS OF ACHIEVEMENT: ORIGINS AND MAINTENANCE

Different theoretical perspectives provide various explanations for the patterns of achievement followed by women and men. The Freudian perspective might say, for example, that women are oriented toward producing and rearing babies because of an unconscious need to make up for their anatomical "inferiority" to men. Horney's version of the psychoanalytic perspective, on the other hand, suggests that men pour their energy into achievement and creativity as a way of sublimating their own unconscious envy of women's ability to bear children. Both of these viewpoints are discussed in Chapter 2. Either one of them may adequately explain behavior in individual cases, but neither one appears to fit the general data reviewed in the previous section, since they both suggest that men and women differ in the basic need to achieve.

One biological perspective, discussed in some detail in Chapter 7, suggests that men and women develop different cognitive styles and that sex differences in some cognitive abilities can be traced to the influence of genes or to the sex differences in the brain mentioned in Chapter 3. Such a perspective would suggest that there may be physiological reasons why men tend to accomplish more than women in fields such as engineering and mathematics, where as women cluster in fields that require verbal and/or social skills. The pros and cons of this perspective are not evaluated here. We note only that even given a limited biological predisposition toward different cognitive styles, men and women would not vary in their achievement patterns as widely as they do unless some other powerful factors were at work.

What other factors *are* at work? This section emphasizes two general ones: the socialization of children and young adults into sex roles and the social structure in which women and men live out their lives.

Sex-Role Socialization

Much of the work on socialization and achievement emphasizes the importance of the parent–child relationship in the development of the achievement motive. Interestingly enough, the conclusions about the best way to socialize a child to be achievement oriented differ for boys and for girls. One child-rearing dimension in which this seems to be particularly true is that of parental warmth versus hostility.* In a recent review of studies in this area, Manley (1977) concludes that parental warmth appears to operate differently on the achievement orientation of boys and girls. In general, studies showed that parental warmth was more often positively related to males' achievement orientation than to that of females. Whereas high levels of maternal warmth and affection were associated with strong achievement orientation in boys, moderate warmth and slight hostility related most strongly to girls' achievement orientation. A number of explanations for this apparently paradoxical situation have been offered. It has been suggested (Crandall et al.. 1960) that the girls who do not receive as much maternal affection turn to achievement as an alternate source of satisfaction (again, the suggestion that girls' achievement motive comes out only when not in conflict with the affiliation motive!). These authors have also suggested that the less nurturant mother may be more involved with her own achievement and thus be providing her daughter with a female achieving role model. Hoffman (1972), on the other hand, points out that some of the research results themselves may be suspect on the grounds that behavior labeled "hostility" when directed toward girls might not be so labeled when directed toward boys. Finally, it must be pointed out that if parental warmth does relate differently to girls' and boys' achievement orientation, the existence of the relationship does not specify causality. It is just possible that whereas parents who see a daughter becoming independent and achievement oriented may withdraw a small portion of their warmth from her, a son exhibiting similar behavior may be the recipient of extra praise and approval. In other words, nurturant parents may be reinforcing accepted cultural definitions of "healthy" behavior for girls and boys. This issue is dis-

*The warmth end of this dimension refers to behaviors that can be characterized as accepting, affectionate, approving, understanding, child centered, and the like, whereas the hostility end is characterized by the opposite type of behavior.

187

cussed further in Chapter 11. In this sphere as in so many others, research has not yet provided all the answers. However, there are indications that this type of pattern is sometimes present in the interactions of children with their teachers. One study of fifth- and sixth-grade children (Sears, 1963, cited in Crandall, 1963) showed that teachers switched from positive ratings of high IQ, task-oriented girls in the fall to negative ratings in the spring on dimensions such as their liking for the student. However, bright girls who were "socially" work oriented (i.e., who worked well in a social context), rather than simply task oriented, received consistently positive ratings. It appears that the teachers were reinforcing female achievement orientation only when it was manifested in a social context. This pattern was not found for boys.

An important factor in the socialization of achievement, which touches on the child's relationship with parents as well as other adults, is the presence of models. It cannot be denied that in our culture, there are fewer female than male role models in many areas of achievement, and this fact may be crucial in producing some of the apparent sex differences in achievement orientation. Where females are provided with achieving female models, their attitudes toward careers, success, and so on seem to be favorably affected. Stein and Bailey's (1973) review of the literature suggests that maternal employment in middle-class families is associated with high educational and occupational aspirations for daughters. Baruch (1972) showed that daughters of working mothers regarded the professional competence of women more highly than did those of nonworking mothers. A study of college women by Stein (1973) found that maternal employment was correlated with high achievement motivation, dominance, and endurance. Finally, Tidball (1973) found that the number of career women a college produces is positively related to the number of faculty women at the school.

The net effect of current "normal" sex-role socialization practices seems to have been the creation and maintenance of a stereotype that views men as more achieving, active, striving, intelligent, powerful, and independent than women (Broverman, Vogel, Broverman, Clarkson, & Rosenkrantz, 1972). This stereotype is seen in action in studies that look at the way people evaluate male and female performance. Goldberg (1968) showed that female college students evaluated articles supposedly written by women lower than the identical articles attributed to male authors. Pheterson, Kiesler, and

Goldberg (1971) found a similar pattern in the judgment of paintings attributed to women or men, except when subjects were told the painting had won a prize (in which case, male and female artists received comparable ratings). More recent studies (e.g., Levenson, Burford, Bonno, & Davis, 1975) have found little evidence that raters of articles are affected by the sex of the author, but this has been interpreted by some as meaning only that the antifemale bias has gone underground (Tavris & Offir, 1977). In particular, there is still evidence to suggest that both men and women who deviate from accepted sex roles in their interests are devalued (Spence, Helmreich, & Stapp, 1975).

What effect does the presence of these stereotypes have on the way women and men react to their own achievements? First of all, it seems to have a differential effect on the two sexes' expectations for success. A series of studies by Crandall (1969) provides ample evidence that females from childhood to adulthood have lower expectancies for success in a variety of tasks than do males. The studies also showed that males tended to overestimate their future performance, whereas females underestimated how successful they would be. More recent studies have documented the same phenomenon (e.g., Bar–Tal & Frieze, 1973; McMahan, 1972), although others (e.g., Feather & Simon, 1971) have failed to show sex differences in expectancies for success. There is some evidence also that expectancies are affected by the sex-role appropriateness of the task. Stein, Pohly, and Mueller (1971) found that presented with the same tasks, girls predicted better performance for themselves when the task was labeled "girls generally do better," and boys expected more success when the task was labeled "boys do better."

If sex-role stereotypes help to create different expectancies of success for males and females, just how do these differing expectations relate to actual achievement? In the first place, a number of studies have shown that people who expect to do better on an achievement task actually do perform at a higher level (Battle, 1965, and Feather, 1966, cited in Frieze, 1975). In the second place, a person's performance expectations probably influence the way s/he assigns causality in trying to explain success and failure. For example, an unexpected outcome is perhaps more likely to be attributed to luck. Such attributions, in turn, seem to influence the individual's response to success or failure: will s/he, for instance, try extra hard next time or give up?

According to Weiner, Frieze, Kukla, Reed, Rest, and Rosenbaum (1971), four frequent explanations for achievement outcomes (success or failure) are ability, effort, luck, and task ease or difficulty. Ability and effort are internal factors, considered to originate within the individual, whereas luck and task ease are environmental factors, external to the individual. Also, ability and task ease are thought of as relatively stable and unchanging, but both effort and luck are unstable factors that can conceivably fluctuate widely.

Frieze (1975) demonstrates the logical implications of various causal attributions within the foregoing framework. She explains, for example, that a person views her success with maximum pride and security when she perceives it as being due to the internal, stable factor of ability, whereas success attributed to external factors produces less pride. She points out also that if lack of ability is seen as the main cause of a failure, there is no tendency to "try again," because the person does not believe that the failure can be changed to success at a future time.

Frieze argues that maximum self-esteem would theoretically be associated with internal, stable attributions for success and external or unstable attributions for failure. She points out, however, that the sexes appear to differ somewhat in their preferred attributional patterns, with women having patterns that are the result of and/or that contribute to low self-esteem. She cites a number of studies that show women making more external attributions than men for both success and failure and notes that men rely more heavily on ability and women on luck to explain success. There is even evidence that suggests a tendency for some women to attribute their failures to lack of ability or other internal factors. Given this negative pattern of cognitions about achievement, it is not surprising that many women do not strive to excel in traditional achievement areas. More recent research (Bar–Tal & Frieze, 1977) shows a sex difference in attribution patterns even among highly achievement-motivated women and men, with the women attributing both success and failure more to effort and luck and the men relying heavily on ability to explain success and on external factors to explain failure.

It seems clear that men and women, even under conditions of equal success, do not experience success in the same way. Men have learned to take credit for success, to be proud of it, and to count on its recurrence. Women have learned to regard their successes as less susceptible to their own control and as less reliable sources of pride.

Frieze (1975) suggests, therefore, that women need more than just an extra "dose" of success to boost their self-confidence. Rather, they need to be reeducated to interpret their successes in ways that boost self-esteem and encourage continued striving.

It is evident that socialization into sex roles is an important factor in determining the achievement orientations of females and males. We have seen that the parent–child relationship appears to be different for high-achieving girls than boys, that the presence of female success-oriented models (although still rare) is positively related to success orientation in girls and women, and that women and men seem to learn to experience success as well as failure differently. Let us assume for a moment that these socialization variables could be controlled so that females and males in our culture received equal parental, peer, teacher, and even media approval and encouragement for success. Would sex differences in achievement patterns quickly disappear? We think not. The basis for this conclusion lies in the way our society is structured, and this issue is explored in the following section.

The World Out There

Properly motivated, prepared, and socialized though an individual may be to succeed in a given area, there are many external obstacles that can prevent, attenuate, or slow down that success. Years ago, Virginia Woolf suggested that great women writers would remain a rare breed until women were routinely granted "rooms of their own" in which to work (Woolf, 1929), and Linda Nochlin (1973) has recently argued that women will not become great artists as long as they are expected to continue with all the tasks that women are usually obliged to perform in our society. Any person who has tried to complete a major intellectual or creative task while keeping an eye on two small children will immediately see the point that these two women were trying to make! It is difficult to accomplish anything worthwhile without a minimum of privacy and uninterrupted time— commodities that are in short supply for the average family woman.

With a little reflection, it can be seen that families, universities, businesses, and other institutions have been structured to support male but not female achievement patterns. Traditionally, the successful male has had a supportive wife who was largely responsible for details such as laundry, meals, baby-sitters, and keeping the house clean while he focused his energy on his career. Today, even the extremely rare career woman who should find herself the lucky participant in a role reversal of this situation would have to contend with reproach and ridicule by her relatives, colleagues, and acquaintances. At best, the married career woman can work out an even split of the household chores with her husband; at worst, she may have to cope with his share of the work as well as his continuous resistance and resentment.

The dual-career couple quickly finds that society is reluctant to make adjustments for it. Large companies routinely transfer their employees with the expectation that their families will automatically be able to follow them. Job sharing and secure, well-paying, part-time employment are innovations regarded as unnecessary by many employers. Adequate maternity and paternity leaves are notoriously unavailable, and finding good day care for preschool children is often a constant headache. In the midst of the struggle to solve these problems, the woman receives frequent reminders that she doesn't *have* to go through this, is asked why she wants to work anyway, and is even scolded for neglecting her children and husband. No wonder so many women decide to set career ambitions aside and stay at home with their children!

If a couple decides to resist social pressure and have the man stay at home while the woman goes out to work, they may have to cope with extra financial problems. Statistics continue to show that women are paid less than men and that it is more difficult for them to get hired for or promoted into the highest paying jobs. It seems that many employers have continued to believe the myth that women are unreliable workers who will probably become pregnant and quit. (Sex discrimination works both ways, however. Men are sometimes not considered for jobs such as typists, receptionists, and switchboard operators, because it is assumed that they will not be satisfied with this type of job and will leave as soon as a better opportunity presents itself.)

What is the solution for the would-be career woman? Some women, after spending their college years wondering how to combine parenthood and a career (an issue, by the way, that is not even slightly problematic for most college men), decide to choose between the two or to take them on one at a time. The woman who decides not to marry or not to have children may fare better in her career without the burdens of family life.* She may, however, lack the emotional support that most career men take for granted and will find virtually closed to her the many aspects of social life that are geared for couples. On the other hand, the woman who decides to have children first and wait until they reach school age before pursuing her own career or education may find that both college programs and jobs are designed to fit the standard male rather than this female career pattern. The situation is undergoing rapid change in some areas; but it is still likely that a woman returning to school in her thirties or forties will find that mature students are not taken seriously, that scholarships are rarely available to part-time students, and that there are serious problems with arranging flexible day care for preschool children or planning an academic schedule into which family responsibilities can be wedged. The system is designed on the assumption that the student has no major responsibilities outside the academic setting. Many jobs are also designed to be filled by employees who have a partner to deal with such emergencies as children's illnesses, unexpected guests, and parent–teacher conferences. Women quickly find that whenever they resolve a conflict in responsibilities in favor of their families (e.g., staying home with a sick child), the incident is likely to be used as one more example of the "fact" that women are not seriously dedicated to their jobs (instead of the fact that there is simply no one else who is willing and/or able to look after the child).

On the whole, it seems that even if a woman is very achievement-oriented and has the advantage of a good education, she is still likely to meet more obstacles in her quest for success than does the average man. Yet many women do pursue careers and do achieve a great deal of success. One wonders what would happen if the external obstacles to female career achievement were removed. Psychologists have invested considerable time and energy studying internal personality factors and socialization processes that have an impact on sex differences in achievement. Though not denying the importance of these variables, we feel that they are inextricably linked with a social structure that simply makes it easier for males than for females to achieve career success. As long as this structure remains

---

*She does, in fact, do better economically. According to data reported by Treiman and Terrell (1975), never-married women earned considerably more than their married counterparts.

essentially unchanged, it will be only the woman who is especially gifted and/or unencumbered with family responsibilities who achieves visible success.

WHAT IS SUCCESS? A QUESTION OF VALUES

Before closing the door on the issue of sex differences in achievement, we must pause to consider the way in which values have been assigned to various achievements. In our society, writing a great novel, hitting a record number of home runs, getting a large research grant, or hitting the million mark in record sales are considered achievements; raising three children is not. The popular definition of achievement has emerged in such a way that success in the traditionally feminine domain of home and family is simply taken for granted rather than treated as an accomplishment. Perhaps nowhere can this be seen more clearly than in the difficult quest for the history of women (e.g., Rasmussen, Rasmussen, Savage, & Wheeler, 1976). A reading of traditional history books might well give one the impression that women had not even been present during most major historical events or at least that they had made no noticeable impact on the way things turned out! In North American history, one reads references to "the pioneer and his wife" (does not the wife also deserve pioneer status?) with the realization that even when working against terrible odds and under the most difficult and dangerous conditions, a woman devoting herself to her home and family is considered merely to be doing her duty rather than accomplishing anything special. Were we to rethink this value system, perhaps we would be more cautious in concluding that men have achieved more than women have.

As researchers, we often find ourselves defining achievement strictly in traditional male terms and then framing questions such as: "Why don't women achieve more than they do?" Although this may sometimes be a valid question, it is important to keep in mind the fact that a woman or man who chooses not to pursue a career outside the home cannot automatically be labeled a "nonachiever."

SUMMARY

The chapter began with a query about why there were so few "great" women. A number of psychological explanations have been put forward for the lack of eminence among women relative to men, and we made an attempt to evaluate them. We noted, first of all, that the sexes do not appear to differ in level of basic achievement motivation. That motivation, however, appears to be aroused under different conditions for males and females. Males respond best to achievement instructions stressing competition and leadership, females to instructions stressing social skills. In trying to account for this fact, some theories have stressed the idea that women have strong affiliation needs that may conflict with or override their achievement needs, whereas for men, achievement needs predominate. Our examination of the evidence for two of these theories—task orientation versus personal orientation and fear of success—leads to the conclusion that it is neither the case that women's stronger affiliation needs are overpowering their achievement drives nor that men—untroubled by a need to be liked and approved of—achieve to their hearts' content. Rather, men obtain social rewards *by* achieving, whereas women sometimes obtain them by avoiding success. Also, both men and women are more likely to obtain approval when succeeding in a sex-role-appropriate area, and more achievement areas are considered appropriate for men than for women. It is likely that the realm of social skills is one of the few in which it is considered appropriately feminine to achieve. Thus, we do not accept the explanation that sex differences in achievement are due to stronger affiliation needs on the part of women.

Two other hypothesized sex differences in achievement-related personality dispositions (male threat from female competence and process versus impact achievement orientation) were mentioned as possible factors relating to sex-differentiated achievement patterns. Both factors present interesting possibilities but as yet are insufficiently researched. At this point, we are not convinced that sex differences in these dispositions actually exist, so they cannot be invoked to explain sex differences in achievement behavior.

On the whole, it seems unlikely that a personality disposition can neatly explain sex differences in achievement behavior. Rather, women and men learn that the same behavior is differentially rewarded according to sex, and they adjust their behavior and cognitions accordingly. We have seen in this chapter as well as others that children are carefully socialized into appropriate sex roles and that their expectations for and attributions about themselves begin to fit these sex roles. Hence, as Frieze (1975) demonstrates, women and men learn to respond differently to their successes, and to their failures. It seems clear that sex-role stereotyping and the socializing processes that feed into it would require some dramatic changes to make female and male orientations toward achievement more similar.

One additional thing seems obvious, however, and it is that attempts to change patterns of sex-role stereotyping without altering the social structure with which they are linked will probably not result in a "great leap forward" for women in nontraditional achievement areas. Even if the psychological barriers that seem to interfere with female achievement in many areas (e.g., fear of success, lack of self-confidence, negative attribution patterns) were removed, external obstacles such as sex discrimination and lack of adequate day-care facilities could continue to deflect the achievement-oriented efforts of many women. This point is underscored by the fact that females consistently achieve better grades than males throughout their school years, before external impediments to achievement become a serious problem (Maccoby & Jacklin, 1974). After their school years, however, women's visible achievements tend to decrease as they encounter the stumbling blocks that come with the traditional wife–mother role.

Researchers searching for the key to increased female achievement outside the home are now focusing on the effects of experiments in family styles that divide housework and child care in new ways (e.g., Boulding, 1976) and on ways in which informal "hidden" discrimination in the work place may keep career women from achieving at their full potential (e.g., Bernard, 1976). Given an increased understanding of the forces involved, future generations may see an attenuation of the current sex differences in achievement patterns.

9 Wendy L. Josephson
& Nina Lee Colwill

MALES,
FEMALES,
& AGGRESSION

Throughout the animal kingdom, males of a species are typically more aggressive than females, and humans seem to be no exception to this general rule (Johnson, 1972). Two recent reviews of two complicated psychological literatures dovetail on this point: Maccoby and Jacklin (1974) concluded that sex differences in aggression are among the most firmly established findings in the sex-differences literature, and Eron, Walder, and Lefkowitz (1971) noted that sex differences are one of the best-substantiated findings in the human aggression literature. Yet the literature is not as simple as it might be because human behavior is complex, and research has not always found men to be significantly more aggressive than women. There are exceptions to the simple rule of greater male than female aggressivity, and that rule rests rather heavily on a matter of definition—which behaviors one decides to include in the category of aggression.

In the area of family conflict, for instance, females are not less aggressive. Wives are not significantly less violent than their husbands (Straus, Gelles, & Steinmetz, 1974), and more mothers than fathers are involved in child abuse (Gelles, 1973). It must also be recognized that the distributions of aggression for males and females overlap, so that there are some females who are more aggressive than some males.

We begin this chapter with a short discussion of these complexities in the phenomenon of sex differences in aggression. Then we survey various theoretical explanations for greater male aggressivity. Evolutionary speculations, various physiological explanations, and learning theories have all been advanced. These "answers" are at least as complicated as the phenomenon itself, and no single one of them provides an entirely satisfactory explanation. However, a number of these explanations, considered together, may provide a reasonable account of the phenomenon.

The definition of aggression is especially important for our purposes, because it has implications for the psychological perspective used and the sex-differentiated behaviors that we are willing to accept as sex differences in aggression. For example, young girls in our society tend to be socially exclusive—to make it difficult for outsiders to join their friendship groups. Feshbach (1969) regards this as the female child's special mode of aggression, yet Maccoby and Jacklin (1974) suggest it might simply be more indicative of girls' preference for smaller friendship groups. Frodi, Macaulay, and Thome (1977) included such diverse behaviors as "approval of violence, appreciation of hostile humor, and willingness to admit hostile feelings" (p. 641) in their discussion of indirect modes of aggression and reported no consistent sex differences in these behaviors. They did, however, find sex differences between nonangered men and women in the "expression of hostile or aggressive attitudes or . . . individual personality traits" (p. 641). Whether one concludes that there are sex differences in indirect aggression clearly depends on which of these measures one includes in one's definition of aggression. Many of even the broadest definitions would exclude *all* of these "indirect" modes of aggression, in fact!

The way in which we deal with the definition of aggression has implications for every area of the literature. It has long been a moot point, for instance, whether or not the greater frequency of male criminality (Mann, 1967) necessarily falls under the general rubric of aggression. Adler (1975) has suggested that the "rise of the female crook" is one of the unattractive but predictable consequences of women's liberation. She points out that many crimes are increasing more dramatically for females than for males—embezzlement, larceny, robbery, burglary, and auto theft. The fact that there is no sex difference in increase in murder over the past fifteen years leads Adler to speculate that the phenomenon represents an increase in status rather than violence: women, it seems, are merely finding their way into more prestigious crime. Whether or not this trend constitutes evidence of a reduction in the gender gap in aggression depends, once again, on what behaviors are considered aggression.

What is aggression, then? Even the coauthors of this chapter, who have trained at the same graduate school, have been unable to reach a definition that is mutually satisfying. Aggression might be defined as: *any physical behavior intended to injure another person.* But need it be *another* person? Can self-punitiveness, masochism, and suicide be termed aggression? Need the injured even be a person? Many would argue that kicking a dog until it yelps, or even kicking a hole in a wall constitute aggression. Perhaps it would be better to define aggression as *any physical behavior intended to injure,* but intent is a slippery issue. Should it be defined with reference to the aggressor, the aggressed upon, or one of several disinterested third parties? Perhaps we should drop the concept of intent and change our definition to: *any physical behavior that injures.* But even this may represent too narrow a definition. Need a behavior be physical in order to be aggressive? What about verbal attack? What about stony silence? Perhaps we should broaden our definition to include: *any behavior that results in injury.* But is the person who aims, shoots, and misses less aggressive than the person whose gun accidentally kills another person? This, of course, brings us back to intent, but now we are talking about intent without injury. Is the wish to see another person dead aggressive? Could the mere positive sanction of aggression be considered aggressive? For purposes of including a variety of relevant material, we are using one of the broadest definitions of aggression: *any nonaccidental act that causes harm to another person, animal, object, or institution.**

*Though simplicity requires that a single definition be used throughout the chapter, it should be noted that all psychologists would not agree with this particular one. In fact, Josephson is more comfortable with a definition of aggression that excludes harm to objects and institutions, and Colwill does not even require that any harm be done.

AN EVOLUTIONARY EXPLANATION OF
SEX DIFFERENCES IN AGGRESSION

If one is willing to assume that aggression has a genetic component, it is possible to construct a rather compelling argument for the idea that sex differences in aggression are one result of human evolution. Assuming that the prehistoric female of the species was often gestating and lactating and that the male of the species was larger and stronger, it may have been very functional for humans to divide labor on the basis of strength. If this was the case, men probably tended to take over the hunting and fighting aspects of human survival. Since these two activities require aggression as well as strength, strength and aggression may have become bound together in the human male. Females, the bearers and sucklers of children, on the other hand, would aid in the survival of the species best through nonaggression, by treating their offspring gently. Furthermore, hunting and fighting require being away from home for long periods of time, preferably unencumbered by a noisy and dependent infant. Yet females who hunted without their infants would return to find their suckling children dead and their line discontinued. Social groups that protected mothers from the dangerous occupations of hunting and fighting probably best guaranteed the survival of their unborn and suckling children.

Conversely, one could argue that the line of *unaggressive* females would be discontinued, for they would not defend their young. It is, of course, possible for females to excel in one very specific type of aggression (i.e., offspring defense), while being unaggressive in most other situations. In the few animal species in which females are more aggressive than males, this appears to be the case: a female's aggression is usually in the interest of survival of her offspring (Johnson, 1972).

It is possible, of course, that men did *not* start out as the stronger sex. They may have been forced to handle the jobs of hunting and fighting, mainly because the women were busily engaged in giving birth to and nursing children. Thus, greater male strength may have been a result of this division of labor rather than a cause.

Whenever we endeavor to explain the behaviors of a complex

species, we must consider the influence of society. Within any group-
ing that constitutes a society, that which contributes to its smooth
functioning is rewarded by its occupants. Therefore, even as the
biological process of survival of the fittest may have caused the selection of the most aggressive males and the most unaggressive females
as those whose genetic line would be continued, another process, a
social one, may have been taking place concurrently. This social process may have incidentally caused aggressive males and nonaggressive
females to be rewarded by the group, thereby strengthening the sex
specificity of their behaviors. The two processes might even have been
intertwined: if nonaggressive females and aggressive males were considered to be more attractive than their opposites, they would have
been more likely to be chosen as mates and hence to reproduce. Thus
although an evolutionary process implies something outside the control of a society, it can easily be aided by a group that recognizes and
rewards certain preferred behaviors that *incidentally* optimize survival.

All of our evolutionary and social evolutionary speculations are,
of course, most applicable to social groups in which long-distance
hunting was an important part of necessary food gathering. Such
cultures would probably benefit greatly from establishing a division of
labor by sex. As anthropologists have often demonstrated, however,
not all cultures display sex differences in aggression (e.g., Mead,
1935), and it seems logical to suppose that such differences may have
evolved in some cultures in response to particular environmental
pressures and their influence on division of labor.

PHYSIOLOGICAL EXPLANATIONS
FOR SEX DIFFERENCES IN AGGRESSION

Psychology has offered many and varied physiological arguments for
sex differences in aggression. This section examines several of these
explanations.

Aggression and the Y Chromosome

The most direct way in which sex differences in aggression could
be genetically based is for aggression to be associated with the Y
chromosome. At the present time scientific knowledge about chromo-

somes is too limited to tell us if this is possible (see, e.g., Hutt, 1972). If aggression were associated with the Y chromosome, however, it might be evidenced in the differential aggression patterns of males with an extra Y chromosome: XYY males.

The female karyotype is XX, the male is XY; and one in 550 males, reports Shah (1970, cited in Johnson, 1972), has an XYY karyotype. The extra Y has been associated with greater body size and with aggression. Lissey, Klodin, and Matsuyama (1973) have put forth the rather simplistic argument that Y is the chromosome of aggression and that doubling Y doubles aggression.

The XYY syndrome has also been associated with abnormally high levels of circulating testosterone, which, as we see in the next section, has also been related to aggression. Wiggins, Renner, Clore, and Rose (1971) suggest that these high levels of testosterone are due to the insensitivity of the testes of XYY males to stimulation by pituitary luteinizing hormones, which—as we have seen in Chapter 3—regulate testosterone production. The anterior pituitary, it is felt, overcompensates with abnormally large quantities of testosterone.

Whatever the speculated cause for the relationship, the argument of extreme aggression in the XYY karyotype has been made on the grounds that the anomaly is found much oftener in institutions for the criminally insane than in the normal population and that these proportions are even higher in maximum-security prisons (Court–Brown, 1967). Although an XYY karyotype argument has been put forth more than once in defense of murder in a court of law (Bartholomew & Sutherland, 1969; Evansbury, cited in Johnson, 1972), it is not a generally accepted position.

Studies of XYY males have been sadly lacking in appropriate control groups. Price and Whatmore's (1967a) careful examination of the literature indicates that although XYY males had criminal convictions at a significantly earlier age, they actually committed fewer crimes overall than an appropriate control group of XY males. Even the finding of younger conviction for XYY males is not a consistent one (Owen, 1972). The two groups were about equally likely to commit crimes against property, but when we consider crimes against persons, the results are actually in favor of a *lower* aggressivity in the XYY males: XY males have a slight edge in murder rates, their assault rate is six times that of XYY males, and their sexual assault rate two and a half times that of XYY males (Price & Whatmore, 1976b). On the whole, it appears that there is little or no evidence to link the XYY karyotype with abnormally high levels of aggression and that one might even effectively argue the opposite.

Probably one of the best arguments against aggression being carried on the Y chromosome is that it precludes aggression in females. Although the female karyotype is XX, we know that females *can* be aggressive. It is possible, of course, that the Y chromosome is a contributing factor, but it appears to be neither a necessary nor a sufficient factor. If one were to insist on a chromosomal interpretation of aggression, in fact, it would probably make much more sense to suggest that the X chromosome *inhibits* aggression, and that females have greater aggression inhibition as a function of having a second X chromosome. Since both sexes have X chromosomes, such an interpretation could better handle sex differences in aggression as we know them to exist.

Male Sex Hormones and Aggression

There has long been an assumption of a link between male sex hormones and aggression. The castration of animals, for instance, though performed for control of breeding, is also used to control aggression.

Gray (1971), in his review of the literature, comes to the conclusion that aggression "is enhanced by the presence of circulating androgen,* but androgen exercises its facilitative effect on aggressive behaviour only in animals which have differentiated sexually as male" (p. 45). "Differentiated sexually as male" is the key point. The phrase refers both to males and to those chromosomal females whose physiological systems have been exposed to testosterone during the developmental stage in which the brain differentiates by sex. Gray's interpretation implies that all adult animals, male and female, can carry within them the genetic predisposition to respond with aggression under the influence of testosterone. However, that predisposition will be realized only if, at an earlier state of development, the animal differentiated sexually as male.

As discussed in Chapter 3, an animal's brain will differentiate sexually as male only if testosterone is present during the particular

---

*Testosterone is an androgen or male sex hormone, but the terms *androgen* and *testosterone* are often used synonymously.

critical period at which the brain differentiates by sex. It is believed that certain neural pathways are established during this critical period. At puberty, the animal's hormonal system will become cyclic if testosterone was absent during the critical period, or noncyclic if testosterone was present. This developmental process occurs naturally through the influence of sex hormones on the hypothalamus during the critical period but can be produced or altered artificially with sex hormone treatments. By introducing cross-sex hormones at this critical stage, we can redifferentiate XX animals as noncyclic and XY animals as cyclic. There is some evidence that when such redifferentiation occurs in lower animals, the cross-sex pattern of aggression is also adopted. Neonatal administration of androgens to female mice (Edwards, 1969), for instance, raises adult aggression, especially if further testosterone treatments are given in adulthood (Edwards & Herndon, 1970).

In higher animals, the critical period of sexual differentiation occurs before birth. For the XX animal to differentiate sexually as male, therefore, it must be exposed to testosterone in utero. As we saw in Chapter 3, this produces mixed sexual characteristics in offspring that would otherwise have been born unambiguously female. This rare phenomenon, known as hermaphroditism, occurs when abnormally high levels of androgen are present in the body of the pregnant mother, but hermaphroditism has been artificially induced by injecting pregnant animals with androgens. Rhesus monkeys treated in this way produced offspring with ovaries, uterus, penis, and empty scrotum (Goy, 1970). These animals were reported to have engaged in more rough-and-tumble play and chasing and threatening behaviors than did their nonhermaphroditic female age-mates. Such behaviors have been described by more than one author as the young male primate's mode of aggression (e.g., Hamburg & Lunde, 1966). Even in primates, however, we cannot assume that correlation implies causation. Primates have a rich social life, and hermaphroditism may accord them differential socialization.

The effects of hormones on humans are somewhat more difficult to assess, since we cannot deliberately interfere with human fetal development. Several years ago, the synthetic hormone progestin was administered to pregnant women to prevent impending miscarriage. The progestin interacted with the women's normal androgen supply in such a way as to produce hermaphroditic children. From this tragic happening evolved a large research project, which tended to the

anatomical, physiological, and psychological needs of these hermaphrodites and collected data on all aspects of their development. Hermaphroditism is discussed in more detail in Chapter 3, but for our
purposes, it is interesting to note that by our definition of aggression,
the described behavior of these children would not qualify as aggression. Money and Ehrhardt (1972) describe them, rather, as more
self-assertive and dominant than their female age-mates. We feel that
even this description should be interpreted with caution. Unfortunately, much of their data was anecdotal, based only on retrospective
self-reports of hermaphrodites and their families, rather than on behavior observed by the investigators. Furthermore, it does not seem
altogether legitimate to draw conclusions about the effects of sex
hormones based on the comparison of hermaphrodites and nonhermaphroditic females. The prenatal administration of sex hormones
may induce other physiological effects, making hermaphrodites non-
comparable in many ways. Even more important, hermaphrodites
must certainly experience dramatic social and emotional effects of
being "born different," and these effects may well overshadow the
influence of early hormonal imbalance. Although Money and Ehrhardt's data do seem to fall into the same pattern as that from true
experiments with lower primates, whether either human or lower
primate hermaphrodites exhibit inordinate *aggression* is a moot point.
In any case, this research provides weak evidence for a sex hormonal
explanation of sex differences in aggression.

Female Sex Hormones and Aggression

The case for a link between male sex hormones and aggression is
not compelling. Can any case be made for a relationship between
female hormones and aggression? Direct experimental evidence, available only in the animal literature, is somewhat confusing. Neither the
injection of estrogen (Gustafson & Winocur, 1960) nor its removal
through ovariectomy (Conner & Levine, 1969) produces any change
in the aggression patterns of female rodents. However, lactating
female rats, which tend to be very aggressive, have demonstrated
docility following estrogen treatments.

How does the human female fit into this picture? As discussed in
Chapter 4, progesterone and estrogen levels are at their lowest during
the premenstrual and menstrual period of the female cycle. Since

unusually high levels of hostility have sometimes been reported during this period (e.g., Ivey & Bardwick, 1968), there has been some suggestion of a causal link between female sex hormones and aggression. Despite the fact that most of the evidence for such a link is based on self-reported feelings of hostility rather than actual aggressive behavior, some investigators have made much of this "aggressive effect" and have developed hypotheses to explain it. Dalton (1969), for example, suggests that the aggressive effect is not as simple as low progesterone and estrogen. The body's low premenstrual progesterone forces the uterus to rob the adrenal glands, leaving them short of the progesterone necessary for corticosteroid production. Corticosteroids are responsible for potassium and sodium regulation, and the imbalance of these chemicals, she believes, results in heightened aggression.

Some support for the idea of a link between the menstrual cycle and aggression comes from the finding that the so-called premenstrual syndrome is less pronounced in women on contraceptive pills that do not allow hormonal levels to drop as they would naturally (Hamburg, Moos, & Yalom, 1968). However, as discussed in Chapter 4, psychologists cannot even agree on what the premenstrual syndrome is, and the assumption that it includes heightened aggression is based largely on studies indicating that higher levels of irritability and hostile feelings are sometimes reported by women during the premenstrual phase. The evidence is somewhat contradictory and related only indirectly to aggressive behavior, and few psychologists currently writing on the subject would agree that a causal link has been established.

Preparedness to Learn Aggressive Responses

It is possible that there are physiological sex differences, not in aggression, but in the *preparedness to learn* aggression. Such a preparedness might, for instance, be associated with the Y chromosome. One implication of this notion is that we enter the world with differing potentials for learning aggression, depending on which genotype we have been dealt in the gender game. A preparedness to learn aggressive responses might also be a sex-limited trait, like baldness, with the genetic program existing in both males and females but requiring testosterone to release it. A third genetic alternative is that the brain is instructed by the sex chromosomes at some critical stage of development to establish different neural pathways for aggression in males and females. All three alternatives predict that males and females would experience differential learning of aggression because they respond differently to the same environmental stimuli. Conversely, one might speculate that X chromosomes, female sex hormones, or brain differentiation by sex might be associated with a preparedness to *inhibit* aggression.

In what appears to be the only study addressing the question of human preparedness to learn aggression, Diener, Bugge, and Diener (1975) found that four- to six-year-old children learned the reinforced response of punching a toy clown in significantly fewer trials if they were reinforced for hitting it hard than if they were reinforced for hitting it softly. However, boys and girls did not differ in the number of trials needed to learn either a hard or a soft response. The results of this study indicate that children are apparently prepared to learn high-magnitude punching, although we can't tell whether this preparedness is biological in origin or related to past learning experiences. (After all, a person does a lot of living before the age of four!) The point that concerns us here is that males and females appear not to be *differentially* prepared to learn this response.

Neural Reaction to Allergens: A Speculation

We have examined several physiological explanations for sex differences in aggression. It is doubtful that any one of these can serve as the definitive explanation. More probably, physiological factors interact with each other and with the environment. Nor are all the possibilities likely exhausted. Physiological explanations of the future may well proceed in entirely new directions. One such possibility is allergy research.

Moyer (1975) believes that allergens can attack the nervous system, causing swelling of brain cells that directly affect behavior. Certain brain centers have been identified as relating directly to aggression. Allergic swelling is thought to cause pressure on these neural areas, deactivating inhibitory areas or activating sites that directly produce aggressive behaviors, which can range from restless irritation to full-blown destructive episodes.

Moyer has presented the hypothesis of "inborn neural networks that are stimulated [by allergens] into activity that results in aggression" (p. 78). We might suggest the possibility that these networks are laid down during the critical period when certain sex-differentiated neural pathways are thought to be established and are thus different for males and females. It is also possible that testosterone interacts in some way with certain foods and substances, causing an allergic reaction. We do know, for instance, that testosterone interferes with the body's carbohydrate tolerance and that it speeds the metabolism of certain drugs (Hutt, 1972), making it a likely suspect for a mediating variable.

LEARNING THEORIES OF AGGRESSION

To this point, we have been discussing explanations that share the common assumption that sex differences in aggression are a built-in feature of our species. We now examine learning theories that have been used to explain how aggressive behavior is affected by the environment.

An Operant Conditioning Model of Aggression

The operant conditioning model provides perhaps the simplest explanation of how aggression is learned. Buss (1971) succinctly expresses this position as: "Aggression pays!" (p. 7). Aggression should increase when it is followed by reinforcements such as goods, services, and social approval, and it should decrease when it has such punishing consequences as retaliation and social disapproval. If an operant conditioning model is to be used to explain sex differences in aggression, we would at least have to assume that the payoff for aggressive behavior is different for males and females.

Females have a disadvantage in size and strength throughout most of their lives (Terman & Tyler, 1954), so any physical aggression in which they do engage is less likely to meet with the reinforcement of success. Boys start out at birth about 5 percent heavier and 1 to 2 percent taller than girls, and this difference is maintained until about age eleven, when the tables are turned for about three years. From age fourteen through adulthood, males are once again larger and heavier. More important perhaps is the difference in strength. Boys have 10 percent more handgrip strength, for instance, by age seven. By the time they are eighteen, their grip strength is 50 to 60 percent greater than that of their female peers. Back and leg strength show a similar pattern.

Physical assault is only one mode of aggression, however. Most definitions, including the one used in this chapter, include a far broader range of behaviors as aggression. It has been argued (by Feshbach, 1970, for instance) that females equal or even surpass males in verbal and indirect modes of aggression. Females certainly ought to be *able* to keep up to males in these areas of aggression, but two recent reviews (Frodi et al., 1977; Maccoby & Jacklin, 1974) have come to the conclusion that different modes of aggression actually account for little if any of the sex differences in aggressive behavior. Sex differences in aggression appear to be more than just a difference in the prerequisite skills. Even without these physical differences, the reinforcement histories of men and women in our society are different because of the different social consequences handed out to male and female aggressors. Studies of child-rearing practices (Sears, 1965; Sears, Maccoby, & Levin, 1957) indicate that whereas mothers almost universally discourage their daughters' aggression, they are at least ambivalent about, and may even encourage, such behavior in their sons.

There is some evidence that male and female aggression is differentially reinforced by peer acceptance. Young children of both sexes increase their aggression in the presence of their peers (Martin, Gelfand, & Hartman, 1971), although the increase is greatest with same-sexed peers. By college age the presence of a male peer observer still increases males' aggression, but a female peer observer significantly lowers it unless the males are given explicit information that she approves of aggression (Borden, 1975). Unfortunately, no female subjects were included in the adult study, but it suggests that males at least see their female peer group as negatively sanctioning aggression and their male peer group as approving it.

It seems, then, that the payoff for aggression is rather different for males and females in our culture, and this probably accounts at least in part for their differences in aggressive behavior. A problem is posed for this model, however, by a study (Eron et al., 1971) in which the relationship between aggression and parents' physical "punishment" was found to be exactly the opposite to what an operant conditioning model (and the parents!) would have predicted. Spanking and slapping did not serve as a *punishment*, since children "punished" more often and more intensely for aggression were the children most likely to act aggressively toward their peers. A social learning model, discussed later, does handle this apparent contradiction. Remember that as parents administer aversive consequences to their children, they are also showing their children how to achieve someone's compliance by administering aversive consequences.

A Classical Conditioning Model of Aggression

It has been suggested (Berkowitz & Frodi, 1977) that aggressive responses have both instrumental and "impulsive" components. The instrumental component may be learned by operant conditioning, but the impulsive component is thought to be affected by a second type of learning: classical conditioning.

A classical conditioning model begins with the assumption that aggression is an involuntary response to certain stimuli in the environment. This involuntary response is called an *unconditioned response* (UCR) to environmental stimuli, which are referred as to *unconditioned stimuli* (UCSs). Noxious stimuli appear to serve as UCSs that elicit such reflexive aggressive responses (UCRs) in nonhuman animals (e.g., Ulrich & Azrìn, 1962).

Classical conditioning involves the repeated pairing of a UCS with some neutral stimulus until the neutral stimulus alone elicits the response. The previously neutral stimulus is now called the *conditioned stimulus* (CS), and the response it elicits is now called a *conditioned response* (CR). Classical conditioning procedures with nonhuman animals, using pain as the UCS, have been moderately effective in establishing "reflexive fighting" as a CR to a previously neutral stimulus such as a light or tone (Vernon & Ulrich, 1966). According to Berkowitz (e.g., 1970), cues such as weapons, which are associated with past aggression, may elicit aggressive behavior in humans on subsequent occasions (Berkowitz & LePage, 1967), especially when subjects are angry ("set to aggress"). However, if the cues are also associated with negative consequences, including the negative emotional reactions that supposedly accompany "excessive" violence, cues may elicit "aggression anxiety" instead, resulting in the inhibition of aggression (Berkowitz, 1962).

Frodi and her colleagues (Frodi et al., 1977) have proposed that differences in aggression anxiety between males and females are partly responsible for sex differences in aggression. In reviewing the literature, they found that women reported greater guilt and anxiety about aggression and were more self-punitive after aggressing than were men.

This literature review also provided some evidence that men and women may be angered differentially by different things. Since anger has an important "priming" function in Berkowitz's model of aggression, this would be expected to result in different patterns of aggression. Berkowitz (1962), in fact, suggested that such differences in anger arousal and aggression pattern might exist between the sexes. However, Frodi and her associates were unable to identify any such patterns.

Frodi and her colleagues have found "scanty but hard to ignore" (p. 654) evidence that although some cues like aggressive humor serve equally as CSs for men's and women's aggression, other stimuli such as weapons and aggressive models may be aggressive cues (CSs) only for men. Recent investigations in Berkowitz's labs (e.g., Berkowitz & Frodi, 1977) indicate that aggression is strengthened when the eliciting cues have been associated previously with reinforced aggressive responses and weakened when the cues have been associated with punished responses. If boys are reinforced for aggression more than are girls, it seems likely that more cues will be associated with reinforced aggression for boys. Extrapolating from Berkowitz's experiments, then, we would expect to find more situations involving cues that would elicit aggression from males. It is also tempting to speculate that men's sensitivity to weapons as aggressive cues may stem from a history of playing aggressive games with toy weapons—traditionally "boys' games" in our society.

A further extension of the classical conditioning model has been made by Hokanson and his colleagues to explain sex differences in aggression. They found (Hokanson & Edelman, 1966; Hokanson, Willers, & Koropsak, 1968) that males' physiological arousal decreased dramatically after they were allowed to give electric shocks to someone who had insulted them. Females showed no such decrease following aggression; in fact, their arousal decreased following a friendly response toward their insulter. The authors hypothesized that this was because a reduction in physiological arousal accompanies any response strategy that successfully removes noxious stimuli. Assuming that aggressive strategies are usually successful for males whereas nonaggressive strategies (such as friendliness) are more successful for females, Hokanson and his colleagues hypothesized that males' aggression and females' friendliness are reliably followed by removal of noxious stimuli.* These responses eventually come, through classical conditioning, to elicit the relief response (reduction of physiological arousal). According to Hokanson, this relief response *reinforces* the response strategy of aggressiveness for males and friendliness for females. However, he and his associates were able to teach the relief response for aggression to their female subjects simply by changing their reinforcement history: reinforcing aggressive responses with nonshock trials and shocking subjects if they made a friendly response.

A Social Learning Model of Aggression

The learning theories discussed so far are concerned more with regulating behavior already in the performer's repertoire than with the acquisition of new behaviors. Classical conditioning involves learning to perform an old response in the presence of new cues. Operant conditioning affects the frequency of established responses in a given situation. Some new behaviors may be acquired through an operant process called *shaping*—the progressive reinforcement of behaviors increasingly. more like the desired response—but such a process is slow and awkward. To better explain the rapid acquisition of complex responses, we turn to Albert Bandura and social learning theory.

Bandura maintains that most novel responses we learn are acquired *before* they are performed, through observational learning (sometimes called modeling, imitative learning, or vicarious learning).

Learning to Perform Novel Aggression. The social learning theory of modeling includes four subprocesses (Bandura, 1971): attention, retention, motoric reproduction, and motivation. Two of these, motoric reproduction and motivation, are performance variables and have

---

*See Chapter 10 for a discussion of this sex-differentiated use of power in the context of family decision making (Kenkel, 1957).

already been discussed under the topic of operant conditioning. It is certainly likely that motoric reproduction (behavioral enactment of the observed responses) is affected by physical sex differences and that motivation differs as a function of different reinforcement/ punishment expectancies for males and females. But what about initial learning? Do females actually acquire fewer aggressive responses?

Hicks (1965) "cancelled out" performance differences (motoric reproduction and motivation) by having children verbally describe (rather than act out) a model's destructive behavior and also by explicitly offering a reward for recalling the model's behavior. Girls recalled significantly fewer destructive ("aggressive") actions against toys than boys did, even under these conditions. This suggests that girls may actually attend less to models' aggressive acts or may retain less. Yet it appears that when the content is not aggressive, females are generally every bit as good as males at learning from observation (e.g., Hale, Miller, & Stevenson, 1968). There seems to be something special about aggressive behaviors that makes females less likely to attend to them or retain them, possibly relating to reinforcement history or even biological preparedness.

It could be argued that people are likely to see more male than female models reinforced for aggressive behavior. This is true both for real-life observations and media models. If males are more aggressive than females, for whatever other reasons, modeling might just preserve the status quo. It has been pointed out (Gerbner, Gross, Eleey, Jackson–Beeck, Jeffries–Fox, & Signorielli, 1977) that when female characters are involved in violent television scenes, they are about twice as likely as male characters to be on the receiving end. According to Bandura (1971), seeing the model reinforced or punished for a response affects attention as well as performance processes. Since violent scenes involving women tend to show negative consequences for (at least television's) female models, perhaps differences in attention account for male and female differences in acquired aggressive behavior. Evidence is sketchy, but we do know that girls' facial expressions show significantly less interest and arousal than boys' expressions if both are watching males engage in violence on television (Ekman, Liebert, Friesen, Harrison, Zlatchin, Malmstrom, & Baron, 1972).

Whether or not the difference in acquisition is attentional, it may (also) be retentional; the information connected with a model's actions may be rehearsed or encoded in long-term memory differently depending on the sex of the observer. For example, power appears to be an important characteristic of a much-imitated model of either sex (Grusec & Mischel, 1966). It may be that an aggressive act is encoded as a power move by males but not by females.

Maintaining Aggressive Behaviors: Facilitation, Inhibition, and Disinhibition. Models who are observed to be reinforced (Bandura, 1965) or who hold high-status positions (Bandura, Ross, & Ross, 1963) can facilitate the performance of previously learned behaviors, especially if the observer has been reinforced for imitating a model in the past (Adams & Hamm, 1973). Related to this is a disinhibitory or inhibitory effect on previously acquired behavior. When a model is punished for some response, that response is inhibited in the observer (i.e., the observer is less likely to perform that response). When a model is observed to receive *no* punishment for a behavior that has been directly punished in the observer's past, disinhibition occurs: the frequency of that behavior increases for the observer (Bandura, 1965). Since aggression belongs in a response class subject to strong inhibitions, it can be disinhibited when observers see it go unpunished. The most important function of disinhibitory modeling as it influences sex differences is probably informative: it is likely that a keen observer could learn the differential consequences of aggression for males and females without ever having to be directly reinforced or punished.

One source of disinhibitory models in our society is thought to be television. Eron, Huesmann, Lefkowitz, and Walder (1974) report that "one of the best predictors of how aggressive a boy will be at age nineteen is the violence of television programs he prefers at age eight" (p. 420). This relationship did not occur for girls, perhaps because the "might is right" message of television's typical violent programs is implicitly qualified with "for men, of course" (e.g., Gerbner et al., 1977). It is tempting to further speculate on what effects programs such as "Charlie's Angels" and "Wonder Woman" might have on girls. Eron et al. (1974) felt that the growing availability of viable aggressive female models might be one reason why the eight-year-olds they studied in the early 1970s did not show the same sex differences in aggression that characterized eight-year-olds in the early 1960s. They point out, however—and reader beware!—that this argument is not good enough to establish a causal relationship between the variables. It could very well be, for example, that girls are becoming more aggressive and that the incidence of aggressive female models in the media (and real life!) is also increasing but that both result from a third factor, such as a changing role for women in North American society.

Maintaining Aggressive Behaviors: The Effects of Self-reinforcement. A particularly unique feature of the social learning approach is that it recognizes the effects of self-reinforcement; individuals do extensively control their own lives by the consequences they produce for their own actions. Bandura (1971) has pointed out that parents directly reinforce children for adopting parental standards for their behavior and that self-reinforcement is also influenced by parental and other models in the environment. Children thus learn to reward or punish their own behavior by imitating models who reward or punish them.

The concept of *identification* has been used by some authors (e.g., Eron et al., 1971) to describe the process by which children adopt the standards of others into their own self-reinforcement systems. Gewirtz and Stingle (1968) have argued that identification is merely generalized imitation of classes of "diverse but functionally equivalent behavior" (p. 379), and this has led some researchers to use imitation as a measure of identification.

Frequency of confessing wrongdoings and guilt, used as measures of internalization of parents' standards, correlated negatively with children's aggression in the study reported by Eron and his colleagues in 1971. The extent to which children imitated their parents' expressive style related to children's aggression in a similar way. For eight-year-old children these identification measures, along with punishment and instigation (such as parental rejection and nonnurturance), were among the best predictors of concurrent aggression against peers. Of these three factors, only identification reliably predicted the children's aggression ten years later. In a later article (Eron et al., 1974), Eron and associates reported that "low identification with both parents is the most potent predictor of aggression, irrespective of the subject's sex" (pp. 419–420). This indicates that parental identification and the self-reinforcement standards it implies seem to have far-reaching effects on behavior.

Furthermore, identification appeared to have modified the effects of punishment on eight-year-old boys' aggression. Although children rarely showed high identification with very punitive parents, those boys who did identify with highly punitive fathers tended to be

quite nonaggressive. The boys who had low or moderate identification with their fathers showed the pattern remarked upon earlier in
this chapter: the greater the punishment for aggression, the more
aggression was shown toward peers. We know now, of course, that
directing an aggressive act as obvious as physical punishment toward a
child has a modeling potential as well as a punishing potential. Eron et
al. concluded that the child who internalized parental standards was
influenced more by the punitive aspect of such an act. From our
self-reinforcement perspective, this would correspond to adopting
the model's reinforcement contingencies into one's own system of
self-reinforcement. The less highly identified child, on the other
hand, responded more to the modeling aspect of the aggressive act.

Hyde and Schuck (1977) suggest that one reason for sex differences in aggression may be the high proportion of female punishing
agents in children's lives: usually their mothers and their elementary-
school teachers. Female children would be expected to identify more
than male children with a female punisher. Girls, argue Hyde and
Schuck, will therefore reduce their aggression as a result of punishment. Boys' aggression should increase as a result of punishment. It
should be noted that Eron et al. (1977) found mothers to be more
effective punishers than fathers for children of both sexes. If girls
identify with the more effective punishers at home and the primary
punishers at school, we should certainly expect them to be less aggressive than boys!

As evidence for their thesis, Hyde and Schuck reported data
showing that girls in kindergarten and nursery-school classes were
less aggressive than their male classmates and that they also identified
more with their (invariably female) teachers than did boys. In addition, boys were significantly more likely than girls to persist in aggressive behavior after aggression had been punished. This correlational
evidence by no means implies causation, however, so this interesting
proposition remains without solid support.

Unfortunately for Hyde and Schuck's identification thesis, little
support for it can be found in the earlier study by Eron and his
associates (1971). Although it appeared that same-sex modeling of
aggression was important (correlations of a child's aggression being
much higher with the aggression score of the same-sex than the
cross-sex parent), there was no evidence that children generally identified more with the same-sex parent. Nonaggression was even more
strongly related to cross-sex parental identification than to same-sex

parental identification. At any rate, high identification with either parent corresponded to low aggressiveness for both boys and girls.

Sex-role identification, measured by preference for the games and activities typically chosen by girls or boys, also showed some relationship with aggression but only on a few measures for either sex. Eight-year-old boys who preferred girls' games were less aggressive than other boys at that time and ten years later. Aggressive eighteen-year-old females showed a preference for televised contact sports and had "masculine" scores on the MMPI Masculinity–Femininity (Mf) Scale. Eron and his associates (1974) had offered this correlational evidence to support the contention that sex-role identification affects aggression. The usual caution against interpreting correlation as causation applies here, of course. An additional cause for concern is the failure of these measures of sex-role identification to relate to aggression consistently. For example, the level of aggression shown by eight-year-old girls was unrelated to their preference for sex-typed activities, and neither preference for televised contact sports nor Mf score predicted eighteen-year-old males' aggression. This may be because the measures lack reliability and/or suffer from some of the other inadequacies of masculinity–femininity measures discussed in Chapter 6. We certainly would not recommend any of these measures! For whatever reason, the evidence implicating sex-role identification in the development of aggression is equivocal, and even if it were not, its correlational nature would render it merely suggestive of such a relationship.

The evidence at hand, then, provides little support for either Hyde and Schuck's "identification with the punisher" explanation or for the "sex-role identification" thesis of Eron and his colleagues. Identification appears to be a powerful variable in determining aggression, but it remains to be seen whether parental identification or sex-role identification affects males' and females' aggressiveness differentially.

SEXUALITY AND AGGRESSION: AN ASIDE

In our review of the literature on sex differences in aggression, we are intrigued by a supposed link between sexuality and aggression, most dramatically exemplified by rape. There are some data that provide a possible neural basis for this relationship. We know that at least in monkeys, electrical stimulation of a certain area of the brain has elicited penile erection, and stimulation less than a millimeter away elicited a rage response (MacLean & Ploog, 1962). There is on record more than one case of brain tumor being held responsible for abnormally high patterns of both aggression and sexual activity in humans (e.g., Mark & Ervin, cited in Johnson, 1972).

The body chemical acid phosphatase, which may provide us with another physiological link between sexuality and aggression, has been implicated in sex differences in aggression. The prostate gland, part of the male's internal sexual apparatus, dramatically increases its production of acid phosphatase during sexual arousal (Mann & Lutwak–Mann, 1951). Since high acid-phosphatase levels have been correlated with anger arousal in male, but not in female, humans (Barclay, 1969), there may be a chemically sex-differentiated link between sexuality and aggression. The reader is reminded that they are describing, not necessarily a causal, but merely a complex correlational relationship.

One of the reasons that sexuality and aggression are linked so strongly in the public consciousness may be that for Freud, the two were considered inseparable biological forces. His analysis of sadism, masochism, Oedipal conflict, and penis envy all reflect this viewpoint (see Freud, 1924/1970). For Freud, aggression could be turned inward or outward, and he explained many of the sex differences in aggression and sexuality through these different mechanisms. Masochism, for instance, was seen as the normal female's aggression turned inward and a necessary part of all female sexual response. Masochism was not seen as normal in males, of course!

It is also interesting to note that Freud believed humor to be repressed aggression, and some of the neo-Freudians have considered humor a purely masculine domain. "Women are less fond of jokes than men" reports Grotjahn (1965), without data: "A witty woman is a masculine woman" (p. 121).

The obvious limitations of the Freudian model of sex differences lead us to search further to explain why sexuality and aggression might be more strongly paired in males than in females. It could be argued, for example, that we evolved differentially by sex in this regard, since the sexual aggressivity of males may have been important, and the sexual aggressivity of females irrelevant, to survival. Such an argument relies on the assumption made by many writers (e.g., Brownmiller, 1975) that males have always forced females to copulate. As we see in Chapter 12, however, this is not a universal assumption (Sherfey, 1966). In any case, an evolved physiological sex difference could be due to one or more of several factors: sex differences in the proximity of "sexual" and "aggressive" areas of the brain, or sex differences in acid phosphatase, sex hormones, or sex chromosomes, to name a few. Even if one were to adopt such a model, however, it would be difficult to discount the effects of learning. As we see in Chapter 12, we are capable of learning a myriad of sexual responses, one of which may be to respond to certain stimuli with both sexual arousal and aggression.

The relationship between sexuality and aggression may well have a social psychological basis. Malamuth, Feshbach, and Jaffee (1977) have suggested that there are taboos against sexual and aggressive responses in our culture, and they have theorized that lowering inhibitions against one of these taboo responses also disinhibits the other. The relationship between sexual behavior and aggression is expected to be stronger than that found with other socially constrained behaviors, partly because of their common linkage in North American popular culture. "In many cultures, the extent and degree of societal concern about and suppression of one of these activities parallel the other" (p. 123). Sexual behavior and aggressive behavior are also believed to be especially well-linked taboo responses because they share physiological and behavioral features. It should be noted that such similarities may promote an actual mislabeling of sexual arousal as anger, or vice versa, as hypothesized by Zillman and his colleagues (e.g., Zillman, 1971).

Malamuth and his associates argue that the sexuality–aggression link is learned equally by males and females. They even report data that indicate that females as well as males become more sexually aroused when inhibitions against aggression were lowered. Why is it, then, that males have a virtual monopoly on rape—the epitome of the sexuality–aggression relationship.

It could be that rape is the inevitable crime of a misogynous society, one that has historically devalued women and exalted men. Coupled with this philosophy is a sex-role prescription for male aggressivity and female passivity, male dominance and female compliance. Russell (1975) suggests, in fact, that the rapist is not a deviant but an overconformer. In the same vein, Brownmiller (1975) contends that we socialize women to be perfect rape victims by teaching them that part of their sexual role is subservient compliance to men's sexual desires. In her best-seller, *Against our will*, Brownmiller's (1975) thesis is simple: rape is not a crime of passion, but a crime of power:

> Man's discovery that his genitalia could serve as a weapon to generate fear must rank as one of the most important discoveries of prehistoric times, along with the use of fire and the first crude stone axe. From prehistoric times to the present, I believe, rape has played a critical function. It is nothing more or less than a conscious process of intimidation whereby *all men* keep *all women* in a state of fear. [p. 5]*

Brownmiller considers rape to be man's strongest means for controlling women: rape, threat of rape, and protection from rape:

> But among those creatures who were her predators, some might serve as her chosen protectors. Perhaps it was thus that the risky bargain was struck. . . . The historic price of women's protection by man against man was the imposition of chastity and monogamy. A crime committed against her body became a crime against the male estate. [pp. 6, 7]

Early laws against rape were thus property laws. Punishment for rape in early Assyria, for instance, was rape of one's own wife. In other parts of the world, financial payment to the victim's "house"— father, brothers, or husband—was extracted from the rapist (Brownmiller, 1975). Since the social position of a woman's house was the determiner of her sexual worth, Anglo-Saxon law set the rapist's fee with reference to her husband's or father's economic worth (Clark & Lewis, 1977).

Although this historical analysis may seem like the rehashing of a long-antiquated perspective, our laws and court decisions still reflect the ideal that a woman's sexuality is the property of some man. Thus the court favors high-socioeconomic-status virgins and monogamous wives over those to whom Clark and Lewis refer as "common property": the unemployed, the separated, the drug user, the alcoholic, the "promiscuous," the "idle."

Physiologically, psychodynamically, and socially, psychologists, philosophers, and political writers have proposed many links between

---

*From *Against Our Will* by Susan Brownmiller, New York: Simon & Schuster and London: Martin Secker & Warburg Limited. © 1975 by Susan Brownmiller. Reprinted by permission of the publishers.

sexuality and aggression. This is not a trivial issue, not an ivory-tower argument, for an understanding of the link between sexuality and aggression may someday help explain the frightening behavior of Jack the Ripper and Son of Sam.

SUMMARY

Males tend to be more aggressive than females. This phenomenon is among the most consistently reported findings of two psychological literatures—the areas of both sex differences and aggression. The distributions of males' and females' aggression overlap, but it seems safe at present to say that the typical male is generally more aggressive than the typical female. It has been suggested, however, that the gender gap in aggression is shrinking.

Our conclusion that males are more aggressive than females and the nature of the evidence we have been examining in this chapter are greatly influenced by the definition of aggression we have adopted: "any nonaccidental act that causes harm to another person, animal, object, or institution."

The explanations for why a sex difference in aggression should exist are far from clear-cut. They may have their source in our evolutionary origins. If division of labor was originally based on gender—either because males started out stronger or because of females' biological role as bearers and sucklers of young—male aggression, but not female aggression, would be one determinant of fitness to survive. Social history may have functioned in a parallel or interactive way.

An evolutionary argument would lead one to expect a physiological basis for sex differences in aggression. The physiological explanations used so far are desperately in need of good human data to support them: explanations linking human aggression with the Y chromosome, male sex hormones, and female sex hormones rely on correlational studies of XYY males, hermaphroditic females, and self-report data of women at different points in their menstrual cycles. In most cases the data are seriously flawed, and in no case do they provide convincing support for a physiological basis for sex differences in aggression. Preparedness to learn aggressive responses has been tested experimentally and yielded no sex differences. Physiological explanations for human sex differences in aggression are obviously in need of a great deal more empirical support than is presently available. One new direction for research in the area is suggested by research into neural reactions to allergens.

Learning theories of aggression are a bit more successful in accounting for sex differences in aggression. The operant conditioning model explains at least part of the difference in terms of differential payoff for aggression, but it is insufficient to explain much of the available data. The classical conditioning model leads us to suspect that differences in aggression anxiety affect males' and females' aggression. Differences in anger arousal may exist between the sexes, but they do not appear to affect aggression in the expected manner. Recent evidence hints at the possibility that some stimuli may serve as aggressive cues for males but not for females. Research by Hokanson and his colleagues has indicated, furthermore, that men experience a reinforcing "relief response" following aggression and that women experience this response following nonaggressive coping responses.

The acquisition of new aggressive responses occurs most commonly through observational learning, according to social learning theory. There are some data indicating that females acquire fewer aggressive behaviors, even when the performance variables of motoric reproduction and motivation are equalized for males and females. Differences in attention and/or retention may be responsible for this acquisitional difference. Children observing media or real-life models may inhibit or disinhibit their aggression according to the reinforcing or punishing consequences experienced by models of their own sex. It has been suggested that identification with same-sex parents and teachers or with one's sex role may mediate sex differences in aggression, but there is little evidence that this is so.

The popularized relationship between sexuality and aggression—epitomized by rape—appears to be stronger for males than for females. A search for clues to the reason for this phenomenon turned up a number of physiological possibilities: sex differences in proximity of "sexual" and "aggressive" areas of the brain, acid phosphatase, sex hormones, or sex chromosomes. There are also evolutionary, social psychological, and sociopolitical explanations available.

10

Hilary M. Lips
& Nina Lee Colwill

THE PARADOX
OF POWER

Men have long been regarded as members of the more powerful sex. In most societies, men rather than women have led the armies, run the governments, and controlled the resources, whereas women have found themselves mainly in service positions. In recent years, advocates of the movement for women's liberation have called repeatedly for changes in the social power structure, with the stated objective of giving women a larger share of the power and, thus, more control over their own lives (e.g., Morgan, 1970). It should not be surprising that men might find such a call threatening, and indeed, some authors have gone so far as to attribute an alleged increase in male impotence (in our society, truly a symbolic loss of power) to the rise of the women's liberation movement (see Julty, 1972). What is somewhat more puzzling than the male reaction is the fact that a large number of *women* are vocal in their opposition to the feminist call for changes in the power relationship between the sexes. If women really do have considerably less power than men in our culture, why should some women oppose a change in the balance? Anti-women's-liberation activists such as Phyllis Schlafly insist that women already have all the power they need and that they actually stand to lose power by becoming "liberated." She and her followers have successfully blocked the passage of the Equal Rights Amendment in a number of American states. Obviously, powerful women can be a very frightening prospect, not only to men—who have traditionally held the power—but to all who have an investment in the status quo. At the turn of the century, Queen Victoria, one of the most powerful women in history, greeted the power gains of the suffragettes with the following proclamation:

> The Queen is most anxious to enlist everyone to join in checking this mad wicked folly of Women's Rights, with all its attendant horrors. . . . Woman would become the most hateful, heartless and disgusting of human beings were she allowed to unsex herself; and where would be the protection which man was intended to give the weaker sex? [Queen Victoria, quoted in Nunes & White, 1973, p. 10.]

Since then, many millions of words have been written by bright and articulate women presenting the pros and cons of giving women a share of society's power. *The feminine mystique* (Friedan, 1963) had hardly become a best-seller before *A sixpence in her shoe* (McGinley, 1964) advocated that woman find her real power in homemade soup and a beautiful, efficient kitchen. Germaine Greer's (1971) strong cry for power in *The female eunuch* was quickly countered by *The total woman*'s (Morgan, 1973) claim of the divine rightness of feminine power through subservience.

It seems that one of the issues at the root of this controversy is the interpretation of the word *power*. What we try to do in this section is to come to grips with the concept of power and to examine the ways that it is achieved, denied, maintained, and extended by men and women in our culture. Central to our discussion is the question of whether men and women achieve and handle power differently.

STYLES OF POWER AND INFLUENCE

When a social psychologist talks about power, s/he generally means the ability of one person to influence another's behavior. The range of behavioral outcomes through which the power holder can move another person is an index of the amount of power held (Thibaut & Kelley, 1959). Using this definition, we begin to see that power can take many forms, some of which might be extremely subtle. Timidity and helplessness are two subtle methods of influence that some people feel women have used to establish a tyranny of weakness. Jean Mundy (1975) has written of such "helpless heroines." She contends that women have been enraged by centuries of oppression and sex-role conflict but have learned that because anger is labeled unfeminine, it is therefore ineffective. Women have therefore rejected the direct expression of their anger as a means of controlling others and have settled on passive aggression. The methods they use, Mundy suggests, may even be below the level of their own awareness. They direct anger inward, becoming sick or depressed and helpless; they develop phobias that inconvenience their oppressors; they withhold sex and household services or give them "generously" in resentful martyrdom.

How well does such passive aggression work as a method of control? There is some evidence that whereas assertive or even verbally aggressive tactics win husbands more influence in decision making, passive or even ingratiating tactics characterize influential wives (Kenkel, 1957). This may mean that both sexes can best influence by the technique with which they are most familiar—male aggression or female passivity. It may also mean that both sexes are easily disarmed by the techniques with which they are unfamiliar. In any case, it appears that modes of influence in our culture are clearly sex typed.

Recently, social psychologist Paula Johnson has developed a theory that relates sex-role stereotypes to power use (Johnson, 1976). She suggests that there are three major dimensions on which power use is affected by sex-role stereotypes: direct–indirect, concrete–personal, and competent–helpless. This three-dimensional model encompasses many of the concepts Mundy identifies as feminine modes of influence. Johnson considers investigation of the different modes of influence associated with the male and female sex roles to be crucial in the understanding of sex differences in power. The mode used has implications not only for the success or failure of the influence attempt but also for the issues of self-esteem, perception of the influencer by others, and degree of success in future influence attempts.

Indirect versus Direct Power

Whereas direct power is demonstrated when a person exerts influence openly, by giving an order or making a request, indirect power is exercised when the influencer obtains the desired outcome while trying to keep the other person unaware of the influence. Indirect power is often called manipulation.

Johnson suggests that in our society, there are many constraints against directness by women and that, consequently, women more than men tend to rely on indirect power. Many feminist writers (e.g., Morgan, 1970) have noted that a woman who uses direct power is quickly labeled unfeminine, castrating, and bitchy. Furthermore, even a casual perusal of the popular magazines devoted to advising women about interpersonal relationships indicates that women are actually instructed to use manipulative, rather than direct, strategies to get what they want (i.e., "Let him think it was his idea").

A further reason why women may rely more heavily than men do on indirect power is that in our culture as well as in virtually every other, men are the holders of authority (Rosaldo, 1974). Authority is a particular type of power in which the power holder is recognized by the society as having a legitimate, abstract right to make decisions and to command obedience. Obviously, a position of authority lends considerable force to any attempt to exercise power directly. Rosaldo notes that a person who tries to exercise a significant amount of power independent of authority is regarded as manipulative, disruptive, and troublesome and is generally not taken seriously as a powerful person, even though s/he may exert considerable actual influence.

In recent years, our society has witnessed the emergence of a movement toward a more honest and direct use of power (e.g., Brown, 1973). This movement can probably best be exemplified by the tenets of assertiveness training—the teaching of assertion as opposed to nonassertion or aggression. Nonassertion can be thought of as the sort of passive aggression Mundy describes as typically feminine. Aggression, in this context, is the power-through-force control technique so often associated with males in our society. Assertion is a direct, confident expression of one's needs and feelings, standing up for one's rights without violating the rights of others. Assertiveness training purports to teach its students to replace the indirect, ineffectual, guilt-producing, power techniques of nonassertion and aggression with the more direct, effectual, and respect-producing, power technique of assertion. Men, of course, can benefit from this type of training, but it is largely women who have embraced assertion as a way to increase their personal effectiveness. They are learning to say what they mean and to calmly insist upon their rights, thus making their mode of influence direct rather than indirect.

The shift toward more direct modes of influence will probably benefit women in the final analysis. Johnson's (1976) article underscores the notion that the use of indirect power, although potentially effective in the short run, may have long-term negative consequences for the user. She points out that when the source of power is concealed, the person wielding the power may not be regarded as powerful, may be kept in a subordinate position, and is not likely to view her/himself as a strong person.

Personal versus Concrete Power

An individual's attempt to exercise power is given weight by the amount and nature of resources under his/her control. The implied threat in any influence attempt is that a refusal will be met by invoking the resources at the power holder's command in order to induce compliance (Kipnis, 1974). Johnson (1976) suggests that resources can be divided into two categories: those that depend on personal relationships, such as liking and approval; and those that are concrete and independent of relationships, such as money, knowledge, and physical strength. She argues that in our society, men have considerably more control over concrete resources than do women and that women therefore rely on personal resources more than men do. Perhaps one reason for this is that women have always operated from a lower physical power base than men. They tend to be physically smaller and weaker than men, and history records that their biological role as the bearers and nursers of babies placed them at even more of a physical power disadvantage for much of their adult lives. At a time when physical strength was all-important in determining survival, the individual woman found it necessary to cleave to a man for food and protection. She had little concrete physical power in such a pairing but bargained with the personal skills of nurturance and sexuality that she possessed. The nature of this relationship may well have been the basis for women's learning of personal and indirect techniques of power attainment and maintenance.

Personal resources are certainly not unimportant. Women have often been known to use the threat of a denial of love, affection, and sex to gain cooperation from men. Perhaps this helps to explain why women—given their relative physical weakness, biological role as mother, and centuries of economic dependence and legally sanctioned inferiority—have not been completely relegated to slave status. Nonetheless, as Johnson points out, this type of power is effective only in those areas of influence that are affected by a personal relationship. Also, it has the disadvantage of leaving the influencer highly dependent on others. Although a woman may hold great personal power in an individual relationship, it is often not of the sort that generalizes beyond the relationship or holds up in a court of law. For example, a woman may hold great personal power over her husband, easily gaining his compliance to her wishes. This same woman could, in many parts of North America, legally be refused credit, denied the privilege of returning to her birth name, and given poorer pension and insurance benefits than her male counterpart.

It should be noted here that there is one concrete resource that women have always had and that is crucial to society—their ability to bear children. However, their perceived and actual control over this resource has varied considerably over the centuries. Before the relationship between sexual intercourse and pregnancy was clearly understood, fertile women were often accorded a unique respect and had, perhaps, some measure of power because of this. In fact, it seems possible that woman, perhaps because of this mysterious power to bring forth new life, was originally the more powerful of the two sexes (Davis, 1971). Later in history, however, it was perceived that the male was also a necessary element in the conception of a new human life. At this point, reproduction lost whatever usefulness it had as a concrete resource for women in power situations. As de Riencourt (1974) so aptly puts it:

> When man became fully aware of his biological role in the creating of new life . . . he was, in fact, in full control of the fate of woman. . . . Just as the farmer plowing the Earth Mother sows his seed purposefully, so does the male penetrate the female and discharge his semen in the full knowledge that an offspring will grow out of it. The identification of the plow with the phallus and of semen with seed became widespread in all agricultural communities. . . . [p. 34]

Men ceased to worship the "Mother Goddess," asserted their own supremacy, and began to force women to bear children. Church and state laws were developed that gave husbands the right to have sexual intercourse with their wives with or without the wife's consent and that forbade wives to take any measures to prevent or terminate pregnancy. Recent technological advances and changes in the law are giving women an increasing measure of control over their own reproductive processes. Perhaps society has now reached a point where the ability to bear children can be used successfully as a concrete resource by women.

Helplessness versus Competence

Johnson (1976) suggests that because women are often in situations where they are not regarded as or do not feel competent, they tend to rely on helplessness as a mode of influence more than do men. By being or acting helpless, women can get men to do the hard heavy work around the house, look after the family's financial affairs, take care of problems with the car, and so on. It should be mentioned, though, that men are not above using helplessness as a power tactic, as many women have discovered when they first asked their spouse to do a laundry, cook supper, or change the baby's diaper.

Johnson suggests that helplessness, though effective in the short run, does not establish its users as strong influencers and may contribute to both low status and low self-esteem.

Sex Roles, Legitimacy of Desired Outcome, and the Dimensions of Power

Johnson's (1976) research on people's reactions to power use in hypothetical situations offers some support for the notion that people in our society view expert, legitimate, informational, and direct forms of power as stereotypic of males and personal reward and sexuality as stereotypic of females. Results for other hypothesized female sources of power, such as helpless and indirect forms of power, were not as strong but were in the predicted direction. Johnson suggests that men are allowed to use many different kinds of power depending on the situation, whereas women are more severely restricted to the less aggressive types. If this explanation is correct, it sheds considerable light on the resistance by many women to the changes in sex roles advocated by feminists. Women may feel that if they are "liberated," their traditional modes of influence may no longer be effective, and yet they do not anticipate being comfortable with or good at the more direct modes. Consequently, they may foresee a "liberation" that results in a net loss, rather than a net gain, of power for women.

There is another aspect to the differential use of the various modes of influence by the two sexes, however. New research reported by Johnson and Goodchilds (1976) suggests that the situation is an important determinant of the type of power that will be used by the participants. For example, the study indicates that in a dating situation when the issue of sexual intimacy occurs, men are seen as using direct methods to influence a woman to have sexual intercourse, and women are perceived as being capable of equal directness in turning a man down. In a reversal of this situation, however, subjects suggested that a woman would be very indirect in her effort to seduce a man and the man would be correspondingly indirect in refusing her. Johnson uses these results to suggest that a person engaging in an out-of-role power manipulation is likely to be less direct than someone operating within his/her role expectations. A more general explanation might be, however, that the more legitimate a person perceives his/her demands to be, the more direct will be the mode of influence used. If this is indeed the case, it would seem that the feminists' struggle to legitimize the demands of women for equal rights will eventually make it easier for women to exercise direct power in a wide range of situations.

Pat Mainardi's (1970) witty essay, "The politics of housework," outlines the helpless and indirect tactics her husband used in his attempts to avoid his share of the housework. Of course, as a man, he was well within the rights of the traditional male role in refusing to do many household chores. However, in the course of their marriage, he had acknowledged the legitimacy of his wife's argument that housework should be shared, and this acknowledgment disallowed him the future use of direct means of influence such as flat refusal. The arguments that he did use were as indirect ("Housework is too trivial to even talk about"), irrelevant ("Women's Liberation isn't really a political movement"), and helpless ("I don't mind doing the housework, but I don't do it very well") as one might ever hope to find.

STATUS AND POWER

It appears that men as well as women make use of the "feminine" modes of influence as the situation requires. Perhaps what appear to be sex differences in power tactics are actually differences between groups of people who perceive themselves as being, respectively, powerful or powerless in a particular relationship or situation. One way to investigate this possibility would be to systematically alter the initial power of men and women in particular groups and watch for changes in the number and type of influence attempts.

Such an investigation was carried out by Marlaine Lockheed and Katherine Hall (1976). They began by noting the existence of a widespread belief that women can work successfully as the equals or superiors of men only if they are modest, quiet, and inconspicuous. Furthermore, in reviewing the research on mixed-sex small groups, they found three general patterns that seemed to support the idea that when working with men, women do tend to behave inconspicuously and modestly. The three patterns are as follows:

1. On the average, men initiate more verbal acts than women.

2. A woman is more likely to yield to a man's opinion than vice versa.

3. Men spend a larger percentage of their interaction time making suggestions and giving orientations and opinions to the group, whereas women spend the larger percentage of their interaction time agreeing with or praising others in the group. [pp. 112-114]

The authors note that these patterns of sex differences in behavior have been attributed to differences in sex-role socialization (e.g., women are taught to be passive). They, however, propose an alternative explanation for the findings—one that is directly relevant to the suggestion that sex differences in influence strategies are the result of perceived differences in initial power and legitimacy. Lockheed and Hall suggest that other factors in a group being relatively equal, sex serves as a status characteristic that influences the expectations of competence for individual group members. Theoretically, the relative power and prestige of group members is determined by their relative status. The authors cite considerable evidence that the male state is more highly valued than the female state in our society. They therefore suggest that the male state carries with it a higher status, which is translated into higher expectations of competence for men, which leads in turn to the occupation by men rather than women of positions of power and prestige in the group. In other words, high-status persons get more respect from the group from the beginning and hence are more likely to become informal or formal leaders. According to this hypothesis, if women's initial status could be raised, their contributions to and level of influence in the group would rise accordingly.

If there were a society in which maleness and femaleness were equally valued, it would be a simple matter to put this hypothesis to the test. However, according to Rosaldo (1974), every known society assigns a higher value to people and tasks classified as male than to those classified as female. The next best test of the hypothesis, then, is to reduce the impact of initial status differences between male and female group members in some way. One method might be to provide the females with prior experience in the task being attempted by the group. Such experience would enhance their perceived competence. This type of experiment was carried out by Lockheed and Hall in an effort to assess their "status" hypothesis. The research used four-person groups that were either single-sex, mixed-sex, or mixed-sex with females having prior task experiences. Their results indicated, first of all, that when in single-sex groups, males and females did *not* differ in terms of verbal activity or task orientation. This finding demonstrates that the sex differences on these dimensions that appear in mixed-sex groups are situational rather than "true." Second, the results showed that in mixed-sex groups, males were seven times as likely as females to emerge as leader *unless* the females had been allowed to develop task-specific expectations for competence. It was found that engaging in the task first with other women significantly increased the number of task-oriented acts initiated by women in later, mixed-sex groups.

Taken as a whole, Lockheed and Hall's findings suggest that the reason women do not often claim leadership positions in mixed-sex groups is neither that women are less task oriented or active than men nor that women and men naturally assume complementary submissive–dominant roles in a work group. Rather, they indicate that initial status characteristics determine the power and prestige of group members unless that determination process is actively interfered with.

The laboratory findings just described may have extremely important implications for power relationships between men and women in the work place. For instance, it is a common complaint of male executives, faced with pressures to hire and promote more women, that women do not want promotions and do not seek responsibility. Perhaps it is true that women, recognizing their lower initial status and realizing that they will have to prove themselves at every step to male colleagues who automatically have higher status, are hesitant to seek promotion. Certainly, it has been documented that in occupational situations, the woman who is a "token" or a part of a small minority is often the victim of subtle put-downs by her male colleagues and is systematically excluded by the "stag effect" at conventions and in other work-related social situations (Bernard, 1976).

Rosabeth Moss Kanter's (1975) research on women in the work place began as an attempt to isolate the variables that separate women from career success. She sought to discover sex differences in personality or background that made women poorer leaders than men. What she found instead were poor leadership and success skills, not in women, but in certain people: people in token positions, people in dead-end jobs, people in powerless positions of leadership. These people were characterized by rigidity and hostility toward outsiders and powerful superiors. They appeared to have more concern for socializing than for advancement. Moss Kanter's observations led her to conclude that when women are fully accepted as colleagues and given realistic chances for advancement, they no longer take the role of low-status persons but interact actively with their co-workers and display ambition and task orientation that is commensurate with their abilities.

Dr. Moss Kanter is not the only writer who has suggested that observed sex differences in approaches to power may be due more to status differences between the sexes than to any biological or learned behavior. Many feminists feel that several of our cultural structures work to maintain sex differences in status, which in turn maintain sex differences in power. One such structure is language:

> Consider reversing the generic term Man. Think of the future of Woman which, of course, includes both women and men. . . . Think of it always being that way, every day of your life. Feel the everpresence of woman and feel the nonpresence of man. Absorb what it tells you about the importance and value of being woman—of being man.

> Recall that everything you have ever read all your life uses only female pronouns—she, her—meaning both girls and boys, both women and men.*

Many feminists believe that our language must be changed in order to remove an important barrier to female power, yet the process is slow. The words *mailperson, journeyperson,* and *countryperson* still stick on the tongue, and only the habit of use will free them readily.

Another way in which the status difference between men and women is reinforced lies in the terms of address we use for them. Men are men, but women are girls or gals (the child-woman), chicks or broads (the sex object). It is not uncommon to hear fifty-year-old women referred to as "the girls." Even a woman's name usually incorporates her marital status (Miss or Mrs.) and the surname of a man (her father, husband, or ex-husband), a carry-over from the days when women were nonpersons under the law and had to be defined as the property of some man. "Thou shall not covet thy neighbour's wife, nor his manservant, nor his maidservant, nor his ox, nor his ass, nor anything that is thy neighbour's" (Exodus 20:17). It is, in fact, considered proper to refer to a woman by her husband's full name prefaced with "Mrs.," as in "Mrs. John Smith." History gives us one analogy to this practice: that of black American slaves being given the names of their white masters.

Communication involves more than words, however, and some authors, including Nancy Henley (1973), have suggested that nonverbal communication is even more influential than language in maintaining the power differential between men and women. She contends that we have worked out nonverbal power games in our culture: certain tones of voice, certain body stances, that communicate, "I am your superior" or "I am your subordinate." Her examples are all the more dramatic, because when pointed out, they are readily recognizable as power-game rules, although they seldom enter conscious thought. Henley believes that much of the nonverbal communication that characterizes male–female relationships adheres to this model, with males communicating superiority messages and females com-

*From "Woman—Which Includes Man, of Course" by Theodora Wells, printed in the Newsletter of the Association for Humanistic Psychology, December 1970. © Theodora Wells 1970, 1972. All rights reserved. Reprinted by permission of the author. (Copies of the complete article are available from Theodora Wells, P.O. Box 3392, Beverly Hills, CA 90212.)

municating subordinate messages. Subordinates and women, for instance, are characterized by their controlled, circumspect behavior and are touched by other people more than are superordinates and men. Henley further suggests that when women break these rules by staring, touching men, or loosening their demeanor, their actions are interpreted not as power plays, which are unacceptable female motives, but as sexual invitations.

Is Henley's analysis insightful or trivial? The evidence mounts that our communications, both verbal and nonverbal, are saying things about us that the listener may not even be aware of hearing and absorbing. The extent to which these communications shape our power hierarchies should be the topic of much future research.

The analysis of power differences by sex as a social status phenomenon suggests that as status differences between the sexes diminish, so too should sex differences in power orientation. It could be argued, however, that sex differences in status *have* been significantly diminished, yet women, as a sex, have still failed to gain power strongholds. Lionel Tiger (1969), a noted anthropologist, tries to explain this by postulating an inherent biological male–male bond, evolving from prehistory, that still somehow causes men to cling together—the better to hunt, to build, to decide, to invent, and to protect their women and children. Within this bond lies the power of society that women, by biological definition, can never share. Tiger, who bases his argument partially on observed behavior in primates and partially on anthropological studies of a number of cultures, claims that women are never likely to play a significant part in politics because males are biologically predisposed to form and maintain all-male groups, particularly when they are involved with matters of consequence. He also suggests that females have a biologically based inability to release the patterns of behavior in subordinates that could be termed "followership." Therefore, he suggests, the evidence points to the conclusion that male dominance is a biologically rooted condition of human nature. In accordance with this position, he predicts that if a powerful body, such as a cabinet, were to become dominated by women, its importance and activity would be reduced. Even if the powerful bodies of a community become dominated by females, he says, the male-centered dominant group will soon recur. This argument is taken to the following conclusion by a historian, de Riencourt (1974):

> It seems clear that men's refusal to include women in their various associations is motivated by something profoundly rooted in biological reality, rather than mere prejudice and desire to discriminate against them. . . . it goes back to the prehuman primates in whose days, millions of years ago, this form of sociosexual exclusiveness ensured the survival of the group. [p. 57]

Needless to say, Tiger's detractors have been legion (e.g., Weisstein, 1971). It can be argued convincingly that his statements are based on insufficient evidence and that his conclusions serve conveniently to let men "off the hook" as far as the issue of sex discrimination is concerned. Nevertheless, his hypothesis is one that is interesting enough to be taken seriously, if only because the implications of accepting it are so far-reaching. If Tiger's argument is valid, we can never expect large numbers of women, however philosophically egalitarian our society becomes, to attain positions of real legitimate power in our present structure. Tiger himself suggests, however, that a radical restructuring of our present society might overcome its alleged biological predisposition toward male dominance. This suggestion moves us back toward the notion that the amount and type of power wielded by each of the sexes is dramatically influenced by our social organization and culture. It seems permissible to assume that whether or not male dominance is rooted to some extent in the biology of the human species, the pattern is amenable to change in response to variations in the social structure.

THE NEED FOR POWER

We have, to this point, limited our discussion of power to its attainment, its maintenance, and its styles. However, most of the research on power has probably been in the area of power motivation: the tendency to seek impact on others (Winter, 1973). There are, of course, individual differences in the need for power (n Power), which is measured by a semiprojective test.

A question worthy of attention in the context of this chapter is whether having a high need for power has different ramifications for men than for women in our culture. In men, n Power is correlated with leadership in small groups, organizations, and institutions; athletic participation; and efforts to manipulate and persuade others. It has also been found that power-motivated men seek relationships with weaker persons who will follow them and avoid conflict, prefer wives who are dependent and submissive, are interested in pornographic magazines, and tend to have more sexual partners (Winter & Stewart, in press). Other research indicates that men who are high in n Power are more likely to have been physically aggressive toward women (Slavin, 1971) and to be separated or divorced from their wives.

Until recently, there has been very little research on women with high power motivation. However, there is now some evidence that many of the correlates of n Power in men also hold for women (Stewart, 1975; Winter, 1975). The major exception to the similarity between the correlational patterns of men and women seems to be that women high in power motivation do not have the same difficulties in their male–female relationships.

Stewart and Rubin (1976) measured sixty-three dating couples on their individual power motivation and their personal satisfaction with their dating relationship. Two years later subjects were contacted to see if the relationships were still intact. The researchers found that the higher a power-motivation score the men received, the less satisfied they were with their relationship at the early testing and the more likely was the relationship to be terminated within the two-year period studied. For women, no relationship was found between power motivation and either satisfaction or stability in the relationship. The data also revealed that highly power-motivated men tended to be more promiscuous and less likely to marry during the two-year period, whereas this relationship did not hold for women. Stewart and Rubin suggested two interesting interpretations. Highly power-motivated women may be more adept than their male counterparts at handling power conflicts and therefore more able to keep the relationship intact. It is also possible, they suggest, that whereas highly power-motivated men are characterized by the "Don Juan syndrome," highly power-motivated women may seek lasting relationships with men in order to possess them. These two interpretations are not inconsistent with each other or with some of the power issues we have discussed in this chapter. It seems quite reasonable to assume that the men and women having a high need for power in this study may have used different modes of influence. This may partially explain the finding that highly power-motivated men had a different effect on intimate relationships than did highly power-motivated women.

SUMMARY

We have seen that power comes in many forms and that women and men tend to use it differently. In our society, men hold more of the positions of authority and control more of the concrete resources, such as wealth, than do women. Thus, men have more opportunities than women to wield power that involves threats or rewards based on these resources and to wield that power openly and directly. Women, on the other hand, may often find themselves in positions where the only way they can exert influence is through subtle manipulation. There appears, however, to be no built-in sex difference in power styles. Rather, the difference is a result of the social structure that awards men higher status and stereotypes them as more competent than women. When women are in positions of authority or are making a demand that is perceived as legitimate, they also use direct power. Mothers, for instance, regularly give orders to their children and use rewards or threats based on concrete resources to influence their behavior.

Research supports the notion that the social situation influences sex differences in power use. As Lockheed and Hall (1976) demonstrated, women's performance in a group can be markedly affected by giving previous experience to enhance their competence and hence, their status. Women whose status had been raised in this way were more able to participate in the group and to exert some leadership influence. In a similar vein, Kanter (1975) showed that the difficulties women have in moving into leadership positions in male-dominated organizations are not specifically linked to their sex but are shared by all people who find themselves in token or dead-end positions. If sex differences in power style exist, they seem to be due to the fact that the resources on which power is based are distributed unequally between the sexes.

This chapter also raised the issue of how differences in power are maintained. We saw that such subtleties as who touches whom and the use of the masculine pronoun to refer to humans in general help to create a climate where power differences between men and women go unquestioned.

Finally, in looking at the need for power, we saw no significant differences between men and women in the strength of this need. However, men and women high in the need for power seem to behave differently in some respects.

It must be remembered, of course, that status hierarchies, power differentials, and dominance–submission are not necessarily "natural" parts of the human condition. Fromm (1973) points out that many so-called primitive hunting–gathering societies are characterized by an absence of dominance or even permanent leadership associated with high-status qualities or skills. This leads him to suggest that the social structure adopted by a group of people determines, in a large measure, their need for power differences and status hierarchies among themselves, and he claims that the psychology of dominance–submission is an adaptation to a social order rather than a natural human condition that generates a particular social structure. This point of view is an interesting one to keep in mind as one speculates on the type of society that might emerge in the course of women's struggle for equal status with men. Men are beginning to complain that the traditional masculine role, with its built-in authority, is often restricting and burdensome (Pleck, 1976). Will some women simply adopt some aspects of this male role and be accepted, in proportion to their numbers, into society's power elite? Will the process of the struggle for equality result in dramatic changes in the social structure itself? Or will the struggle prove so exhausting and futile that women and men will eventually resume their traditional power modes and relationships, with very little lasting change?

11 Nina Lee Colwill, Judy Conn, & Hilary M. Lips

WIVES & HUSBANDS, MOTHERS & FATHERS

There are sound reasons why we have allowed the subject of marriage and the family to occupy an entire chapter in a book on the psychology of sex differences. The roles of spouse and parent, which consume such a large portion of adulthood for most people in our society, are highly sex differentiated. Nowhere are the stereotypes that shape and define the responsibilities and rights of women and men more obvious than in the expectations surrounding the roles of wife, husband, mother, and father. These roles are highly complex, yet are fairly standardized from family to family, and many of their subtleties are understood by the youngest child (e.g., Emmerick, 1959). So central are they to our lives that actions that deviate from them can fill us with guilt and self-doubt. Indeed, the ultimate argument produced by critics of the feminist movement is that "women's liberation" will result in the destruction of the family.

There is no doubt, of course, that changes in sex roles will affect the family or that significant alterations in family structure, size, or means of livelihood will influence sex roles in general. A better understanding of such changes requires an examination of men's and

women's familial roles and the sex differences, real and assur
which they are based.

Perhaps the most important reason for us to study husban
wives, fathers, and mothers is to try to determine whether their roles
really must be sex dependent. A very good case could be made for
keeping women in the home and out of the job market, for instance, if
women could be shown to have a unique aptitude for nurturance.
There is little point in discussing alternative life-styles that allow parents to share employment, housework, and child care if men are
incapable of the latter.

This chapter examines the roles that our society prescribes for
women and men in the family. We investigate the bases of these roles
and consider the degree to which the evidence suggests they can be
altered. Finally, we take a brief look at some emerging alternatives to
the traditional family.

"I NOW PRONOUNCE YOU MAN AND WIFE"

The implications of the wedding ceremony are far more profound
than sharing life and home together, raising children together, and
growing old together. Marriage and the preparation for marriage
open a whole new world of sex roles.

Traditionally, the man "pops the question" by giving his bride-
to-be an engagement ring. Social events are held in her honor by
female friends and relatives who give, expressly to the bride, gifts that
are later to be used for the maintenance of their joint home. The
groom is often honored in a less formal social function known as the
"stag"—his last night out with the boys—his last night of freedom.

The bride's parents usually assume financial responsibility for the
wedding—probably a throwback to the dowry. The wedding arrangements are typically the responsibility of the bride and her
mother, a considerable task in a society where weddings are such big
business.

The bride's parents usually are "pleased to announce" the engagement of their daughter through a local newspaper and the mar-

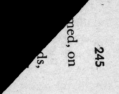

hter through the wedding invitation. On the day of
bride is beautiful in a ritualistic way, wearing a
il to symbolize virginity. She is adorned with flow-
is enhanced by her bridesmaids. She and everyone
r must be beautiful. Ann Landers has more than
upon to solve the dilemma of the bride with a
egnant best friend who expects to be chosen as a
bridesmaid.

The music begins; the guests stand and turn to watch the bridal
attendants' procession, followed by the bride on the arm of her father.
She is "given away" by him to the groom, whom she may promise to
obey. They are pronounced man and wife.

"You may now kiss the bride."

In the reception following, the bride is toasted by a friend or
relative of her family. The groom responds with thanks to the parents
of the bride for their lovely daughter. The bride says nothing, no one
toasts the groom, and his family remains unrecognized.

This marriage ritual indicates that in some ways, the woman is a
member of the more revered sex in our society. She has, since childhood, been the recipient of male chivalry, a throwback to the days of
knights and ladies and the cornerstone of the romantic ideal. We are
all familiar with romantic love as the basis for North American marriage. The myth of romantic love is spread by fairy tales such as
Cinderella, Sleeping Beauty, and Snow White, in which the handsome
male overcomes obstacles to marry the beautiful maiden with whom
he has fallen in love (Rubin, 1973).

The romantic ideal introduces an interesting paradox, for it demands that deference be paid to the sex that is least powerful in terms
of authority and control over resources. In most societies, deference is
a ritualistic acknowledgment of power (D'Andrade, 1966), and in
most measurable ways, males are the more powerful sex in our society
(see Chapter 10). We do have mechanisms through which wives pay
deference to their husbands, however. The marriage tradition de-
crees that though the man is still a man, the woman becomes a wife.
This role assumes that she will adopt not only her husband's surname
but his credit rating and status in the community. Old friends cannot
trace her whereabouts without knowledge of his name. In exchange
for this deference, he will assume the responsibilities of husbandhood.

The Responsibilities of Husbandhood

One of the prime functions of a responsible husband in our society is economic support of his wife and children. In a study of suburban housewives, nearly 65 percent of the subjects stated unequivocally that the most important function of their mate was breadwinning. Their role as father came second and husband, a poor third (Brenton, 1966).

Our society is structured in such a way that whereas wives may, with varying degrees of difficulty, choose between paying careers, nonpaying careers, or some combination thereof, husbands have seldom felt free to exercise the same range of options. Job opportunities, wage differentials, and children have combined to create a situation in which the male partner has been the principal family breadwinner. Working to earn the family's living is usually considered an obligation of husbandhood. This obligation is more than a financial one, for the prestige of his chosen occupation will largely determine the status his immediate family enjoys in the community (Udry, 1971). "The man freed from his kin obligations," says Skolnick (1971), "must support his wife and children in the style to which they aspire to become accustomed. He is caught between demands to achieve and succeed, in the difficulty of joining security and satisfaction on the job, whether he works as a janitor or corporate president" (p. 22).

It has been suggested (Gould, 1973) that our society goes so far as to define a man's masculinity by the size of his paycheck. Single men are able to buy masculinity by owning powerful cars and entertaining women lavishly. For husbands, masculinity is attained through the provision of their family's financial security. Life insurance advertisements have long capitalized on this definition of masculinity. Gould feels that the relationship between masculinity and primary financial support is well dramatized by the husband who objects to his wife's seeking employment when the family income needs to be increased. Even more threatening is the wife whose salary provides for more than the "little extras."

Brenton (1976) discusses the financial obligation of husbands in terms of the high psychic costs to men and their families. Paradoxically, because bearing financial responsibility for the family often entails long hours away from home, the husband does not reap the emotional benefits of enjoying the family that he so nobly supports.

Physical strength, so long considered integral to the definition of masculinity (Gagnon, 1976), continues to play a role in the responsibility of husbandhood. Gagnon contends that in our society, female deference demands perpetuation of the illusion of men's superior physical strength. Whether or not the husband is stronger than his wife, his few household responsibilities consist of the "heavy" work: moving furniture, lifting packages, and opening jars. Implicit in this concept is that the husband should display skills in carpentry, mechanics, and plumbing, whether or not he has any such aptitude or interest.

The husband's responsibility as physical protector of his family is typified by the courtesies "gentlemen" pay to "ladies" in our society; a man traditionally walks on the street side of the sidewalk and physically guides his partner with a firm, gentle hand on her back. The "my-dad-can-beat-up-your-dad" syndrome typifies his children's perception of this protection. Men are also responsible for protecting home and country by going to war. Few countries draft women into their armed forces, and few servicewomen ever see front-line action. It is man's duty to defend. Bednarik (1970) typifies the general social attitude toward this male obligation when he says:

> Today she can even go to war—certainly the most perfidious idea men ever thought up. We are tempted to believe that only sadistic rapist-killers or women-hating homosexual generals could be behind such a measure. . . . A society which tolerates conditions in which individual men no longer defend and protect women, must be regarded as considerably emasculated. [p. 10]

Another responsibility of husbandhood suggested by Gagnon (1976) is the initiation and guidance of the sexual act. Bernard (1968) discusses this in terms of females' recent demands for sexual satisfaction, their new-found orgasmic capacity, and well-publicized statistics describing "average" sexual performance (e.g., Kinsey, Pomeroy, Martin, & Gebbard, 1953). Woman's sexual expectations continue to rise. Says Brenton (1976) of this phenomenon:

> . . . there has come into being a sort of sexual standard which defines female sexual satisfaction solely in terms of the orgasm—not only the orgasm, but the orgasm every time; not only the orgasm every time, but the orgasm attained solely via coitus; not only the orgasm reached every time strictly during coitus itself, but an explosive kind of orgasm closely

approximating the male's; and not only an explosive orgasm achieved directly as a result of intercourse on every occasion that intercourse takes place, but this selfsame orgasm achieved simultaneously with the man's climax. [p. 165]

All this and taking out the garbage too! How much can a human bear?

Clearly, the responsibilities of husbandhood are legion. The average husband is expected to be the breadwinner and protector of his family, to do all the jobs that require physical strength, and to be the chief determiner of the couple's sex life. We might also mention that in many families, he is expected to handle all the money and to make virtually every major decision. The advent of these responsibilities with husbandhood suggest some reasons why men occasionally refer to marriage as a "ball and chain" arrangement.

Why Do We Marry?

Given the amount of deference women are expected to pay to their husbands and the rather onerous responsibilities that descend upon men at marriage, one might certainly wonder why such a large proportion of our population marries. For many, it appears, it is the least negative of several unappealing alternatives. Gove's (1976) review of the literature indicates that single people are less happy than married people on many dimensions, probably as a function of their relative isolation and lack of close interpersonal ties (Gurin, Veroff, & McEachern, 1960, cited in Gove, 1976).

There are few sex differences in mental illness or general satisfaction among single people, a fact that Gove interprets as a result of their role similarity. For married people, however, he argues that role inequities result in the married woman's higher rate of mental illness. It must be remembered, for example, that all the responsibilities of husbandhood described in the previous section constitute not only unpleasant duties but also means of exercising control over other family members. The wife in a traditional marriage may well feel that she has little status and little control over her own life. As Bernard (1972) succinctly put it, "We must make women sick in order to fit them for marriage" (p. 158). The work done by Gove and Bernard, combined with Ambert's (1976) evidence that husbands are the least interested party in the marital relationship and are less likely than wives to equate marital happiness with overall happiness, suggests strongly that women are at a disadvantage in marriage. Several authors (e.g., Gove, 1976) have placed blame for this inequity on the wife's role of housekeeper, although one might equally fault the dual working roles that so many women fill. Let us now examine two of the most common roles played by women in our society—the roles of housewife and employed wife.

THE WORKING WIFE

It is indicative of a misogynous society that women who work inside their homes are not called working women. Regardless of the length of the housewife's day or the number of responsibilities involved, the title *working woman* is reserved for her sister gainfully employed outside the home.

Women as Housewives

Who are the housewives in our society?—nearly all married women, employed or otherwise. Employed wives spend as much as eighteen hours weekly doing housework (Meissner, Humphreys, Meis, & Scheu, 1975, cited in Ambert, 1976), certainly qualifying housewifery as one of their occupations. The husbands of employed women, on the other hand, average one hour of housework weekly.

In spite of the fact that most women are housewives for a goodly portion of their lives, a role that demands that they *work* by almost any definition of the word, there is argument about whether or not housewifery should be considered an occupation (Eichler, 1976a, versus Coser, 1974). Eichler argues that the structural anomalies inherent in housewifery and responsible for its nonoccupational status are present in many other occupations, the status of which goes unquestioned. Housewifery's lack of fixed hours, for instance, is shared by farmers, artists, and academics. Many occupations other than housewifery require no licensing. A third anomaly, lack of generally accepted work procedures, is shared by many of the artistic professions.

Eichler further suggests that although a housewife draws no minimum wage, she has entered into a specific economic relationship with an employer—her husband. However, use of the term *employer* implies that the husband defines the parameters of the job and the way in which the job should be carried out, which is ideally not the case in this special economic relationship. More accurately, it seems, the relationship can be considered a division of labor that the two spouses have deemed to be the most efficient for the financial and structural running of their household. Certainly this ideal is not always attained; family income, for example, is not always equally available to both spouses (Eichler, 1976b). To the extent that the arrangement is a choice on the part of both partners and to the extent that they share equally in the fruits of labor, it can be seen as a partnership and housewifery as an occupation within that partnership.

No discussion of occupation is complete without the consideration of status, and so it is with housewifery. In Eichler's (1976a) study of occupational status, subjects gave housewives an average score 46.3 from a list of ninety-three occupations, the extremes of which were physician at 93.6 and newspaper peddler at 10.8. When subjects were told the sex of the housewife, variations occurred. Female housewives were accorded a prestige score of 53.9, falling between female funeral directors and airplane mechanics, whereas male housewives* were accorded a prestige score of 35.5, which fell between male file clerks and sewing machine operators.

Eichler was also able to alter the prestige score of the female housewife by providing her husband's occupation. The status of a housewife married to a physician was rated 81.5, higher than the status of a female veterinarian, airplane pilot, or architect. A housewife whose husband was an elevator operator was accorded a prestige score of 37.1, lower than that of a female office clerk, teller, or truck driver. This provides evidence for the assertions of one of our male colleagues—although men must work hard for many years to gain prestige, women need only marry well.

Although Eichler's (1976a) research indicates that a housewife married to a man in a high-prestige occupation does not occupy a status position quite on par with that of her husband, her status does come very close to the status of his female colleagues. Housewives married to physicians, for instance, though 11.1 prestige points behind their husbands, are only 4.8 prestige points behind female

*Eichler used the term *male housewife* rather than *househusband* because she felt subjects might not know the meaning of the latter word.

physicians. This pattern changes as husbands move down the prestige scale. Housewives married to plumbers (a middle-status occupation) enjoy greater prestige than their husbands' female colleagues and only slightly less prestige than their husbands. Housewives married to elevator operators (a low-status occupation) enjoy greater prestige than either their husbands or their husbands' female colleagues.

What does all this indicate? For one thing, Eichler's subjects obviously perceived housewifery as an occupation, one that was seen as giving the incumbent a certain status in our society. Second, as in other occupations typically filled by one sex, lower prestige was accorded to people who chose this occupation in defiance of sex-role norms. Third, the housewife's status was largely determined by the occupation of her husband. We do not know that this is unique to housewifery, or even to women. Male accountants married to physicians may enjoy a very different status than male accountants married to newspaper peddlers. Since the income of housewives is so dependent upon the income of their spouses, however, the spouse influence is probably greater for them than for people in other occupations.

The status of housewives is a very important feminist issue today, as it has been throughout the history of feminism. More than a century ago, authors sought to improve the lot of women by elevating the status of housewifery (e.g., Beecher & Stowe, 1869, cited in Williams, 1977), and phrases like *domestic engineering* and *domestic science* were coined. However, from the eighteenth century until the present day, there have been feminists who have considered housework to be the chief cause of female oppression and have viewed attempts to upgrade its status with suspicion (Rossi, 1968; Williams, 1977). So, although it has been suggested that housewives should be paid a living wage by their federal governments in order to raise the status of the occupation, to guarantee financial support to people who choose it, and to increase its attractiveness for men, not all feminists agree that women would benefit in the long run from such an arrangement (Ambert, 1976). It can be argued that a federally administered wage, especially if men were not lured into home care, would actually serve to increase female oppression by providing a rational argument for keeping women out of the external job market. This might, in turn, lower general acceptance for the equal education of young women, an idea still in its tenuous infancy. If all women were guaranteed paid occupations as housewives, would we begin to view expensive training for other occupations as a luxury?

Perhaps the financial independence of housewives could be better attained through laws outlining the specific rights of people who choose to take full responsibility for their family's caretaking. The at-home partner could, for instance, be guaranteed equal access to the family income and part-time training for another occupation.

It is likely that this formal restructuring of the family will not soon occur on a legal level but that each household will find its own solution. If inflation continues, few families will be able to afford the total unemployment of one of its adult members. The fact that women are having fewer children and having their last child at a younger age (Lopata, 1971) decreases the necessity for one long-term, full-time houseworker for each family. Housewifery as we know it may gradually disappear. Will employed women continue to serve as the family's caretaker? Will spouses learn to share home care equally? Or will we expand our vocabulary to include the word *housespouse*?

Women in the External Job Market

Women's economic productivity dates back as far as economics. Only since the Industrial Revolution has the employment of women been commonplace, however, by the 1850 American census, 24 percent of the employed were female (Nye, 1975). Unique to this century is the employment of large numbers of married women, many of whom are mothers (Nye, 1975).

It has been said often enough to constitute a truism that the employment of women is a direct result of effective birth control. Seldom has it been considered, however, that the reverse may be true. Access to effective birth control may be one result of a female-employing society. Birth control has been with us for centuries, but access to the simplest, most comfortable, and least risky means was blocked by modern law long after their discovery. One must ask why these laws were finally repealed.

The cause–effect relationships between economics, sociocultural values, and normative behaviors can seldom be determined. Today we place a high value on small families, economic independence, material goods, specialization of labor, and nondifferential treatment by sex. We cannot be certain, however, whether these factors are responsible for, or a result of, married women's newfound tendency to seek outside employment.

The employment of women raises many social issues seldom considered to be relevant to the employment of men. Foremost among these is child care. Millions of words have been written about the risks posed by maternal employment to the social and emotional development of the child. Hoffman's (1975) review of this literature indicates that maternal employment is associated with children's positive evaluations of female competence, approval of material employment, and lack of sex-role stereotyping. There is also evidence that maternal employment has positive effects on daughters' aspirations, achievements, and even IQ. Hoffman's paper outlines many of the complex intervening variables that limit generalizations about the effects of maternal employment. Factors such as the family's socioeconomic status, the amount of time the father spends with the children, the age of the children, the reasons for the woman's employment, and the husband's attitude toward the wife's employment all seem to contribute to the way in which maternal employment affects children. It is difficult, therefore, to make a general statement about how a mother affects her children by working outside the home, except to say that there is no evidence for the existence of the overall negative effect that is assumed by so many people.

Perhaps the most important question we can ask of the entire maternal employment literature is: "Why are mothers the only subject of concern?" No one seems worried about the usual dearth of contact between *fathers* and children. Is mother necessarily the all-important variable in child development, or can the father or some other adult take her place? Do women have unique capabilities for child rearing? Are women really more nurturant than men? The next section deals with these issues.

NURTURANCE: A FEMALE STRONGHOLD

Perceptions of Sex Differences in Nurturance

Our literature abounds with notions of mother nurturance. As Ashley Montagu (1952) tells us, "The sensitive relationships which exist between mother and child belong to a unique order of humanity, an order in which the male may participate as a child, but from which he increasingly departs as he leaves childhood behind" (p. 142). Mothers are perceived to be the most nurturant parent in our culture by children (Emerick, 1962) and college students alike (Heilbrun, 1964), and females of all ages rate nurturance as a more desirable trait than do males (Ahammer, 1971). The concept of female nurturance as an instinct (the maternal instinct) has received a great deal of mileage in poetry and novels. Few would dare suggest, as has Rollin (1970), that women become mothers, not in an attempt to satisfy their instinct to nurture, but in compliance to social pressure.

The presence of volumes of literature supposedly concerned with parental influences, which in fact deal only with maternal influences, suggests, however, that fathers are not considered to be very important. One might wonder if they are even considered to be parents. It has even been acceptable scientific practice for researchers to measure father nurturance through a questionnaire to the mother (e.g., Sears, 1970).

Sex-role stereotypes and division of labor by sex have combined in our society to assure that the responsibility of child bearing is left largely to mothers. Fathers seldom work their trade at home, as was once so common, and few men spend as many hours with children as do women. To children, then, spending their preschool years in a world of women, nurturance becomes synonymous with women. To the small child, the listener, the protector, the supporter, the feeder, and the trainer is usually female. Even if mother works full time, there is very little likelihood that the caretaker will be male.

Children's perceptions of parental differences in nurturance have been examined empirically. Emmerick (1959) has shown that children as young as three and a half portray mother as nurturant and father as controlling in a doll-play situation. Landreth (1963) demonstrated a variant of this pattern when she examined nurturance perception among children in two social classes (manual labor and professional) in two countries (Berkeley, California, U.S.A. and Wellington, New Zealand). She showed four-year-olds pictures of children in situations requiring either caretaking or companionship and asked which parent would fill the role. Overall, mother was chosen most often for caretaking and father for companionship, but some interesting deviations occurred. In the Berkeley professional group, boys chose father most often for care, and in the Wellington professional group, girls chose mother more often for companionship. Mother was perceived as caretaker more often than companion by all but the sons of professionals. It appears, then, that children perceive parents as filling very different roles in their parent–child relationships. However, these results suggest that even fifteen years ago, at least among some professional families, these roles may have been shifting.

Sex Differences in Nurturance

Obviously, the stereotype of mother nurturance is very well established in our culture. The word *maternal* has come to be almost synonymous with *nurturant*, whereas *paternalism* connotes overbearing and control. Our interest in sex stereotypes is only incidental to our overall interest in sex *differences,* however, and our main concern is not whether females are *perceived* to be more nurturant than males but rather whether they *are.*

This brings us to the familiar issue of definition. Nurturance has been operationally defined, in the many studies that have examined it, as everything from asking information of a young child (Radin, 1972) to the father's hugging and kissing of his teenage son (Greenstein, 1966). For our purposes, nurturance is *the affectionate behavior one shows for another in caretaking,* thus encompassing both behaviors examined in Landreth's study. Caretaking can encompass a wide range of behaviors: fighting off enemies, preparing and serving food, and the teaching of etiquette, for example. Since caretaking can be accomplished without affection and since not all affection takes place in a context of caretaking, both conditions must be satisfied to constitute nurturance.

One way the question of sex differences in nurturance has been approached is through the observation of the nurturing behaviors of lower primates. The assumption behind this approach is that primates are equivalent to nonsocialized humans and their behaviors are therefore "natural." As was made clear in the first chapter, however, primates are neither human nor nonsocialized. To complicate the issue, sex differences in nurturance vary among primate species, and even within the same species there are individual differences (Mitchell, 1969) that vary from violent hostility toward infants to complete and affectionate caretaking. The males of some primate species demonstrate strong nurturance in their natural habitat, and in others, male nurturance has been learned with very short infant contact—

fifteen minutes in one study (Chamove, Harlow, & Mitchell, 1967). Although many researchers have counted on primates to provide evidence of innate sex differences in nurturance, they have failed to do so (see Lynn, 1974, for a review). It has been argued that they have not even provided us with evidence of sex differences in nurturance, innate or otherwise (Linton, 1971).

Conceptually aligned to primate research on the biological nature of sex differences in nurturance is the evolutionary argument. Mothers whose lines were continued, this argument might go, carried within them and passed on to their daughters a preparedness to respond with nurturance to the sight and sound of a human infant. We know, however, that women do not always respond to infants in the way this model would predict: they sometimes respond with affection, sometimes with indifference, and sometimes, the newspapers tell us, with violence. In any case, if there *is* a biological program for a nurturant response to human infants, there is no reason to believe that it exists only in females. We know that any such preparedness must be modified by the environment, or no woman could neglect or batter a child. It seems reasonable to assume that this preparedness is modified differentially for males and females as a function of their different socialization experiences. Whether or not a biological preparedness for child nurturance exists as part of the human experience, socialization may still account for sex differences in nurturance.

A third way that "true" or "natural" sex differences have been explored is through cross-culture research. Are there consistent sex differences in nurturance in all cultures under a variety of socialization processes? If not, there is strong evidence for nurturance being part of a learned sex role. Mead's (1935) study of three primitive New Guinea societies, probably the most famous cross-cultural research to address this issue, concluded that nurturance is learned and can readily be taught to members of either sex, as the society deems appropriate. For example, in one of the tribes Mead studied, both males and females treated children with hostility and neglect. In another, parents took an equally nurturing role, surrounding the child with physical and emotional affection. In a third, the father's sole function in child rearing was impregnation of the mother.

Mead's research indicates that very different sex-role patterns of nurturance may have occurred as a function of three vastly different socialization processes. But how differently *are* children socialized in various cultures? In an attempt to answer this question, Barry, Bacon, and Child (1957) examined the consistency of children's socialization in 110 cultures. Although socialization pressures toward nurturance for girls were present in 82 percent of these cultures, not one society stressed nurturance for boys. One might speculate that girls the world over exhibit a predisposition for nurturance that parents the world over reinforce and that boys never indicate a desire to nurture. We know, however, that this is not the case; boys do show affectionate caretaking behavior. Why, then, did Barry, Bacon, and Child find that only girls were reinforced for nurturing behaviors? Social functionalism can explain this at least as well as biology. Teaching females and only females to nurture has been the most functional way for societies to operate. Before pasteurized milk, it was essential that women be willing to nurse their babies. If the mother was to be at home anyway, it was much more efficient for the father to do what could best be done without the child: hunting, fishing, and fighting. In our society, where few mothers nurse their few children past infancy and where division of labor by sex is no longer necessary, the utility of sex-differentiated training in nurturance has passed into history. Surely we can use all the nurturers we can get.

It would be very difficult to argue that women tend to be less nurturant than men in our society or even that there is no sex difference in nurturance. By our definition of nurturance, women *are* more nurturant, as a function of their role as caretaker-with-affection. That this is the way things *must* or *should* be, however, is a completely different issue. Men who are finally making themselves heard on the issue of sex-role socialization do not believe that nurturance is necessarily specific to women. Biller and Meredith (1975), for example, believe that we have paid a high price for punishing our boys and rewarding only our girls for nurturance.

One reason we may have trouble relating to a concept of male nurturance is that we tend to think of "masculine" and "feminine" traits as precluding each other. Can people socialized into competence, competitiveness, effectiveness, and action orientation (men, in our society) be socialized into nurturance? Peskin's (1968) study of thirty-year-old mothers indicated that those who were rated the most "masculine"—possessing the four traits just mentioned—were also rated as the most maternal. What we call "masculinity" did not preclude nurturance in this study, then, at least for women. It seems logical to assume that the same would hold true for men.

To understand the implications of Peskin's findings and the

complexity of the issues presented in the next section, we must come to grips with the concept of *androgyny*, discussed at greater length in Chapter 6. The *androgynous* person behaves not as his or her sex role dictates, but as the situation dictates. Sandra Bem (1974), who has written extensively on the subject, adheres to an androgyny model wherein people possess a relatively stable constellation of traits to which psychologists usually refer as personality. For the androgynous person, however, as for Peskin's females, these traits are not clustered at a feminine or masculine pole but may equally include traits we see as appropriately masculine or feminine.

Most sex-role liberationists would probably agree that not all, or even most, of the traditionally sex-typed traits are undesirable. What *is* undesirable is the rigid assignment of these traits to one sex. That "masculine" and "feminine" traits are not antithetical to each other is demonstrated to Peskin's (1968) research. The fact that a child learns assertiveness, objectivity, independence, and competence does not preclude the possibility that s/he will be tender, verbally articulate, and artistically inclined.

The Effects of Father Nurturance

We have examined some evidence for the idea that fathers and mothers *could* play equally nurturing roles in their parent–child relationships. Let us now examine some of the effects of father nurturance. Most of the literature on this issue addresses the effects of father nurturance on the male child. One such study indicates that it is to a boy's advantage, socially, to be the son of a nurturant father. Leiderman (cited in Heise, 1972) has shown that fourth-grade boys who have high acceptance among their peers are more likely to have had warm relationships with their fathers. If they have modeled their fathers' nurturance, it appears that they may have an even greater social advantage. Adinolfi's (1970) most highly accepted (as opposed to low-choice or rejected) college freshmen were characterized by their comforting, sympathetic, affectionate natures and, almost paradoxically, by their sympathy seeking and protection seeking. One might speculate that the heritage of the nurtured son is a combination of nurturance, which he has modeled, and nurturance seeking, for which he has been reinforced by his father's nurturance.

In a society characterized by what Lehne (1976) calls

homophobia—fear of homosexuality—it is to be expected that male nurturance may be viewed with suspicion. Our Freudian heritage has created a climate wherein a strong masculine influence in child rearing can be seen as a potential threat to sex-role development, including the development of heterosexuality. Needless to say, this is not universally viewed as problematic. Not all parents see their children's sexual preference as a matter for concern, much less see male nurturance as molding homosexuality.

In any case, what *is* the effect of father nurturance on the sex-role development of children? Many studies (e.g., Freedhein, cited in Lynn, 1974; Mussen & Distler, 1959, 1960; Sears, 1970) have indicated that nurturance by the father aids the process of sex-role socialization for both boys and girls. It may seem paradoxical that a father's exhibition of the traditionally feminine trait of nurturance should aid in the masculine sex-role development of his son. Mussen and Rutherford (1963) offer an explanation based on the assumption that a boy is motivated to imitate the personal qualities, characteristics, behaviors, and interests of the person with whom he shares both gender and affection. This reinforcing relationship with his father further motivates the boy to emulate other men to whom his admiration has generalized. Interestingly, Mussen and Rutherford found preference for the masculine role to be unrelated to mother–son relationship, masculinity of the father, femininity of the mother, or parental encouragement of specifically sex-typed activities. As long as the father was nurturant, then, the son's masculine-role preference developed, whether or not the father was an outstanding example of masculinity or exerted any pressure toward the masculinization of his son.

One is reminded at this point of Lynn's theory of sex-role socialization, discussed in detail in Chapter 2. Lynn believes, as did Freud (1924/1970), that children very early take on the traits and values of their parents through the process of parental identification. Most models of sex-role socialization suggest that initial parental identification is with the mother for both boys and girls (e.g., Lazowich, 1955). Most sex-role theorists also believe that for boys, the early childhood shift from maternal identification to masculine sex-role identification is a dramatic and traumatic transition. Masculine sex-role identification is accomplished in the relative absence of male models, through the punishment of feminine behaviors, and the long and aversive trial-and-error learning of a very stereotypical male role (Lynn, 1966).

The repercussions of boys' initial maternal identification and its resultant social punishment, Lynn feels, are far-reaching. He uses this model to explain the male's stronger opposite-sex hostility (Brown, cited in Lynn, 1966) and greater difficulty in, and anxiety about, sex-role identification (Hartley, 1959).

But if maternal identification is fraught with problems for boys, why need it ever take place? Why can't boys make their parental identification with fathers rather than mothers? We know from social learning theory that the three important model characteristics influencing imitation learning are power, similarity, and nurturance (Mischel, 1971). Since fathers are perceived as more powerful* in our society and are at least anatomically similar to their sons, mother nurturance may account for mother identification in little boys. If Mischel's model can correctly be applied to sex-role learning, then, the nurturant father should be in a position to facilitate father identification in his male child.

This may appear to be less than a perfect situation to the reader who feels that the last thing this society needs is stronger sex typing. Are sex-role liberationists caught in a "catch-22"? Will father nurturance perpetuate the very sex typing that sex-role liberationists, including many nurturant fathers, would help to see die? There are reasons why this should not be a cause for concern.

In the first place, just because sex typing as we know it today encompasses every facet of our existence, we need not assume that it must be that way. It is probable that sex typing can occur in a climate wherein very few traits are considered more appropriate for one sex than the other. Gorer (1968) studied such social climates in his analysis of three primitive, nonwarring societies. He was impressed by the fact that several of *our* social phenomena were completely lacking in these cultures: homosexuality, sex-role identity conflict, and social pressure for sex-role socialization. Sex typing, a joyous learning experience, focused mainly on the sexual. There were some other skills and aptitudes thought to be more characteristic of one sex than the other, but there was no pressure to conform to these stereotypes. From the struggles of the past decade, however, we know that *we* will not wake up some morning to find that our social sex roles have

*As discussed earlier, Emmerick (1959) has shown children to portray father as controlling a doll-play situation. See Chapter 10 for a fuller discussion of sex differences in power.

suddenly become that simple. Rather, we will probably continue to drop specifications from the roles until someday they are reduced to a manageable size.

A second reason why we should not fear that nurturant fathers will produce rigidly sex-typed children is that the research upon which this prophecy is based may be inadequate. At the time these studies were done, the choice available to sex-role researchers was to label behaviors "masculine" or "feminine." We will not go into the criticism of the projective measures used in most of this research, except to say that more sophisticated tools may have yielded more sophisticated conclusions. It is possible that the children of equally nurturant parents tend to androgyny, for instance, but that research- ers of the 1960s and early 1970s, when most of these studies were conducted, had no way of extracting this information.

Third, it is very probable that parental nurturance acts as a gen- eral aid to emotional development. If emotional health was defined in a rigidly sex-typed manner in the 1960s, that was the direction in which the nurtured child matured. It is hoped that the equally nur- turant parents who today define emotional health as androgyny will be blessed with androgynous children.

A climate in which children are raised by equally nurturant par- ents might set the stage for a society in which emotional development is independent of chromosomal composition. The redefinition of nurturance as sex-role appropriate for males could do more to liber- ate the sexes than any other change we might effect. Allowing males to nurture would free men to parent, to teach, and to care for children—children who would not learn that women are "supposed" to be the nurturant sex.

ALTERNATIVES TO TRADITIONAL MARRIAGE

Skolnick and Skolnick (1971) have observed that we perceive strange- ness only in deviations from the familiar. Thus, they question our interest in: "Why did couple X get divorced, rather than why does couple Y stay together?" (p. vii); or "What harm comes to children from mothers who work, rather than how are children harmed by long hours in the total power of their mothers, out of sight of any other eyes?" (p. viii).

Questioning the fairness and utility of traditional marriage and family structures is not new to our decade or even to this century. Rossi (1974) has compiled a large collection of sex-role liberationist papers dating back to the eighteenth century, many of which question—implicitly or explicitly—the rigidity of the roles we play in the family. Never before have so many questioned so vocally and so vehemently, however, and never have so many been prompted to explore alternative life-styles. Thus group marriages, homosexual marriages, nonmonogamous marriages, role-reversal marriages, and trial marriages, none of which is new to our generation, have received much press and interest in the past decade. It is beyond the scope of this chapter to detail all these variations on the marriage theme, but the interested reader will find a comprehensive overview in Skolnick and Skolnick (1971).

Probably the alternatives to traditional marriage that are being most widely tried at this time in history are those that do not change the number and/or sex of the adult participants but try instead to move away from the kinds of stereotyped roles and expectations that have been outlined in this chapter. A case in point is the model presented in the best-seller *Open marriage* (O'Neill & O'Neill, 1972).* One thesis of this book is that marital sex roles can be discarded, leaving the institution of marriage intact and even stronger than before. According to the O'Neills, there is no reason, for instance, why the husband must always initiate sex or feel obligated to be the sole breadwinner in the family. Similarly, they suggest that the wife need not always defer to the husband in matters of decision making or the choice of friends. Perhaps most importantly, they remind us that two people married to each other can and must retain a significant degree of independence and autonomy and need not always operate as a couple. Each partner should have his/her own friends and interests.†

---

*From *Open Marriage: A New Lifestyle for Couples* by Nena O'Neill & George O'Neill, M. Evans and Company, Inc., New York, NY 10017. © 1972 by Nena O'Neill & George O'Neill. Reprinted by permission of the publisher and Mary Yost Associates, Inc., New York.

†The phrase *open marriage* has become associated with the license to engage in extramarital sexual relationships. However, this idea actually plays a relatively minor role in the book.

Such a suggestion runs somewhat contrary to the popular ideology of togetherness in marriage and to the practice of inviting people as "couples" to all social gatherings. Nonetheless, it would certainly seem to be a practical way to reduce some of the dissatisfaction arising from the traditional husband–wife relationship.

Probably one of the most pragmatic ideas to emerge from the open marriage movement of the past few years has been the concept of a partnership contract (Brown, 1973). Such a contract outlines the rights and responsibilities of each member of the couple and may touch on virtually anything, including the division of household chores, the allocation of income, and questions of sexual exclusivity. Although the legality of the partnership contract has not been universally established, many couples have sought to define the parameters of their unique relationship with such a document. In a time when every "rule" of the male–female relationship is being questioned, many couples do not choose to marry, and others feel that their marriage is inconsistent with traditional ideals. The marriage contract, as it has come to be called, can obviously be applied to any interpersonal relationship where the parties feel a need to express their economic and emotional expectations in their own written agreement (Warner & Ihara, 1977).

In a society where marriage is based on romanticism (Rubin, 1973), the idea of documenting marital expectations may be offensive to some. No marriage is without a contract, however, The state never fails to impose its legal contract, the terms of which the couple may not know. Most people may be completely unaware, for instance, that a couple cannot legally make an agreement to waive sexual exclusivity. This contract is actually more binding than most in that in most parts of North America, it cannot be terminated or substantially changed by the simple mutual consent of the two parties involved. Moreover, the signing parties must abide with changes the state imposes on them through law reform, and only the state can break the contract. Thus, if a married couple in North America wants a divorce, they can obtain it only through a judge's ruling and usually only by one spouse suing the other for some violation of the legal contract (e.g., adultery, cruelty).

There is another contract operating in every marriage. In every interpersonal relationship, there is an unwritten, and probably unspoken, agreement defining acceptable behavior within that relationship: the "unconscious contract, agreed to by default, in the sense that it is unwitting" (O'Neill & O'Neill, 1972, p. 51). Unfortunately, there may be two such "agreements," as we have all experienced from time to time when our assumptions about what we felt were mutual expectations of our relationship were violated. Partnership contracts, whether or not they are legally binding, may serve to eliminate some of these ambiguities.

Thinking through the marriage contract could also help a couple to examine the extent to which their sex roles govern division of labor in their household. One of the major disadvantages of the rigid sex-role pattern inherent in traditional marriage is that it leaves both partners dependent on the skills, advantages, and responsibilities associated with the other's role. Hetherington, Cox, and Cox (1977) have demonstrated that divorce in the traditional family leaves the woman without status identity and the man without the basic skills necessary to shop, cook, and keep house for himself. Making the transition from married to single life is no small feat for anyone, but combined with the pressures of learning to perform the ex-partner's unfamiliar role, it may be particularly traumatic.

If it has no other advantages, then, perhaps the sex-role-liberated marriage can better prepare us for divorce or the long absences, illnesses, or death of a spouse. Despite our very real and necessary concern over the form our interpersonal relationships should take, each one of us is first and foremost an individual with primary responsibility for her- or himself.

SUMMARY

To know that someone is a spouse or a parent gives us very little information about the family roles s/he plays. To know that someone is a wife, a husband, a mother, or a father, however, is much more telling. The marital roles provide us with an interesting microcosm of our general sex-role structure: men in our society protect, create, initiate, and decide, and women care for and defer to others.

Even as marriage is a miniature of our sex-role structure, so the marriage ceremony exemplifies these ideas. People weep, whether in joy or sorrow, as a beautifully adorned woman is given to one man by another. The patterns of deference established the day she changes her surname from that of her father to that of her husband may continue throughout the life of their marriage.

Husbands, however, have many responsibilities, and men pay a high price for the privileges inherent in this role. In addition, society grants them fewer options than are available to many wives. The woman who seeks a role reversal by rejecting her caretaking function in favor of an economic support function receives considerably more psychological backing in a money-oriented society than does the man who assumes responsibility for the care of his home and children. Whereas the employed woman is adhering to an important ideal of our society—that of high achievement—the househusband deviates from our ideals of both achievement and masculinity. For, in spite of the lip service paid to the importance of housework and childcare, housewives enjoy little prestige, and househusbands even less.

It has been suggested repeatedly in this chapter that rigid marital sex roles contribute strongly to the negative side of traditional marriage. It follows from this argument that marriage would be more functional if the roles of men and women within it were less defined, more likely to overlap, and more interchangeable. We have tried to show here that such role freedom is a real possibility and not just a feminist fantasy. For example, we have attempted to debunk the notion that women are naturally more nurturant than men and must therefore play the major role in child care. Although our review of the literature indicates that females are *perceived* to be more nurturant than males, there is little evidence that they have any innate advantage or that mother nurturance is superior to father nurturance. It appears that mother nurturance, though real and important, is part of a socially prescribed role and that father nurturance exerts a profound influence on the emotional development of children that has long gone unrecognized. We have argued that equally nurturant parents who support the ideas of sex-role liberation will probably be the parents of a new generation of androgynous adults.

If men choose to nurture and women choose to share financial responsibility for the family, what will constitute the marriage of the future? There is little evidence that male–female unions are on the decline or that we are entering a marriageless era in our history. To the contrary, if the popularity of books on the subject is any indication, we have never before been so interested in marriage. We predict that the existing structure will continue to be revamped to suit couples who are more interested in meeting their individual needs than in adhering to rigid sex-role prescriptions.

12 Nina Lee Colwill
& Stephen W. Holborn

SEX &
SEXUALITY

An analysis of the psychology of sex differences would certainly be incomplete without an examination of human sexuality. So inextricably intertwined are gender and sexuality that we use one word—*sex*—to refer to both. This linguistic generality might lead the casual observer to speculate that the Anglo-Saxon heritage defines sexuality in very general terms. However, as we shall soon see, our definition is relatively narrow—usually restricted to adult heterosexual relationships.

However narrow our definition, we do view sexuality from many perspectives. Evolution, physiology, psychodynamics, learning, and social psychology all serve as explanatory frameworks in this chapter.

SEXUALITY AS THE NORTH AMERICAN SEES IT

We tend, in our culture, to view sexuality in terms of intercourse and accompanying behaviors. Thus, sexuality usually refers to the behaviors associated with adult male–female relationships in which intercourse or the expectation of intercourse plays a vital role. We seldom think of young children's behaviors as sexual, for instance, in spite of the major public impact of Freud's view of infant sexuality. We have many rules governing who should feel what, with whom, and under what conditions; and we tend not to acknowledge as sexual, feelings that do not fall into the prescribed patterns.

Newton: The Trebly Sensuous Woman

Recently, feminists have been speaking out against our narrow definition of female sexuality. Niles Newton (1971), for instance, suggests that female sexuality encompasses *three* reproductive partnerships (intercourse, childbirth, and breast-feeding) that share several psychological and physiological similarities. Breathing patterns, facial expression, uterine and abdominal contractions, clitoral engorgement, lowered inhibitions, increased physical strength, greater flexibility, and increased insensitivity to external stimuli are similar in both intercourse and childbearing, although they may differ in intensity. Immediately after birth and orgasm there is typically a sudden return of sensory acuity and a strong feeling of joy and well-being. Intercourse and breast-feeding also have several physiological similarities: uterine contractions and nipple erection, for instance. Further, orgasm may cause milk secretion in lactating women, and breast-feeding can trigger orgasm.

Why have these associations generally gone unrecognized? Certainly, our romantic myths surrounding intercourse are very different from our romantic myths surrounding childbirth and breast-feeding. The epitome of this separation is seen in the Christian belief that Christ, the son of God, was born of a virgin. Newton suggests that our ignorance of the three reproductive partnerships is due largely to the fact that female sexuality has been defined according to adult male needs, and adult males do not enter into the reproductive relationships of breast-feeding and childbearing.

If *female* sexuality has been separated from reproduction, it is a minor split in comparison to the degree that *male* sexuality has been separated from reproduction. The male contribution to reproduction has suffered from the most rigid and limiting definition possible: the moment of conception. Whereas some societies see both sexual partners as pregnant and as participants in childbirth, this is typically not the case in North America. Although the Lamaze method of childbirth, introduced to North America in the 1960s, includes very specific roles for both parents, it has not become common practice. Few men are even present at the birth of their children.

It is this narrow definition of male reproduction that makes it legally possible for an unmarried woman to have a baby and put it up for adoption without the father's knowledge. Certainly, it is seldom considered that the father might have equal rights and responsibilities—that he might, for instance, keep the child himself or share the baby's upbringing with the mother. Perhaps our views are slowly changing. More hospitals are permitting fathers to be present at the birth of their children, and more courts are recognizing the equal rights of fathers to care for their children as single parents.

Rotkin: Phallocentrism and Vagina-Centered Female Sexuality

Karen Rotkin (1976) contends that society's male-oriented approach to sexuality, which she labels phallocentrism, defines even female sexuality in terms of the penis. Unlike Newton, she clearly and vehemently differentiates between the sexual and the reproductive. What is sexual for females is clitoris-centered in the same way that what is sexual for males is penis-centered. She deplores the common practice of teaching sexuality to children by equating the penis with the vagina. The vagina is part of the reproductive system, and the clitoris is sexual, just as the testicles are part of the reproductive system, and the penis is sexual. She does not imply that the entire body is not involved in the sexual act for both males and females, merely that the clitoris is to a woman what the penis is to a man.

In spite of her very different approach, Rotkin comes to the same conclusion as Newton: our definition of female sexuality has been shaped by male needs. Thus, female sexuality has been defined in terms of the vagina—that which gives direct pleasure to men.

The phallocentrism of which Rotkin speaks affects not only our definition of *female* sexuality. It is also the basis of the failure label we attach to impotency and premature ejaculation:

> His penis-centeredness blinds him to the sensuality of sex not connected to the penis. A hard penis is not necessary for sexual enjoyment. Some

cultures have, in fact, developed a rich and varied sex life for large groups within [them] without ever having intercourse. . . . Most men feel free to say "I'd really like to lay her" but do not feel free to say "I'd really like to lay *by* her." We become "pressure-cooker lovers." When the pressure is off the hard penis the focus on the rest of the body—on caressing, on sensual games like toe-touching under water or finger-sucking—tends to be greater. Redefining impotency, then, means eliminating the pressure on the penis to be upwardly mobile. [Farrell, 1975, pp. 54, 55, 57]

Farrell's emphasis on sensuality is what we would call a broader definition of sexuality—a definition that would not attach a failure label to the male's premature ejaculation or to the female's orgasm attained through direct manual stimulation of the clitoris. The death of phallocentrism may have positive implications for providing a new sexual environment free from achievement standards.

Sherfey: The Evolution of Female Sexuality

Newton and Rotkin suggest, then, that female sexuality has been defined by a male-oriented society. Mary Jane Sherfey (1966) goes a step further with her suggestion that the female sex drive has actually been suppressed by men. She reasons that the female's capacity for multiple orgasms is indicative of her biologically determined sexual need. Because a woman rarely attains orgasmic satiation, she must will herself into satisfaction, a state called satiation-in-*insatiation*. Satiation-in-*satiation*, on the other hand, describes orgasm to the point of physical exhaustion. Because of woman's great orgasmic capacity, Sherfey sees her as possessing a much stronger sexual need and sexual capacity than man, although in civilized societies, this typically is not manifested in sexual acts.

With the rise of an agricultural civilization, Sherfey reasons, woman's sexual drive had to be tamed if she were to provide adequate maternal care in a world where large families were beginning to emerge. Property inheritance demanded that a child's parentage be known, and it became important, therefore, for a woman to restrict her sexual activity to one man. Thus, with the agricultural society's need for large families to work the inherited land and to be cared for by a nurturing parent, woman's "inordinate" sexual drive was brought under strict control.

Sherfey contends that men, having tamed the female sex drive, moved on to create and conquer, secure in the knowledge of a home and family cared for by a monogamous woman. Although women gave up their aggressive sexuality, the vestiges remained, in the form of a biologically determined capacity for multiple orgasm.

If Sherfey's analysis were to achieve popular acceptance, the implications for women might not be as liberating as she would hope. In fact, her argument could be used to justify a continuing suppression of female sexuality, for—some might argue—if the rise of civilization required woman to be subjugated, her liberation might herald its crumble. One could argue, of course, that we have advanced so far in evolution, technology, and social structure that we could now cope with the full expression of female sexuality. Both possibilities provide for interesting speculation.

In any case, it is important to remember that Sherfey's reasoning is highly speculative. One could equally well argue that males were at one time endowed with an insatiable sexual capacity and that it took women centuries to tame it. With the emergence of the family, man's sexual drive had to be curbed if he were to provide material support for woman, who was often encumbered by pregnancy and nursing. Sexual exclusivity was also much to woman's advantage: she would not have to continually vie for a sexual partner and provider. And so, the argument might go, men gave up their inordinate sexual drive in return for the comforts of home. One might further speculate that nocturnal emission, indicating a drive so strong that it is manifested unconsciously in sleep, is the remaining vestige of the male's insatiable sexual capacity.

Our alternative to the evolution of sexuality is probably based on no weaker ground than Sherfey's. Our aim is not to create an evolutionary theory, however, but to remind the reader that our definition of sexuality has probably affected both men and women. Surely female sexuality has been no more restricted by our ideal of orgasm through vaginal intercourse than has male sexuality by our vision of man, the phallic pursuer.

Our narrow definitions of male and female sexuality are really not very surprising. They are certainly not incongruent with the general sex roles operative in our society. Nowhere is the stereotype of male aggressivity and female passivity, male dominance and female nurturance, as evident as it is in our patterns of male and female sexuality. Our very language reinforces these roles. Men "lay" women; seldom the reverse. Women "submit" to men; seldom the reverse.

In this chapter we will consider sexuality in its broadest sense to include a wide range of responses. Toward this end, we will examine the perspectives of physiology, learning, and social psychology. We hope that this will enable you to more fully appreciate the broad range of human sexual behavior and to reexamine your views of the sexual roles of males and females.

The distinction we have made between female and male sexuality may be leading the reader to assume that there are many dramatic sex differences in sexual response. To explore that possibility, we begin with a brief study of the physiology of sexuality. What happens when we are sexually aroused, and how does that differ as a function of our sex?

THE PHYSIOLOGY OF SEXUAL RESPONSE

Until the past decade, we knew surprisingly little about human sexual response. But in 1966 Masters and Johnson made *orgasm* a household word by publishing in popular, albeit technical, form the results of years of research on human sexuality. They had painstakingly measured and recorded every minute detail of physiological response in the volunteers who engaged in intercourse and masturbation in their laboratory.

Masters and Johnson categorized physical response to sexual stimuli into four progressive phases: *excitement, plateau, orgasmic,* and *resolution.* Although the duration and intensity of these four phases differ among individuals of both sexes, the pattern is amazingly consistent. For both males and females, orgasm represents a reliable progression of physiological events.

Excitement Phase

The first, *excitement,* phase may be initiated by any of several sexual responses: a smell, a sight, a touch, a sound, a taste. If stimulation continues, the genital organs become congested with blood (vasocongestion). In females this is manifested by the lubrication, lengthening, and swelling of the vagina; in males, by penile erection. The male testes begin their elevation into the body, and in both sexes, nipples harden and erect. Although physiologically, this phase is the same for males and females, their anatomies dictate somewhat different physical and social consequences. The erect penis cannot be ignored as easily as the moist vagina.

Plateau Phase

If sexual stimulation continues with sufficient intensity, the excitement phase soon gives way to a second, *plateau*, phase characterized by elevated blood pressure, hyperventilation, rapid heart rate, and genital lubrication. In females the clitoris retracts, the vaginal opening narrows, and the uterus elevates. In males the circumference of the penis is increased, and the testes are fully elevated. Both sexes may demonstrate skin changes as well. The upper body may flush (the "sex flush"), and the female labia minora (inner lips surrounding the vaginal opening) and, less often, the male glans (head of the penis) may deepen in color. If sexual stimuli are withdrawn at this point, the sexually stimulated person does not reach orgasm, and s/he enters directly into the resolution phase. Without orgasm, the resolution phase progresses much more slowly than it would after orgasm and may be quite uncomfortable. Men call this condition "blue balls." In spite of the fact that many women (51 percent in Hite's [1976] sample) rarely or never reach orgasm, they have not formalized this condition with an equivalent joking phrase. Perhaps women do not consider unrelieved sexual tension to be a laughing matter.

Interestingly, vasocongestion, which occurs in the reproductive organs during sexual tension, also occurs during the female's premenstrual and early menstrual days, causing the same physiological reactions. Vasocongestion is thought to account for much of the discomfort and bloated feeling experienced by women premenstrually. Since menstrual symptoms include some of the physiological symptoms of sexual tension, it is not surprising that orgasm often provides relief. Some women report heightened sexual desire at this time. Bardwick (1971) interprets this arousal as due to hormonal changes, but we would suggest that women could be labeling their menstrual symptoms as sexual arousal.* In any case, many women have discovered orgasm through intercourse or masturbation to be a way of quickly relieving premenstrual congestion and uterine tension.

Orgasmic Phase

After the first two stages of sexual response have been examined, the importance of orgasm becomes obvious. This third, *orgasmic*, phase lasts only seconds. Blood pressure, vasocongestion, heart rate, breathing, and muscular tension, which have all reached a peak, undergo a sudden and involuntary return to homeostasis, accompanied, in the male, by ejaculation. Whether or not the sexual partners experience simultaneous orgasm or whether there even is a partner, orgasm is the same physiological process. For females, however, there is greater individual variation in duration and intensity of orgasm than there is for males. Also, female masturbatory orgasm appears to be more intense than orgasm from intercourse, probably as a function of the female's greater physical control of her body during masturbation. Obviously, women attach much importance to the more subjective components of orgasm, however, as masturbation has not threatened to replace intercourse. Partnership sex is much more emotionally satisfying to most people than is solo sex (Hite, 1976), and for many, masturbation is still equated with moral turpitude.

Resolution Phase

Following orgasm, the body enters a fourth, *resolution*, phase. The entire sequence of physiological events that took place during the excitement and plateau stages is now reversed, as though a film were being quickly rewound. In this phase, a notable sex difference in sexual response occurs: males experience a refractory period, during which they typically cannot be restimulated to a higher level of sexual tension, whereas females may experience a series of orgasms.

---

*Similarly, one could argue that women escape pain from sexual tension by *not* labeling their physiological condition as painful. The concept of labeling is discussed in greater detail later in this chapter.

Recently, sex researchers have reported multiple orgasms in some men (Robbin & Jensen, cited in Tavris & Offir, 1977). These data should be cautiously interpreted in view of the fact that only thirteen males were included in the sample. Moreover, orgasm was defined in terms of physiological responses independent of ejaculation, a definition that not everyone might consider acceptable. Nevertheless, these data should serve to remind us that we are not yet fully knowledgeable about male or female sexuality.

The Myth of the Double Orgasm

One of the most popular misconceptions about orgasm, arising from Freudian theory, is that females can experience two distinct kinds of orgasm. This belief, the myth of the double orgasm, differentiates between the "immature, inferior" orgasm produced by direct manual stimulation of the clitoris and the "mature, superior" orgasm produced by penile stimulation of the vagina during intercourse. Probably the greatest contribution made by Masters and Johnson was showing that females do not experience two physiologically different kinds of orgasm.

The vagina is a relatively insensitive organ. Were this not the case, it would be impossible for women to use tampons, and childbirth would be an excruciatingly painful experience. The vagina is, however, sensitive to pressure, and it is this sensitivity that makes insertion of the penis so pleasurable (Barbach, 1976). The clitoris, which (as we saw in Chapter 2) grows from the same fetal structure as the penis, is an exquisitely sensitive organ—so sensitive, in fact, that direct contact can be painful. (This is probably why the clitoris retracts during the plateau phase of sexual arousal.) Vaginal intercourse can indirectly stimulate the clitoris to orgasm, and that in fact is what vaginal orgasm really involves.

What has been the impact of this knowledge on the pleasure derived from sexual relationships? For some sexual partners, it may have been their first knowledge that the clitoris existed. For others, it may have represented freedom from the distinction between appropriate and inappropriate orgasm (Byrne & Byrne, 1977). It is hoped that such information will enhance the sexual pleasure of women and their sexual partners. Small wonder that Byrne and Byrne have suggested that we erect on the outskirts of St. Louis, where Masters and Johnson set up their laboratory, a plaque enscribed: "Site at which the clitoris was discovered—1966."

HOW DO OUR GENES CONTRIBUTE TO OUR SEXUAL BEHAVIOR?

In the next two sections of this chapter, we evaluate the evidence for genetic and learning interpretations of sex differences in human sexual behavior. However, though we may choose to examine the effects of one or the other of these categories of variables in relative isolation, the inevitable joint interaction of genetics and environment should not be forgotten.

Harlow's Research on Sex Differences in Monkey Sexuality

Harlow is well known for his social-deprivation experiments with monkeys: isolating infant monkeys from their parents and peers at birth to eliminate the process of socialization. In relation to the development of sexual behaviors, Harlow argues that biologically mediated, sex-differentiated responses maintain themselves, at least partially, in the face of severe social deprivation.

In describing the behavior of a previously socially isolated male in the presence of a receptive female partner, Harlow (1975) states:

> The basic heterosexual heritage of socially inexperienced or socially isolated infant monkeys [is] often appropriate in intent, though hopeless in achievement. This is demonstrated by a male . . . . he mounted the female laterally and thrust sidewise, a posture which left him totally at cross purposes with reality. At least the motions were made, even if the behavior was meaningless. [p. 90]

Similarly, he describes a socially isolated female's responses to a sexually experienced male:

> Unfortunately throughout the affair, she looked lovingly into the male's eyes while sitting flat on the floor. This was a posture in which only her

heart was in the right place, but at least it was a feminine heart. Thus it is perfectly obvious that even immature and abnormal sex patterns may differentiate the two sexes. [p. 90]

Though Harlow wrote in a humorous vein, his anthropomorphizing may not be considered a welcome addition to the sex-role-liberation movement or to the scientific study of sexuality. As discussed in Chapter 1, there are many problems in animal-to-human generalizations.

Harlow reports that infant pelvic thrusting (also observed in human infants) was found to be much more common in male than in female monkeys. A female pattern of passivity and a male pattern of threat were well developed within the first three months of life. Later-developing sexual behaviors were also differentiated on the basis of biological sex; e.g., more grooming occurred in females and more rough-and-tumble play in males.*

What can we infer about generalizations to humans and the interactions of heredity and environment? Harlow answers:

> I have often been asked if monkey data generalizes to man. It is impossible to prove this is true and equally impossible to prove that it is not true. The best I can do is to let you make your own judgments. . . .
>
> Once significant bisexual signposts have been biologically achieved, they tend to be formalized and accentuated by cultural variables. Biology, however, is always first and culture is always second. [p. 90]

A Genetic Basis for Homosexuality?

The possibility that homosexual behavior is genetically controlled has captured both public and professional interest for some time. As you will more fully appreciate after reading about homophobia in a later section of this chapter, research studies appear to have focused exclusively on *male* homosexuality.

The classic study in this area is Kallman's (1952) twin study of male homosexuals. He compared pairs of monozygotic (identical) twins with dizygotic (nonidentical) twins and found strong concordance for homosexuality among the monozygotic pairs but not among

---

*It is interesting to note that Hamburg and Lunde (1966) view rough-and-tumble play as the young primate's mode of *aggression*. It is obviously very difficult to generalize from monkeys to humans when psychologists do not even agree on the definitions of monkeys' behavior.

the dizygotic pairs. However, Rosenthal (1970) has convincingly argued that the results are vitiated by sampling bias and experimenter bias. Acosta (1975) in fact concludes, in a penetrating analysis of the available research, that there is scant evidence to support any biochemical or genetic model of homosexuality.

Eysenck's Heritability Analyses of Sexual Traits of Women and Men

Employing a personality questionnaire and heritability estimates (statistical tools of population genetics), Eysenck (1976) found a heavy genetic involvement in libido (sexual drive), with a markedly greater sexual drive being exhibited by men than by women. In contrast, the heritability of sexual satisfaction was lower than that for sexual drive; i.e., sexual satisfaction was less directly influenced by genetics and more directly influenced by environment. In addition, the heritability of sexual satisfaction in women was marginally greater than in men.

This sex difference in sexual satisfaction may seem puzzling. We know from Hite's (1976) data, for instance, that many women seldom or never experience orgasm. Should that not manifest itself in low sexual satisfaction? There are at least three reasons why this might not be so. First, the sex differences in sexual satisfaction were slight, and as Eysenck readily acknowledges, his research is best regarded as "preliminary exploration of uncharted water unlikely to provide definitive results but perhaps capable of suggesting likely conclusions" (p. 192). Second, a personality questionnaire only measures what it questions, and Eysenck does not seem to have inquired about orgasm directly. Third, many women remain uniformed about the nature of female sexual satisfaction (Barbach, 1976) and may not have answered the questionnaire adequately.

The foregoing comments should not lead you to completely dismiss Eysenck's research. He does offer some tentative evidence suggesting a heritable sex difference in sex drive.

Biological Preparedness and Human Sexuality

As you will recall from Chapters 1 and 9, biological preparedness refers to a facilitation of learning via genetic mechanisms. Is there any evidence for a biological preparedness to learn sexual behaviors? In a manner reminiscent of Harlow, Money and Ehrhardt (1972) have enunciated a "biological clock" model of sexuality for both human males and females. They argue that there are separate, genetically programmed biological clocks determining the onset of puberty and the onset of "love" in teenagers. The sexual alarms for the onset of both puberty and love are set to go off about two years earlier in females than in males, they contend, although the clocks for puberty and love are not necessarily synchronized. Although supportive biochemical data may be proffered for the "puberty clock," we wonder about what seems to be the complete circularity of the "love clock" conception. We know of no evidence for a love clock independent of the behavioral evidence that teenagers fall in love.

Some ethological investigators have taken a very bold [but shaky; see Hinde, 1970] stand favoring sexual stimulus releasers in humans. Stimulus releasers are environmental stimuli that produce genetically programmed behavioral responses: in the present case, sexual reactions. Eibl–Ebesfeldt (1970) proposes sex differences in human stimulus releasers: females are presumed to be genetically programmed to find such features as width of male shoulders and narrowness of male hips sexually attractive, whereas males are viewed as genetically responsive to female breasts, buttocks, legs, and lips. The major problem is of course to determine whether social learning is not the better interpretation of the data.

Stronger evidence for biological preparedness has come from the area of conditioning, discussed in detail in the next section. Seligman (1971) has argued that conditioned responses that (1) can be conditioned in one trial, (2) are highly resistant to extinction, and (3) are relatively impervious to cognitive modification are likely to represent biologically prepared associations. Sexual responses, at least in adolescent males, appear to qualify. Gebhard (1965) reports a case where a male teenager at puberty underwent one-trial sexual conditioning with long-lasting results, which were not changed by cognitive insight:

> The other case is that of a boy who was already in what one might call the flush of sexual excitability which accompanies puberty in most males. During some childhood game he fractured his arm and was taken to a neighborhood physician who, noting the rapidity of swelling, decided to "set" the fracture at once without anesthesia. The physician's attractive nurse felt very sorry for the boy. During the reduction of the fracture and for some time afterwards she held and caressed him with

his head pressed against her breasts. The boy experienced a powerful and curious combination of pain and sexual arousal. Considerably later in life this man began to notice that he was unusually attracted to brunettes with a certain type of hair style—attracted to an extent meriting the label of fetish. Some sadomasochistic tendencies also existed. After much introspection the man recalled that the hair style which was his fetish was the style in which the nurse had worn her hair. This insight did not destroy the fetish. [pp. 489–490]

HOW DOES LEARNING CONTRIBUTE TO OUR SEXUAL BEHAVIOR?

In contrast to the genetic model, the learning model of sexual behavior is both conceptually persuasive and eminently well documented by basic and applied research. The general theory of learning that places the behavior (in our case, sexual behavior) of the human being in the context of his/her social environment is called the social learning (O'Leary & Wilson, 1975) or sociopsychological (Ullmann & Krasner, 1975) approach.

The Social Learning Approach

The social learning model postulates that both adaptive and maladaptive sexual patterns of responding are primarily produced by the conditions of learning instituted by the social environment. These social conditions may vary greatly with the individual, producing a wide range of sexual behaviors. Each society selects out particular sexual behaviors as appropriate or inappropriate for males and females, and "The range of behaviors considered appropriate cross-culturally is essentially the total range of observed sexual responses" (Ullmann & Krasner, 1975, p. 420). We consider less appropriate or less adaptive behaviors simply as variations in learned behavior.

When sexual behaviors become problematic for the individual, they may be modified in the same manner that they were originally acquired, through the processes of learning. New, more adaptive sexual behaviors may be substituted for old, less adaptive sexual behaviors. Social learning therapy focuses on sexual behaviors *per se* as the problem and on the conditions for changing the problem behaviors. The therapy emphasizes the stimuli controlling behavior and the related techniques for instituting more functionally adaptive behavior. Typically, relatively few therapeutic sessions are required, and results are enduring.

As we soon see, social learning is implicated in the development of adaptive and maladaptive emotional feelings about sexuality, in verbal and motor sexual activities, and in cognitions concerning sexuality. As a result, the social learning model underlies many of the conceptions considered throughout this chapter. For now, we concentrate on developing a basic understanding of some of the important processes and principles of learning as applied to human sexual behavior. For this purpose, we use the tripartite conceptual organization of learning provided by Bandura (1969): (1) classical conditioning, (2) operant conditioning, and (3) cognitive mediation.

Classical Conditioning of Human Sexual Behavior

The classical conditioning paradigm is often illustrated through Pavlov's (1927) research, which involved the salivary reflex in dogs.* However, the power of classical conditioning is perhaps best revealed by its extension to human emotions—in our case, to sexual feelings.

We use the development of a fetish as a major example of the classical conditioning of sexual emotions, because not only is it interesting in its own right but it also may be considered to simulate the acquisition of sexual arousal to "normal" sexual stimuli. Sexual fetishism may be defined as sexual behavior that is completely under the control of a culturally inappropriate conditioned stimulus. Fetishistic stimuli range from motorcycles to handbags and beyond. An object becomes a sexual fetish only when it is both detached from accompaniment to "normal" sexual activity and a sexual stimulus in its own right. Fetishism is usually considered a behavioral problem only if the object leads to compulsive sexual responses at inappropriate times or places (Ullmann & Krasner, 1975).

Since culturally appropriate sexual arousal can be stimulated by a wide range of objects, it is not surprising that fetishism is rarely reported (Rimm & Masters, 1974). That the reports are virtually exclu-

*You will recall that conditioning was previously discussed in Chapter 9.

sive to males (O'Leary & Wilson, 1975) is less easily explained. It is possible that there is a sex difference in biological preparedness to learn sexual associations, or simply that there is a sex difference in the cultural acceptability of reporting sexual fetishism to therapists.

Rachman (1966) and Rachman and Hodgson (1968) produced a boot fetish in a small group of male subjects by classically conditioning sexual arousal to a previously neutral stimulus, a pair of women's black knee-length boots. The classical conditioning procedure involved presenting the neutral or *conditioned stimulus* (CS) to the subject, followed immediately by the *unconditioned stimulus* (UCS), that reliably elicited the *unconditioned response* (UCR) of sexual arousal (as measured by penile erection on a penile plethysmograph). The CS was a colored slide of the boots, and the UCS consisted of a series of slides of attractive nude women. Obviously, pictures of nude women do not evoke sexual arousal unless the individual's past history of experience has already produced conditioned sexual arousal to the pictures, a highly likely phenomenon for males in our society.

Over the course of the trials in both experiments, eight male subjects acquired a conditioned response (CR) of sexual arousal to the slide of the boots. This arousal generalized to other similar stimuli: for example, black shoes, or, in the second study (Rachman & Hodgson, 1968), brown boots and even gold sandals! The arousal was extinguished by successive presentation of the CS without the UCS. In all cases, the response showed spontaneous recovery (regained some of its capacity to elicit arousal) after a week, necessitating a second series of extinction trials. Rachman (1966) concluded that three criteria of conditioning had been met: acquisition, generalization, and spontaneous recovery.

Although in this instance the fetish was extinguished by a simple process of extinction, in actuality this is rarely the treatment of choice. When a condition has become problematic and change is desired, a commonly used form of treatment is aversion therapy, which is an illustration of classical counterconditioning (Wolpe, 1973). Counterconditioning is based upon the principle of *reciprocal inhibition*, which presupposes that a high-potency emotional response (e.g., nausea) will dominate and eventually supplant a low-potency emotional response (e.g., sexual arousal). If the elicited nausea is stronger than sexual arousal in the presence of the relevant CS (the fetishistic object), with repeated pairings the object becomes aversive; and the fetishist no longer pursues it as a source of sexual satisfaction.

A classic example of aversive counterconditioning is that of Raymond (1956), in which he describes the treatment of a perambulator (baby carriage) and handbag fetishist. The patient had been arrested several times for physically attacking (e.g., slashing) perambulators before being presented for treatment. During treatment, he was presented with a collection of perambulators, handbags, and colored illustrations of the two immediately after receiving an injection of the nausea-producing drug apomorphine. Pairing the fetish objects with the onset of nausea eventually produced a loss of interest in the fetish. Subsequent studies (e.g., Feldman, 1966) have focused upon electric shock as a more effective and controllable aversive stimulus.

As you may have anticipated from our discussion of aversive counterconditioning, just as classical conditioning provides a useful model to explain how sexual arousal becomes attached to specific objects, it also reveals how anxiety becomes attached to what usually would be considered sexually arousing stimuli. In this latter situation, anxiety, if very strong, will overpower sexual arousal to these stimuli. Any facet of a sexual situation, either directly or through stimulus generalization, can become a cue that elicits conditioned anxiety, thereby inhibiting satisfactory sexual activity. This model has been used to explain female orgasmic dysfunction (Brady, 1966), male impotence (Dengrove, 1971), and heterophobia (LoPiccolo, 1971). Heterophobia is a frequent component of male homosexuality and involves an intense fear of women and heterosexual intercourse. This extreme anxiety inhibits a sexual response to women. Treatments that include only aversive conditioning of homosexual stimuli without removing the heterosexual anxiety could conceivably leave the patient without any sexual outlet (LoPiccolo, 1971), a highly undesirable outcome! Therefore, steps must be taken to ensure replacement arousal to heterosexual stimuli (Barlow & Abel, 1976) if a homosexual client wishes to change his sexual preference.

If anxiety is a conditioned emotional response, then logically, a counterconditioning (Wolpe, 1973) procedure may be used to overcome it. Brady (1966) describes a particular counterconditioning procedure, *systematic desensitization* (Wolpe, 1973), used to treat orgasmic dysfunction in several women. The technique of systematic desensitization consists of replacing anxiety with relaxation in a series of graded steps. In Brady's procedure, anxiety-producing sexual scenes were ranked in an ascending hierarchy, and while the client was deeply relaxed, low-ranking items (least anxiety) were presented repeatedly until they elicited little or no anxiety, i.e., were inhibited by relaxation. Gradually, more anxiety-producing items were introduced until the anxiety response was completely eliminated and sexual activity was no longer dysfunctional.

Operant Conditioning of Human Sexual Behavior

Operant conditioning (Skinner, 1938) emphasizes the relationship between an organism's behavior and the environmental events that follow it. Events that increase the probability of responses that they follow are called *reinforcers*, and events that decrease the probability of responses that they follow are called *punishers*.

We illustrate the application of the operant conditioning model to human sexual behavior by describing some of the environmental conditions leading to the development of homosexual behaviors in a client treated by the second author. The client reported being caught by his parents at twelve years of age in the midst of sexual activity with his girl friend in his parents' bedroom. He was greatly embarrassed and was severely whipped by his father for his supposed wrongdoing. Plans were then made for him to be shipped off to an all-male boarding school. Shortly after his arrival at the boarding school, he was initiated into performing oral sex on upperclassmen for rewards such as comic books and candy bars.

Although these experiences may not capture all the environmental influences determining the client's homosexual behavior, the embarrassment, whipping, and withdrawal of parental affection (via the boarding school) all represent *punishment* for heterosexual behavior. Similarly, the comic books, candy bars, and presumably the male social camaraderie all represent *reinforcement* for homosexual behaviors. Thus, from these consequences, heterosexual behavior decreased in frequency (probability), and homosexual behavior increased in frequency. In accordance with the client's wishes, social learning therapy was used to increase heterosexual and decrease homosexual behavior.

A second major feature of the operant conditioning model concerns the *stimulus control* of behavior by environmental events that regularly precede responses and their consequences. These preceding events are called *discriminative stimuli*, for they signal which behaviors will lead to which consequences and thereby enable an individual to *discriminate* as to the course of action s/he should take. In the case of the homosexual client, he presumably learned that when a female was present as a discriminative stimulus, sexual behavior would be punished. Alternatively, with a male, sexual behavior was more likely to be rewarded.

Discriminative stimulus control must become relatively precise, however. Obviously, not all males would deliver reinforcement for sexual advances, so those males who likely would must be discriminated from those males who likely would not.

Three critical components of the operant conditioning model have been isolated: the *responses*, the *consequences* (reinforcements or punishments), and the *discriminative stimuli*. We now consider each separately in order to demonstrate their involvement in human sexuality.

As Ullmann and Krasner (1975) have indicated, there are two main classes of operant responses that are important in sexual behavior: (1) behaviors in the actual sexual situation, and (2) behaviors (social skills) that are prerequisite to arriving in a sexual situation. We often think of sexual behaviors as only involving those in the first class. However, the second class of behaviors is equally, if not more, important. Most of us have probably seen Charlie Brown in the "Peanuts" comic strip, sitting alone eating his peanut butter sandwich and gazing longingly at the little red-haired girl across the gym. What Charlie Brown needed in learning terms was training in social skills:

> ... that factors such as how to dress, where to circulate, how to talk; how to interpret small gestures, hints, and invitations; how to offer gently, and how to accept rejection without overgeneralizing to all people on all occasions, become the burden of much of the treatment. From our own clinical work and from the reports of our colleagues we would conclude that it is not any particular mode of dress or physical attractant that is crucial, but rather it is the demonstration of interest in the other person as an individual. The key advice may be: relate, don't overwhelm or impress. In summary, before an individual will alter a pattern of behavior, he must be able to do so realistically. This often requires training in skills that are typically considered social rather than sexual. [Ullmann & Krasner, 1975, p. 428]

Turning to the consequences that shape behavior, we have already indicated that reinforcements and punishments may alter sexual operants. However, we should not overlook the fact that pleasant sexual feelings, most notably orgasm, are among the most powerful of reinforcers. To illustrate, a young female client sought assistance from the second author because of continually increasing verbal abuse from her boyfriend. The abuse had begun in private but had generalized to public places such as restaurants. Careful behavioral analysis revealed that yelling and arguing were consistently followed by sexual reinforcement. The couple argued because it was so much fun making up. When they learned to reprogram the contingencies so that more desirable behaviors were rewarded with sexual closeness the problem disappeared.

The last concept of the operant conditioning model to be considered in the context of sexuality is the discriminative stimulus. As Schimel (1971) remarks: "For me all such sexual complaints as 'impotence,' 'frigidity,' 'premature ejaculation,' and so forth are undefinable abstractions until I know with great specificity to what behaviors the patient is attaching these words and in what *contexts* they occur" (italics ours) (p. 24). Masters and Johnson (1970) attempt, with what they call their *sensate focus* technique,* to place sexual behavior under the control of physical and social stimuli that facilitate rather than interfere with sexual arousal. Obviously, any of the discriminative stimuli with which we deal are cognitive (internal) in nature, and this leads us nicely into the next section of the chapter.

Cognitive Mediation of Human Sexual Behavior

In comparison with external events, cognitive stimuli and responses present an immediate problem to the social learning specialist: they are difficult to verify directly through observation and measurement. Thus, considerable operational ingenuity is required. Although private internal events are more difficult to measure than public external events, the social learning theorist assumes that they follow the same laws of behavior (Martin & Pear, 1978). Thus, we now are considering sexual behavior in the context of classical and operant conditioning where all or some of the stimuli and responses are cognitive events.

---

*This sexual therapy technique focuses on developing and maintaining stimuli which produce positive sensual and emotional experiences rather than on evaluating sexual performance. A couple gradually moves toward more advanced sexual responses as positive feelings gain dominance over performance anxiety.

Cognitively mediated classical conditioning is considered first. One of the best examples of cognitive classical conditioning is *orgasmic reconditioning* (Davison, 1968; Marquis, 1970). This technique has been used with males to transfer sexual arousal from an "inappropriate" to an "appropriate" sexual object through imagination. Davison (1968) treated a twenty-one-year-old college senior who reported masturbating about five times a week, exclusively to sadistic fantasies of torturing women. Davison's client stated that he was never sexually aroused by other images and had only kissed a woman twice in his life.

With Davison's technique, the client was instructed to masturbate to sadistic fantasies up until the point of ejaculatory inevitability (the point at which ejaculation is involuntary). At this point, the client was to switch to a "normal" erotic fantasy. The fantasy switch was gradually moved earlier in the sequence until the erotic fantasy was able to be used throughout masturbation.

Davison conceptualizes his technique as one of classical counterconditioning (Wolpe, 1973) in which positive sexual arousal (orgasm) overcomes anxiety previously conditioned to "normal" erotic fantasies. In any event, in the way we have described it, both the original CS (sadistic fantasy) and the replacement CS (erotic fantasy) are cognitive in nature.

Davison (1968) also employed *covert sensitization* (Cautela, 1966; 1967), a procedure in which an aversive thought (US) is paired with an attractive thought (CS) in order to make the latter less appealing. Davison paired a nausea-inducing US with the sadistic fantasy CS in order to decrease the attractiveness of the sadistic fantasy.

With the operant conditioning paradigm, any or all three basic elements—discriminative stimuli, responses, and consequences—may be cognitive in nature. Later in the chapter, we consider cultural and personal labels affecting sexual behavior. From the operant conditioning perspective, these labels may be considered to be cognitive discriminative stimuli.

There is a large number of covert procedures based on operant conditioning techniques; for example, covert reinforcement, covert punishment, covert extinction, and covert modeling (Craighead, Kazdin, & Mahoney, 1976). One of the present authors makes good use of *covert reinforcement* by rewarding the performance of morning exercises with five minutes of uninterrupted sexual fantasy (a powerful covert reinforcement!).

THE SOCIAL PSYCHOLOGY OF SEXUALITY

In the first section we discussed the narrow definition our society has applied to sexuality: heterosexual intercourse and its concomitant behaviors. We then discussed the physiology of sexual arousal and the ways in which psychologists believe we become sexual beings. In this section we explore the social psychology of sexuality. How does our social environment decree what is and what is not sexual? How does this affect our views of the sexual behaviors of others and of ourselves? This section examines our labels: the broad cultural labels that define the "appropriateness" of sexual behaviors and our personal, idiosyncratic labels that help to determine for us as individuals whether or not we are sexually aroused.

Homophobia: A Cultural Label

In 1935 Adolph Hitler outlawed homosexual fantasies (Lauritsen & Thorstad, 1974, cited in Lehne, 1976). What social perspective could lead a government to pass such an obviously unenforceable law against such a seemingly harmless behavior? Lehne (1976) believes this action to be indicative of a widespread sociosexual phenomenon he calls *homophobia:** " the irrational fear or intolerance of homosexuality" (p. 66). Lehne describes homophobia as almost exclusively masculine in character: perpetuated by men against men.

What is the evidence for sex differences in homophobia? Few women who have been denied employment, housing, or child custody on the basis of their sexual preference or who have been rejected by their families would be willing to accept the suggestion that acknowledged lesbians are not discriminated against in our society. We would posit, however, that we do not look for lesbians behind every bush or infer homosexuality from a woman's every sex-role-inappropriate action.

Colwill's (see Anderson, 1974) study of attributions of homosex-

---

*Phobias are usually considered to be extreme anxiety reactions occurring in a small percentage of the population. *Homophobia*, as Lehne uses the word, refers to a general, pervasive social attitude—a mechanism for the control of both sex role and sexual behavior. We use the word here according to Lehne's meaning.

uality speaks directly to sex differences in homophobia. She found that male and female subjects both attributed homosexuality to males who held social attitudes that subjects had prejudged as "feminine," yet neither males nor females attributed homosexuality to females with "masculine" attitudes. We interpret these findings as an indication that homophobia is manifested by attributions of homosexuality, is socially transmitted by both sexes, and applies chiefly to male homosexuality.

It should not be particularly surprising that homophobia is practiced by both sexes against one sex. It is probably another reflection of antifemale prejudice, which is exhibited by both men and women in North America. To be female in our culture is to be subordinate. To be male is to be superordinate. To emulate woman's role is more than to emulate sex-inappropriate behavior; it is to emulate culture-inappropriate behavior (Broverman, Broverman, Clarkson, Rosenkrantz, & Vogel, 1970). Achieving females may not appreciate being considered masculine, and the dubious compliment "You think like a man" is seldom accepted with grace; but when someone calls a man effeminate, no one doubts that an insult was meant. The emulation of superordinates is a natural phenomenon in an achieving society, but the emulation of subordinates smacks of perversion.

The superordinate position of males in our society manifests itself in some rather frightening pressures on men and boys to keep constantly achieving masculinity, a process that is usually fraught with anxiety (Lynn, 1966). Homosexuality is often a fear for male adolescents and young adult males—fear that they or their friends are homosexual (Henshel, 1973). "What are you, a fag?" is a common taunt even in elementary school. The seven-year-old boy may not know what the word means, but he soon learns which behaviors will elicit it. These behaviors may have nothing to do with physical contact with other boys—more likely, they are behaviors that his peers have deemed "feminine."

Because a male's sexuality is such a strong element in our definition of his masculinity, it has been tempting to create a link between his social behaviors and his sexual behaviors. For whatever reason, we have attached strong negative social sanctions to homosexual behavior, and by associating homosexuality with "inappropriate" sex-role behaviors, we manage not only to control homosexuality but also to discourage males from exhibiting "feminine" behavior.

Homophobia is thus a powerful social mechanism for maintaining the sex-role status quo.

In spite of the fact that the American Psychiatric Association (APA) has removed homosexuality from its categories of "mental illness," this change has had little public (and we wonder about professional) impact. As a society we view homosexual behavior as a highly aversive mental illness. In contradiction, *The Wolfenden Report* (1964) is emphatic in its assertion that psychiatric abnormalities of homosexuals are a product of what Lehne would call a homophobic society and do not exist in cultures where homosexuality is viewed as a completely acceptable mode of sexual preference.

In our society, however, homosexuality is seen as much more than a sexual preference. It has evolved into an implicit theory of personality. We apply the label *homosexual* to *people* and not merely to acts. Ann Landers (1977) was recently chided for insulting people who choose sexual partners of both sexes. Her reply reinforced for millions the belief that homosexuality is an extremely aberrant behavior and that we can all be meaningfully classified on the basis of sexual orientation into three distinct nonoverlapping camps: the homosexuals, the heterosexuals, and the bisexuals. Notice particularly the degree of commitment reflected in Ann Landers's closing statement:

> I view homosexuals as individuals who have a *severe personality disorder*. [APA notwithstanding; italics ours]. My adjectives "weird, bombed, stoned, kinky or a little cuckoo" described HETEROSEXUAL students who would go in for bisexual shenanigans just for the heck of it. These people are not gay, they are college students with normal and natural sexual preferences who are simply looking for a new kind of trip.
>
> I thought a long time before I wrote that response and I wouldn't take back a word of it. [p. 30]

We believe that our society has paid a high price for our homophobic labels. We have created sympathetic ears for Anita Bryant's plea for discrimination on the basis of sexual preference. We are raising our children in a society where people are called "queer" (and worse) on the basis of their choice of a sexual partner. And if, as Lehne has argued, homophobia serves to maintain sex-role stereotypes, we are, by indulging our prejudices, postponing our sex-role liberation.

The Double Standard: A Cultural Label

The notion that males have a greater desire for and need of sexual activity than females is one of the most firmly established in our sociosexual lore: the infamous "double standard." This notion touches every facet of our sexual lives. It establishes women as the gatekeepers of sexual relationships. It establishes men as the initiators, the pursuers, and the sexual teachers. It implies that men ask for sexual favors and that women refuse, or comply and learn.

Driscoll and Davis (1976) examined how individuals use sociosexual stereotypes in evaluating the sexuality of others. It will come as no surprise that their subjects rated males as more sexually aggressive than females. What is perhaps more interesting is that their female subjects rated men as more sexually aggressive than men rated either themselves or other men. Furthermore, men saw themselves as less sexually aggressive than their same-sex peers. Warnings that men are "only after one thing" seem to be having their effect; women place great faith in the dictum, and men believe it of other men.

But aren't we in the midst of a sexual revolution? Is the double standard still alive and well and living in North America? We know that the sex-differences gap in sexual behaviors is closing, particularly among young adults. For example, Kinsey (1953) reported that less than one-third of young (under age 25), then-single white females had engaged in premarital intercourse, whereas 71 percent of then-single white males had done so, a difference of approximately 40 percent. Hunt's (1974) comparable figures are 75 percent for females and 95 percent for males, a difference of only 20 percent. Turning to extramarital intercourse, Kinsey (1953) reported an 8 percent incidence for young white females and a 24 percent incidence for young white males, a gap of 16 percent. Twenty years later (Hunt, 1974) the figures are 24 percent for females and 26 percent for males, a mere 2 percent difference. While the maximum incidence of extramarital intercourse appears to have changed little over the intervening years (24 to 26 percent), presumably because of prevailing cultural sanctions, females have certainly caught up to males.

It is tempting to treat these figures as the sexual gospel. Unfortunately, however, there may be a tendency for males to overreport and for females to underreport sexual activity, consistent with our double standard of sexual behavior. In any case, direct comparison of Kinsey's and Hunt's data is very difficult. Kinsey sought out sexual informers at a time when sexuality was a taboo topic, and in spite of his brilliantly designed and administered questionnaire, he may have had difficulty obtaining completely honest responses. Probably more importantly, his respondents, by agreeing to discuss their sexual habits, showed themselves to be a rather daring segment of North American society in the late 1940s. Kinsey also actively sought out low-statistical-frequency individuals such as divorced people and overrepresented them in order to attain more nearly equal subsamples. Hunt's respondents may have represented an even more biased sample: people who chose to respond to the *Playboy* questionnaire. The biased sampling may be tapping males and females who not only exhibit atypical sexual behavior but who also show a high degree of similarity in their sexual attitudes and behaviors.

Kinsey's and Hunt's data are not directly comparable on age, race, marital status, and socioeconomic status. Although both researchers provided important pioneering contributions to the study of sexuality and although Hunt has gone to considerable pains to attain statistical comparability with Kinsey, we should still be cautious in our comparisons. Nevertheless, it does seem reasonably safe to conclude that although more males than females currently report engaging in nonmarital intercourse, the gap has closed appreciably over the decades.

If our analysis of Kinsey's and Hunt's data has left you with the impression that everyone in our society is engaging in sexual intercourse at every opportunity, we have certainly misrepresented the data. To make it into the "premarital intercourse" group in Hunt's study, for instance, one need only to have had premarital sexual intercourse once. Although the media may give the impression that rampant sexuality is the order of the day, most sexual-standard researchers (e.g., Hunt, 1974) would probably agree that sexual restraint is still no stranger in North America.

Does the increasing similarity of male and female sexual behaviors indicate, as Hunt has suggested, "a radical break with the double standard" (p. 263)? Some psychologists believe (e.g., Gordon & Shankweiler, 1974) that the double standard has merely been rewritten to conform to the language of the sexual revolution. So although more females are having sexual intercourse and although responses to sexual-attitudes questionnaires indicate increasing sexual equality (see Perlman, in press, for a review), the underpinnings of sexism in sexuality still persist. As Gordon and Shankweiler (1971) have suggested, recently publicized female sexuality is merely being "poured into old bottles of male–female relationships" (p. 174). They accuse even "J," (1969), of *The sensuous woman* fame, of teaching women not to enjoy their own sexuality but merely to perfect their techniques for the pleasure of men.

And so we return to an earlier idea—male-centered sexuality. As one of Hite's (1976) respondents complained:

> Men have been raised in an environment where sex is seen as something *they need*, and that they must trick and seduce women into letting them have, against the woman's better judgment. Thus when a woman really chooses to have sex with a man, he doesn't see it that way. Rather he thinks he has won something, and proceeds to use it. [p. 469]*

This seems like a very negative sociosexual situation. How did it come about, and how is it maintained? Laws and Schwartz (1977) feel that our social history has moved through three dominant "sexual scripts," or labels, in the past few decades. The first was the standard of abstinence, which read that sexual intercourse was permissible only between spouses. We might add that the most extreme form of this script advocated only procreative sex. Overlapping this standard for many segments of society was a second script: the double standard—which read, explicitly or implicitly, that the standard of abstinence *really* only applied to females. A third standard emerged during the 1960s: permissiveness with affection (Reiss, 1960), which allowed premarital intercourse between partners in love.

The dilemma comes, say Laws and Schwartz, with our difficulty in defining love and in knowing under which of the three still-present standards one's partner is operating. Also, these standards may overlap, and when the double standard overlaps the permissiveness-with-affection standard, women are not permitted to be "in love" too often. Thus, Schwartz (1973, cited in Laws & Schwartz, 1977) has shown that although male undergraduates reported that they would not lose respect for a sexually experienced woman, ten lovers exceeded their level of acceptable experience and caused their respect to decline. Unfortunately, we do not know whether or not this finding supports the existence of a double standard, because women may feel the same way about men.

To this point, our discussion has focused on the disadvantages to females of a double standard of sexuality. The disadvantages to males are finally being voiced, however (e.g., Farrell, 1975). The role of sexual initiator, pursuer, and teacher entails considerable responsibility and interpersonal risk. Although males undoubtedly learn with experience to read cues (discriminative stimuli) that would help minimize the risk, Lester (1973) remembers, with pain, his reaction to the sociosexual institution of teenage dating:

> That meant risking my ego, which was about as substantial as a toilet-paper raincoat in the African rainy season. But I had to thrust that ego forward to be judged, accepted, or rejected by some girl. It wasn't fair! Who was she to sit back like a queen with the power to create joy by her consent or destruction by her denial? [p. 271]

Masters and Johnson (1974) make a passionate plea against the double standard, which they feel creates wariness and mistrust between males and females and creates a situation in which women are constantly reinforced for not touching. This is a very important component of women's sociosexual development, they believe. To be the one touched simultaneously affirms one's desirability and places responsibility on the shoulders of the toucher. It is as if one person must lose for the other to win.

Have we learned our sexual sex roles so well that the double standard will follow us to our graves? Not if we are to believe writers such as Farrell (1975) and David and Brannon (1976), who have breathed optimism into sexual sex-role liberation. There are more desirable alternatives, and we can attain them. We have learned certain sexual sex-role responses, and we can learn to replace them with new responses. We can learn to view males and females as sexual equals: equals in sexual privilege and equals in sexual responsibility. We can learn that women may initiate, pursue, and teach and that men may refuse or comply and learn. Someday soon, *sexy* may have an entirely new meaning devoid of the sex-role restrictions of female passivity and male dominance, female compliance and male achievement, so familiar to us all.

The Labeling of Individual Sexual Response

To this point, we have been discussing labeling in a broad cultural sense: what does our society define as sexual? But labeling is also a very important aspect of individual sexual response. A woman may label the arousal associated with her breast being sucked by her infant as nurturance and by her lover as passion. Yet both may elicit the same physiological response. We know, in fact, from Newton's (1971) research on "the trebly sensuous woman" presented in the first section of this chapter that the physiological responses associated with breast-feeding and orgasm are highly similar.

The social psychological approach of labeling, which fits under the general rubric of attribution theory (Jones & Davis, 1965), is usually credited to Schacter and Singer (1962), who were the first to provide experimental evidence that we label our physiological arousal with reference to cues in the environment. However, Valins (1967) was probably the first to bring the idea of labeling to the study of sexual arousal. He showed male subjects slides of seminude females while playing to them tapes of sounds they believed to be their heartbeats. Subjects he had prerated on the basis of psychometric tests as "emotional" (and *only* those subjects) judged females whose pictures were accompanied with "heart-rate change" as more attractive than females whose pictures had not been accompanied by this "change." The effect was sustained for an appreciable length of time. Two months later, when offered nude photographs as a reward, subjects were more likely to choose photographs of the "heart-rate changers." The interpretation has been that male subjects predisposed to emotionality, when given no better explanation, labeled their heart-rate change as sexual arousal and the woman who caused the arousal as sexually attractive.

It is tempting to attribute the cause of the inferred sexual arousal in Valins' research to cognitive change: the labeling in and of itself. However, Wolpe (1976), in the context of anxiety reduction, emphasizes that cognitive events can change emotional reactions only if they have autonomic effects, e.g., *actual* rather than false changes in heart-rate. A test of Wolpe's hypothesis in the context of sexual arousal would involve monitoring subjects' autonomic arousal during periods of differential heart-rate feedback. According to Wolpe, false heart-rate-change feedback should produce sexual arousal only when accompanied by autonomic change. If this turns out to be true, it would further substantiate the theory (Schacter & Singer, 1962) that both autonomic arousal and labeling are necessary components for the experience of emotion.*

What are the implications of this physiological research for the differential sexualities of males and females? Berscheid and Walster (1974) have suggested that because our double standard prescribes that a woman is "supposed" to feel sexual arousal only when "in love," her labels for physiological arousal may be very different from the labels of a man in a similar situation. There is some research to bear out their contention. Using tapes of erotic and romantic literature and measures of genital blood volume response, Heiman (1977) found that women are *physiologically* aroused by sexually explicit material but that many do not label themselves as *sexually* aroused. Men are much more likely to call a spade a spade, in this situation at least. This sex difference was especially evident when males and females listened to nonerotic but romantic material. Although all males rated themselves as experiencing sexual arousal during their largest blood volume response, 42 percent of females did not. One possibility is that females may be less willing than males to *report* sexual arousal in an experimental situation. Or, as they could not label themselves "in love" in that situation, they did not see themselves as sexually aroused.

An interesting commentary on the double standard is that male and female subjects both experienced greater arousal with tapes of erotic literature than with tapes of nonerotic, romantic literature. What is more, both sexes experienced female-initiated, female-centered sexual interaction as the most arousing. Even if males are perceived as the initiators of sexual activity in our culture, then, we need not assume that that pattern is a necessary precondition of sexual arousal for either sex or that it is minimally arousing.

It appears, then, that there is some empirical support for Berscheid and Walster's model: that given the chance to label their physiological arousal as romantic, women may do so. Because of the double standard, men may have little to lose by labeling or reporting their physiological arousal as sexual; on the other hand, they may have no choice. A man may have difficulty labeling his erect penis as

---

*We are indebted to R. W. Tait for his suggestion that "heart-rate change" feedback may merely have led to increased attention to the photographs. Those photographs that received more attention and therefore became more familiar may have been rated as more attractive. The mechanism may have been increased attention rather than increased sexual arousal.

indicative of anything but sexual arousal, whereas a woman may over-look vaginal lubrication. Perhaps if women learn to read their bodies with greater sensitivity, the more subtle physiological changes that they experience will be more readily interpreted and acted upon as sexual.

SUMMARY

In our study of sex differences in human sexuality, we have examined this most basic of responses from a variety of psychological perspectives. We began by considering how both female and male sexuality was defined and dominated by the penis. In opposition to this ideology are the views of Newton, Rotkin, and Sherfey. Newton argues for a broader definition of female sexuality that would include childbirth and breast-feeding as well as intercourse; Rotkin deplores our penis-and-vagina-centered orientation; and Sherfey contends that a patriarchial society has suppressed not only the definition, but also the expression, of female sexuality.

The physiology of sexuality, as described by Masters and Johnson, was then compared for males and females. Both sexes progress through four stages of physical responsiveness: excitement, plateau, orgasmic, and resolution. Although the progression is similar for males and females, there are large individual differences in duration and intensity and, of course, sex differences in the anatomical structures involved. A particular myth exploded by this research was the long-held belief that females experience two distinct types of orgasm: clitoral and vaginal.

We next examined several hypothesized genetic mechanisms in human sexual behavior. Learning models, it appears, offer a much more fruitful approach. We presented a social learning approach to human sexual behavior that postulates that both adaptive and maladaptive sexual responses are produced by the social environment. Three learning models—classical conditioning, operant conditioning, and cognitive mediation—were used to analyze the development, maintenance, and modification of human sexual behaviors.

Our final analysis was of the cultural and idiosyncratic labels we attach to our sexual behaviors. Through this social psychological approach, we examined homophobia, the double standard, and self-attributions of sexual arousal.

As we researched for and wrote this chapter, paramount in our minds were sex differences in sexuality. What were the differences, and how could we best explain them with the various psychological tools at our disposal? We answered some of those questions and raised some new questions of our own. Our emphasis on sex differences over similarities may have suggested a separation of the sexes rather than a joining together, which is what sexuality means for most people—part of an important sharing relationship. This is the way we would like to think of the two sexes—as sharing together—sharing in their differences and in their similarities.

References

ACOSTA, F. X. Etiology and treatment of homosexuality: A review. *Archives of Sexual Behavior*, 1975, *4*, 9–29.

ADAIR, J. G. *The human subject: The social psychology of the psychological experiment.* Boston: Little, Brown and Co., 1973.

ADAMS, G. R., & HAMM, N. H. A partial test of the "contiguity" and "generalized imitation" theories of the social modeling process. *The Journal of Genetic Psychology*, 1973, *123*, 145–154.

ADINOLFI, A. A. Characteristics of highly accepted, highly rejected and relatively unknown university freshmen. *Journal of Counselling Psychology*, 1970, *17*, 456–464.

ADLER, F. The rise of the female crook. *Psychology Today*, 1975, *9*(6), pp. 42; 46; 48; 112; 114.

AHAMMER, I. M. Desirability judgments as a function of item content, instructional set and sex: A life span development study. *Human Development*, 1971, *14*, 195–207.

ALLPORT, G. W. The historical background of modern social psychology. In G. Lindzey & E. Aronson (Eds.), *The handbook of social psychology* (Vol. 1) (2nd ed.). Reading, Mass.: Addison–Wesley, 1969, pp. 1–80.

301

ALPER, T. Where are we now? Discussion of papers presented in the 1975 AERA symposium on sex differences in achievement motivation and achievement behavior. *Psychology of Women Quarterly*, 1977, *1*(3), 294–303.

AMBERT, A.–M. *Sex structure.* Don Mills: Longman Canada, 1976.

ANASTASI, A. Heredity, environment, and the question "how?" *Psychological Review*, 1958, *65*, 197–208.

ANDERSON, N. *A stereotypical association between sex role appropriateness, sexual orientation and sex drive.* Unpublished B.A. thesis, Universtiy of Western Ontario, 1974.

ATKINSON, J. W. (Ed.). *Motives in fantasy, action and society.* Princeton, N.J.: Van Nostrand, 1958.

ATKINSON, J. W. *An introduction to motivation.* Princeton, N.J.: Van Nostrand, 1964.

ATKINSON, J. W., & FEATHER, N. T. (Eds.). *A theory of achievement motivation.* New York: Wiley, 1966.

BAKAN, D. *The duality of human existence.* Chicago: Rand McNally, 1966.

BALL, D. W. Toward a sociology of toys: Inanimate objects, socialization, and the demography of the doll world. *Sociological Quarterly*, 1967, *8*, 447–458.

BANDURA, A. Influence of model's reinforcement contingencies on the acquisition of imitative responses. *Journal of Personality and Social Psychology*, 1965, *1*, 589–595.

BANDURA, A. *Principles of behavior modification.* New York: Holt, Rinehart and Winston, 1969.

BANDURA, A. *A social learning theory.* New York: General Learning Press, 1971.

BANDURA, A., ROSS, D., & ROSS, S. A. A comparative test of the status envy, social power, and secondary reinforcement theories of identificatory learning. *Journal of Abnormal and Social Psychology*, 1963, *67*, 527–534.

BARBACH, L. G. *For yourself: The fulfillment of female sexuality.* Garden City, N.Y.: Anchor Books, 1976.

BARCLAY, A. The effects of hostility on physiological and fantasy responses. *Journal of Personality*, 1969, *37*, 651–667.

BARDWICK, J. *The psychology of women: A study of bio-cultural conflicts.* New York: Harper and Row, 1971.

BARGLOW, P., & BROWN, E. Pseudocyesis. To be and not to be pregnant: A psychosomatic question. In J. G. Howells (Ed.), *Modern perspectives in psycho-obstetrics.* New York: Brunner/Mazel Publishers, 1972.

BARLOW, D. H., & ABEL, G. C. Sexual deviation. In W. E. Craighead, A. E. Kazdin, & M. S. Mahoney (Eds.), *Behavior modification: Principles, issues and applications.* Boston: Houghton Mifflin, 1976.

BARRY, H., BACON, M. K., & CHILD, I. L. A cross-cultural survey of some sex differences in socialization. *Journal of Abnormal and Social Psychology,* 1957, *55*, 327–332.

BART, P. Depression in middle-aged women. In V. Gornick & B. Moran, (Eds.), *Women in sexist society.* New York: Basic Books, 1971.

BAR-TAL, D., & FRIEZE, I. H. *Achievement motivation and gender as determinants of attributions for success and failure.* Unpublished manuscript, University of Pittsburgh, 1973.

BAR-TAL, D., & FRIEZE, I. H. Achievement motivation for males and females as a determinant of attributions for success and failure. *Sex Roles,* 1977, *3*(3), 301–314.

BARTHOLOMEW, A. A., & SUTHERLAND, G. A. A defense of insanity and extra Y chromosome, R vs. Hannel. *Australian and New Zealand Journal of Criminology,* 1969, *2*, 29–37.

BARUCH, G. K. Maternal influences upon college women's attitudes toward women and work. *Developmental Psychology,* 1972, *6*, 32–37.

BAXENDALE, H. V. *Are children neglecting their mothers?.* New York: Doubleday & Company, Inc., 1974.

BAYNE, N. E., & PHYE, G.D. Age and sex differences in induced hierarchical organizational ability. *Journal of Genetic Psychology,* 1977, *130*, 191–200.

BAZIN, N. T. The concept of androgyny: A working bibliography. *Women's Studies,* 1974, *2*(2), 217–236.

BAZIN, N. T., & FREEMAN, A. The androgynous vision. *Women's Studies,* 1974, *2*(2), 185–215.

BECKER, H. S., & STRAUSS, H. Careers, personality and adult socialization. *American Journal of Sociology,* 1956, *62*, 253–263.

BEDNARIK, K. *The male in crisis.* New York: Alfred A. Knopf, 1970.

BELOTE, B. Masochistic syndrome, hyterical personality, and the illusion of a healthy woman. In S. Cox (Ed.), *Female psychology: The emerging self.* Chicago: Science Research Associates, 1976, 335–348.

BEM, S. L. The measurement of psychological androgyny. *Journal of Consulting and Clinical Psychology*, 1974, *42*, 155–162.

BEM, S. L. Sex-role adaptability: One consequence of psychological androgyny. *Journal of Personality and Social Psychology*, 1975, *31*, 634–643.

BEM, S. L. Beyond androgyny: Some presumptuous prescriptions for a liberated sexual identity. In J. Sherman & F. Denmark (Eds.), *Psychology of women: Future directions of research*. New York: Psychological Dimensions, in press.

BEM, S. L., & LENNEY, E. Sex-typing and the avoidance of cross-sex behavior. *Journal of Personality and Social Psychology*, 1976, *33*(1), 48–54.

BEM, S. L., MARTYNA, W., & WATSON, C. Sex-typing and androgyny: Further explorations of the expressive domain. *Journal of Personality and Social Psychology*, 1976, *34*(5), 1016–1023.

BERKOWITZ, L. *Aggression: A social psychological analysis*. New York: McGraw–Hill, 1962.

BERKOWITZ, L. The contagion of violence: An S–R mediational analysis of some effects of observed aggression. In W. Arnold & M. Page (Eds.), *Nebraska Symposium on Motivation* (Vol. 18). Lincoln, Nebraska: University of Nebraska Press, 1970, pp. 95–133.

BERKOWITZ, L., & FRODI, A. Stimulus characteristics that can enhance or decrease aggression: Associations with prior positive or negative reinforcements for aggression. *Aggressive Behavior*, 1977, *3*, 1–15.

BERKOWITZ, L., & LEPAGE, A. Weapons as aggression-eliciting stimuli. *Journal of Personality and Social Psychology*, 1967, *1*, 202–207.

BERNARD, J. *The sex game*. Englewood Cliffs, N.J.: Prentice–Hall, 1968.

BERNARD, J. The paradox of the happy marriage. In V. Gornick & B. K. Moran (Eds.), *Women in sexist society*. New York: Basic Books, Inc., 1971.

BERNARD, J. *The future of marriage*. New York: World, 1972.

BERNARD, J. Where are we now? Some thoughts on the current scene. *Psychology of Women Quarterly*, Fall 1976, *1*(1), 21–37.

BERSCHEID, E., & WALSTER, E. A little bit above love. In T. L. Huston (Ed.), *Foundations of interpersonal attraction*. New York: Academic Press, 1974, pp. 355–381. Also, in edited version in D. Byrne & L. A. Byrne (Eds.), *Exploring human sexuality*. New York: Thomas Y. Crowell Company, 1977, pp. 238–258.

Bible, English (King James Version). Authorized, 1957.

BILLER, H., & MEREDITH, D. *Father power.* Garden City, N.Y.: Anchor Books, 1975.

BING, E. Effect of childrearing practices on development of differential cognitive abilities. *Child Development,* 1963, *34*, 631–648.

BLOCK, J. H. Conceptions of sex role: Some cross-cultural and longitudinal perspectives. *American Psychologist,* 1973, *28*, 512–526.

BLUMER, H. Sociological implications of the thought of George Herbert Mead. In G. P. Stone & H. A. Farberman (Eds.), *Social Psychology through Symbolic Interaction.* Toronto: Ginn–Blaisdell, 1970, 282–293.

BLUMER, H. Society as symbolic interaction. In J. G. Manis & B. N. Meltzer (Eds.), *Symbolic interaction, a reader in social psychology.* Boston: Allyn and Bacon, 1972, 145–153.

BOCK, D. R. Word and image: Sources of the verbal and spatial factors in mental test scores. *Psychometrika,* 1973, *38*, 437–457.

BOCK, D. R., & KOLAKOWSKI, D. Further evidence of sex-linked major-gene influence on human spatial visualizing ability. *American Journal of Human Genetics,* 1973, *25*, 1–14.

BORDEN, R. J. Witnessed aggression: Influence of an observer's sex and values on aggressive responding. *Journal of Personality and Social Psychology,* 1975, *31*, 567–573.

BOSTON WOMEN'S HEALTH COLLECTIVE. *Our bodies, ourselves.* New York: Simon and Schuster, 1971.

BOULDING, E. Familial constraints on women's work roles. *Signs,* 1976, *1*(3), 95–117.

BRADY, J. P. Brevitat relaxation treatment of frigidity. *Behaviour Research and Therapy,* 1966, *4*, 71–77.

BRAGINSKY, D. D., & BRAGINSKY, B. M. Surplus people: Their lost faith in self and system. *Psychology Today,* 1975, *9*(3), 68–72.

BRENTON, M. *The American male.* Greenwich, Conn.: Fawcett Publications Inc., 1966.

BRENTON, M. The breadwinner. In D. S. David & R. Brannon (Eds.), *The forty-nine percent majority: The male sex role.* Reading, Mass.: Addison–Wesley Publishing Company, 1976, pp. 92–98.

BROVERMAN, D. M., KLAIBER, E. L., KOBAYASHI, Y., & VOGEL, W. Roles of activation and inhibition in sex differences in cognitive abilities. *Psychological Review,* 1968, *75*, 23–50.

BROVERMAN, I. K., BROVERMAN, D. M., CLARKSON, F. E., ROSENKRANTZ, P. S., & VOGEL, S. R. Sex role stereotypes and clinical judgments of mental health. *Journal of Consulting and Clinical Psychology*, 1970, *34*(1), 1–7.

BROVERMAN, I., VOGEL, S., BROVERMAN, D., CLARKSON, F., & ROSENKRANTZ, P. Sex-role stereotypes: A current appraisal. *Journal of Social Issues*, 1972, *28*(2), 59–78.

BROWN, H. *How I found freedom in an unfree world.* New York: Avon Books, 1973.

BROWNMILLER, S. *Against our will.* New York: Simon & Schuster, 1975.

BUFFERY, A. W. H., & GRAY, J. A. Sex differences in the development of spatial and linguistic skills. In C. Ounsted & D. C. Taylor (Eds.), *Gender differences: Their ontogeny and significance.* Baltimore: Williams & Wilkins, 1972.

BUSS, A. H. Aggression pays. In J. Singer (Ed.), *The control of aggression and violence: Cognitive and physiological factors.* New York: Academic Press, 1971, pp. 7–18.

BUSS, A. H. *The psychology of aggression.* New York: Wiley, 1961.

BYRNE, D., & BYRNE, L. *Exploring human sexuality.* New York: Thomas Y. Crowell Company, 1977.

CAUTELA, J. Treatment of compulsive behavior by covert sensitization. *Psychological Record*, 1966, *16*, 33–41.

CAUTELA, J. Covert sensitization. *Psychological Reports*, 1967, *20*, 459–468.

CHAMOVE, A., HARLOW, H. F., & MITCHELL, G. Sex differences in the infant-directed behavior of preadolescent rhesus monkeys. *Child Development*, 1967, *38*, 329–335.

CHAPPELL, N. L. *Work, commitment to work, and self-identity among women.* Unpublished Ph.D. thesis, McMaster University, Hamilton, Ontario, Canada, 1978.

CHERRY, F., & DEAUX, K. *Fear of success versus fear of gender-inconsistent behavior: A sex similarity.* Paper presented at a meeting of the Midwestern Psychological Association, Chicago, 1975.

CHESLER, P. Patient and patriarch: Women in the psychotherapeutic relationship. *Journal of Marriage and the Family*, 1971, *33*, 746–759.

CHESLER, P. *Women and madness.* New York: Avon Books, 1972.

CLARK, L., & LEWIS, D. *Rape: The price of coercive sexuality.* Toronto: The Women's Press, 1977.

COLWILL, N. L., & PERLMAN, D. Effects of sex and relationship on self-disclosure. *JSAS Catalogue of Selected Documents in Psychology*, 1977, *7*, 40, MS. 1470.

CONNELLY, M. P., & CHRISTIANSEN-RUFFMAN, L. Women's problems: Private troubles or public issues? *The Canadian Journal of Sociology*, 1977, *12*, 167–178.

CONNER, R., & LEVINE, S. Hormonal influences on aggressive behavior. In S. Garatti & E. Sigg (Eds.), *Aggressive behavior*. New York: Wiley, 1969.

CONSTANTINOPLE, A. Masculinity–femininity: An exception to a famous dictum? *Psychological Bulletin*, 1973, *80*(3), 389–407.

COOLEY, C. H. Primary group and human nature. In J. G. Manis & B. N. Meltzer (Eds.), *Symbolic interaction, a reader in social psychology*. Boston: Allyn and Bacon, 1972, 158–160.

COSER, L. A. *Greedy institutions*. New York: The Free Press, 1974.

COURT-BROWN, W. *Human population cytogenetics*. New York: Wiley, 1967.

COX, S. *Female psychology: The emerging self*. Chicago: Science Research Associates, 1976.

COZBY, P. C. Self-disclosure: A literature review. *Psychological Bulletin*, 1973, *79*, 73–91.

CRAIGHEAD, W. E., KAZDIN, A. E., & MAHONEY, M. J. *Behavior modification: Principles, issues, and applications*. Boston: Houghton Mifflin, 1976.

CRANDALL, V. J. Achievement. In H. W. Stevenson (Ed.), *Child psychology: Sixty-second yearbook of the National Society for the Study of Education*. Chicago: University of Chicago Press, 1963.

CRANDALL, V. J. Sex differences in expectancy of intellectual and academic reinforcement. In C. P. Smith (Ed.), *Achievement-related motives in children*. New York: Russell Sage, 1969.

CRANDALL, V. J., KATKOVSKY, W., & PRESTON, A. A conceptual formulation for some research on children's achievement development. *Child Development*, 1960, *31*, 787–797.

DALTON, K. *The premenstrual cycle*. Baltimore: Penguin Books, 1969.

D'ANDRADE, R. G. Sex differences and cultural institutions. In E. E. Maccoby (Ed.), *The development of sex differences*. Stanford, Calif.: Stanford University Press, 1966, pp. 173–203.

DAVID, D. S., & BRANNON, R. *The forty-nine percent majority: The male sex role*. Don Mills; Canada: Addison–Wesley and Reading, Mass.: Addison–Wesley Publishing Company, 1976.

DAVIS, E. G. *The first sex.* New York: Putnam, 1971.

DAVISON, G. C. The elimination of a sadistic fantasy by a client-controlled conditioning technique: A case study. *Journal of Abnormal Psychology,* 1968, *73,* 84–90.

DEAUX, K. *The behavior of women and men.* Belmont, Calif.: Brooks/Cole, 1976.

DE BEAUVOIR, S. *The second sex.* New York: Alfred A. Knopf, 1952.

DENGROVE, E. Behavior therapy of impotence. *Journal of Sex Research,* 1971, 7, 177–183.

DE RIENCOURT, A. *Sex and power in history.* New York: Delta Books, 1974.

DICKASON, A. Anatomy and destiny: The role of biology in Plato's views of women. In C. C. Gould & M. W. Wartofsky (Eds.), *Women and philosophy: Toward a theory of liberation.* New York: G. P. Putnam's Sons, 1976, 45–53.

DIENER, E., BUGGE, I., & DIENER, C. Children's preparedness to learn high magnitude responses. *The Journal of Social Psychology,* 1975, *96,* 99–107.

DOERING, C. H., BRODIE, H. K., KRAEMER, H., BECKER, H., & HAMBURG, D. A. Plasma testosterone levels and psychologic measures in men over a 2-month period. In R. C. Friedman, R. M. Richart, & R. L. VandeWiele (Eds.), *Sex differences in behavior.* New York: Wiley, 1974, 413–432.

DRISCOLL, R. A., & DAVIS, K. E. Sexual restraints: A comparison of perceived and self-reported reasons for college students. *Journal of Sex Research,* 1971, 7, pp. 253–262. Reprinted in J. L. McCasy & D. R. Copeland (Eds.), *Modern views of human sexual behavior.* Chicago: Science Research Associations, Inc., 1976, pp. 37–43.

DUFTY, W. F. *Sugar blues.* Radnor, Pa.: Chilton Books Co., 1975.

DYER, K. Female athletes are catching up. *New Scientist,* Sept. 22, 1977, 722–723.

EDWARDS, D. A. Early androgen stimulation and aggressive behavior in male and female mice. *Physiology and Behavior,* 1969, *4,* 333–338.

EDWARDS, D. A., & HERNDON, J. Neonatal estrogen stimulation and aggressive behavior in female mice. *Physiological Behavior,* 1970, *5,* 993–995.

EHRHARDT, A. A., & BAKER, S. W. Fetal androgens, human central nervous system differentiation, and behavior sex differences. In R. C. Friedman, R. M. Richart, & R. L. VandeWiele (Eds.), *Sex differences in behavior.* New York: Wiley, 1974.

EIBL-EIBESFELDT, I. *Ethology: The biology of behavior.* New York: Holt, Rinehart and Winston, 1970.

EICHLER, M. *The prestige of the occupation housewife.* Paper presented at The Working Sexes Symposium, Vancouver, B.C., October 1976. (a)

EICHLER, M. *The industrialization of housework.* Paper presented at the National Council on Family Research, meetings, New York, 1976. (b)

EISENBERG, L. The *human* nature of human nature. *Science,* 1972, *176,* 123–128.

EKMAN, P., LIEBERT, R. M., FRIESEN, W. V., HARRISON, R., ZLATCHIN, C., MALMSTROM, E. J., & BARON, R. A. Facial expressions of emotion while watching televised violence as predictors of subsequent aggression. In G. A. Comstock, E. A. Rubinstein, & J. P. Murray (Eds.), *Television and social behavior (Vol. 5): Television's effects: Further explorations.* Washington, D.C.: U.S. Government Printing Office, 1972, pp. 22–43.

EMMERICK, W. Parental identification in young children. *Genetic Psychological Monographs,* 1959, *60,* 257–308.

EMMERICK, W. Variations in the parental role as a function of parents' sex and the childs' sex and age. *Merrill–Palmer Quarterly,* 1962, *8,* 1–11.

ERICKSON, E. H. *Identity, youth and crisis.* New York: W. W. Norton and Company, 1968.

ERIKSON, E. H. Womanhood and inner space (1968). Reprinted in J. Strouse (Ed.), *Women and analysis.* New York: Dell Publishing Co., 1974.

ERNEST, J. *Mathematics and sex.* Booklet published at the University of California at Santa Barbara, 1974.

ERON, L. D., HUESMANN, L. R., LEFKOWITZ, M. M., & WALDER, L. O. How learning conditions in early childhood—including mass media—relate to aggression in late adolescence. *American Journal of Orthopsychiatry,* 1974, *44,* 412–423.

ERON, L. D., WALDER, L. O. & LEFKOWITZ, M. M. *Learning of aggression in children.* Boston: Little, Brown and Co., 1971.

EXLINE, R. V., GRAY, D., & SCHUETTE, D. Visual behavior in a dyad as affected by interview content and sex of respondent. *Journal of Personality and Social Psychology,* 1965, *1,* 201–209.

EYSENCK, H. J. *Sex and personality.* Austin: University of Texas Press, 1976.

FARRELL, W. *The liberated man.* New York: Bantam Books, 1975.

FAY, T. L., & SECHREST, L. *Masculinity–femininity: Test validation and construct definition.* Paper presented at meeting of Midwestern Psychological Association, Chicago, May 1973.

FEATHER, N. T., & SIMON, J. G. Attribution of responsibility and valence of outcome in relation to initial confidence and success and failure of self and others. *Journal of Personality and Social Psychology,* 1971, *18,* 173–188.

FELDMAN, M. P. Aversion therapy for sexual deviations: A critical review. *Psychological Bulletin,* 1966, *65,* 65–79.

FENNEMA, E., & SHERMAN, J. Fennema–Sherman Mathematics Attitudes Scales: Instruments designed to measure attitudes toward the learning of mathematics by females and males. *JSAS Catalog of Selected Documents in Psychology,* 1976, *6*(2), 31, MS. 1225.

FESHBACH, N. D. Sex differences in children's modes of aggressive responses toward outsiders. *Merrill–Palmer Quarterly,* 1969, *15,* 249–258.

FESHBACH, S. Aggression. In P. H. Mussen (Ed.), *Carmichael's manual of child psychology* (Vol. 2). New York: John Wiley & Sons, Inc., 1970, pp. 159–259.

FREUD, S. [*A general introduction to psycho-analysis*] (J. Riviere, Ed. and trans.). New York: Pocket Books, 1970. (Originally published, 1924.)

FREUD, S. Some psychical consequences of the anatomical distinction between the sexes (1925/1974). *The standard edition of the complete psychological works of Sigmund Freud,* The Hogarth Press Ltd. & The Institute of Psycho-Analysis, London. Also in *The collected papers of Sigmund Freud,* Basic Books, Inc., New York.

FRIEDAN, B. *The feminine mystique.* New York: Dell Publishing Co., 1963.

FRIEDL, E. *Women and men: An anthropologist's view.* New York: Holt, Rinehart and Winston, 1975.

FRIEZE, I. H. Women's expectations for and causal attributions of success and failure. In M. Mednick, S. Tangri, & L. Hoffman (Eds.), *Women and achievement.* New York: Wiley, 1975.

FRODI, A., MACAULAY, J. & THOME, P. R. Are women always less aggressive than men? *Psychological Bulletin,* 1977, *84,* 634–660.

FROMM, E. *The anatomy of human destructiveness.* Greenwich, Conn.: Fawcett Publications Inc., 1973.

GAGNON, J. H. Physical strength, once of significance. In D. S. David & R. Brannon (Eds.), *The forty-nine percent majority: The male sex role.* Reading, Mass.: Addison–Wesley Publishing Company, 1976, pp. 169–178.

GEBHARD, P. H. Situational factors affecting human sexual behavior. In F. A. Beach (Ed.), *Sex and behavior*. New York: John Wiley & Sons, Inc., 1965.

GELLES, R. J. Child abuse as psychopathology. *American Journal of Orthopsychiatry*, 1973, *43*, 611–621.

GERBNER, G., GROSS, L., ELEEY, M. F., JACKSON-BEECK, M., JEFFRIES-FOX, S., & SIGNORIELLI, N. TV violence profile no. 8: The highlights. *Journal of Communication*, 1977, *27*, 171–180.

GERTH, H., & MILLS, C. W. *Character and social structure*. New York: Harcourt, Brace & World, 1953.

GEWIRTZ, J. L., & STINGLE, K. G. Learning of generalized imitation as the basis for identification. *Psychological Review*, 1968, *75*, 374–397.

GITTER, A. G., BLACK, H., & MOSTOFSKY, D. Race and sex in the communication of emotion. *Journal of Social Psychology*, 1972, *88*, 273–276.

GOFFMAN, E. The arrangement between the sexes. *Theory and Society*, 1977, *4*, 301–331.

GOLD, D. P. Effect of experimenter in eyeblink conditioning. *Psychonomic Science*, 1969, *17*, 232–233.

GOLDBERG, P. Are women predjudiced against women? *Trans-action*, April 1968, 28–30.

GOLDENBERG, N. R. A feminist critique of Jung. *Signs*, 1976, *2*(2), 443–449.

GORDON, M., & SHANKWEILER, P. J. Different equals less: Female sexuality in recent marriage manuals. *Journal of Marriage and the Family*, 1971, *33*, 459–465. Reprinted in A. Skolnick & J. H. Skolnick (Eds.), *Family in transition*. Boston: Little, Brown and Company, 1974.

GORDON, R. E., KAPOSTINS, E. E., & GORDON, K. K. Factors in postpartum emotional adjustment. *Obstetrics and Gynecology*, 1965, *25*(2), 158–166.

GORER, G. Man has no "killer" instinct. In M. F. Montagu (Ed.), *Man and aggression*. New York: Oxford University Press, 1968, pp. 27–36.

GORHAM, D. The Canadian suffragists. In G. Matheson (Ed.), *Women in the Canadian mosaic*. Toronto: Peter Martin Associates, 1976, 23–56.

GOUGH, H. G. Identifying psychological femininity. *Educational and Psychological Measurement*, 1952, *12*, 427–439.

GOULD, R. M. Measuring masculinity by the size of a paycheck. *Ms.*, 1973, *1*(12), 18–21.

GOVE, W. R. The relationship between sex roles, marital status and mental illness. In A. G. Kaplan & J. P. Bean (Eds.) *Beyond sex-role stereotypes:*

Readings toward a psychology of androgyny. Boston: Little, Brown and Company, 1976, pp. 282–292.

GOVE, W. R., & TUDOR, J. F. Adult sex roles and mental illness. *American Journal of Sociology,* 1973, *78,* 812–832.

GOY, R. W. Experimental control of psychosexuality. In G. W. Harris & R. G. Edwards (Eds.), *A discussion on the determination of sex.* London: Philosophical Transactions of the Royal Society, 1970.

GRAY, J. A. Sex differences in emotional behaviour in mammals including man: Endocrine bases. *Acta Psychologica,* 1971, *35,* 29–46.

GREEN, R. *Sexual identity conflict in children and adults.* Baltimore: Penguin Books, 1974.

GREENSTEIN, J. M. Father characteristics and sex typing. *Journal of Personality and Social Psychology,* 1966, *3,* 271–277.

GREER, G. *The female eunuch.* London, England: Granada Publishing Limited, 1971.

GRIFFIN, P. S. *Perceptions of women's roles and female sport involvement among a selected sample of college students.* Unpublished manuscript, University of Massachusetts, 1972.

GROTJAHN, M. Interview in L. Freeman & M. Theodores (Eds.), *The why report.* New York: Pocket Books, Inc., 1965.

GRUSEC, J. E., & MISCHEL, W. Model's characteristics as determinants of social learning. *Journal of Personality and Social Psychology,* 1966, *4,* 211–215.

GUILFORD, J. P., & ZIMMERMAN, W. S. Fourteen dimensions of temperament. *Psychological Monographs,* 1956, *70*(10, Whole No. 417).

GUSTAFSON, J. E., & WINOCUR, G. The effect of sexual satiation and female hormone upon aggressivity in an inbred mouse strain. *Journal of Neuropsychiatry,* 1960, *1,* 182–184.

GUTMANN, D. Ego psychological and developmental approaches to the "retirement crisis" in men. In F. M. Carp (Ed.), *Retirement.* New York: Behavioral Publications, 1972.

HALE, G. A., MILLER, L. K., & STEVENSON, H. W. Incidental learning of film content: A developmental study. *Child Development,* 1968, *39,* 69–77.

HALL, C. S. & LINDZEY, G. *Theories of personality.* New York: Wiley, 1957.

HAMBURG, D. A., & LUNDE, D. T. Sex hormones in the development of sex differences in human behavior. In E. E. Maccoby (Ed.), *The development of sex differences.* Stanford, Calif.: Stanford University Press, 1966, pp. 1–21.

HAMBURG, D. A., MOOS, R. H., & YALOM, I. D. Studies of distress in the menstrual cycle and the postpartum period. In R. P. Michael (Ed.), *Endocrinology and human behavior*. London: Oxford University Press, 1968.

HAMPSON, J. L., & HAMPSON, G. H. The ontogenesis of sexual behavior in man. In W. C. Young (Ed.), *Sex and internal secretions*. Baltimore, Md.: Williams and Wilkins, 1961.

HARLOW, H. F. Lust, latency and love: Simian secrets of successful sex. *Journal of Sex Research*, 1975, *11*, 79–90.

HARRIS, S. Influence of subject and experimenter sex in psychological research. *Journal of Consulting and Clinical Psychology*, 1971, *37*, 291–294.

HARTLEY, R. E. Sex-role pressures and the socialization of the male child. *Psychological Reports*, 1959, *5*, 457–68. Reprinted in J. H. Pleck & J. Sawyer (Eds.), *Men and masculinity*. Englewood Cliffs, N. J.: Prentice-Hall, 1974, 7–13.

HATHAWAY, S. R., & McKINLEY, J. C. *The Minnesota Multiphasic Personality Inventory*. New York: Psychological Corporation, 1943.

HEILBRUN, A. B. Parental model attributes, nurturant reinforcement and consistency of behavior in adolescents. *Child Development*, 1964, *35*, 151–167.

HEILBRUN, C. *Toward a recognition of androgyny*. New York: Harper & Row, 1973.

HEIMAN, J. R. A psychophysiological exploration of sexual arousal patterns in females and males. *Psychophysiology*, 1977, *14*, 266–274.

HEISE, D. R. (Ed.). *Personality and socialization*. Chicago: Rand, McNally & Company, 1972.

HENLEY, N. Power, sex and nonverbal communication. *Berkeley Journal of Sociology*, 1973, *18*, 1–26.

HENLEY, N. M. *Body politics: Power, sex, and nonverbal communication*. Englewood Cliffs, N. J.: Prentice-Hall, 1977.

HENSHEL, A. M. *Sex structure*. Don Mills, Ontario: Longman Canada Limited, 1973.

HENSHEL, A.–M. Swinging: The sociology of decision-making. In S. P. Wakil (Ed.), *Marriage, family and society: Canadian perspectives*. Scarborough: Butterworth and Co., 1975.

HETHERINGTON, E. M., COX, M., & COX, R. Divorced fathers. *Psychology Today*, 1977, *10*(11), 42–46.

HICKS, D. J. Imitation and retention of film-mediated aggressive peer and adult models. *Journal of Personality and Social Psychology*, 1965, *2*, 97–100.

HINDE, R. A. *Animal behavior: A synthesis of ethology and comparative psychology* (2nd ed.). New York: McGraw–Hill, 1970.

HINKLE, R. C., & HINKLE, H. J. *The development of modern sociology*. New York: Random House, 1954.

HIRSCH, J. Behavior-genetic analysis and its biosocial consequences. *Seminar in Psychiatry*, 1970, *2*(1), 89–105.

HITE, S. *The Hite report*. New York: Macmillan; Australia: Collier Macmillan Australia; & London: Franklin Talmy Ltd., 1976.

HOFFMAN, L. W. Early childhood experiences and women's achievement motives. *Journal of Social Issues*, 1972, *28*(2), 129–155.

HOFFMAN, L. W. Psychological factors. In L. W. Hoffman & F. I. Nye (Eds.), *Working mothers*. San Francisco: Jossey–Bass Publishers, 1975.

HOKANSON, J. E., & EDELMAN, R. Effects of three social responses on vascular processes. *Journal of Personality and Social Psychology*, 1966, *3*, 442–447.

HOKANSON, J. E., WILLERS, K. R., & KOROPSAK, E. The modification of autonomic responses during aggressive interchange. *Journal of Personality*, 1968, *36*, 386–404.

HOLMES, D. S., & JORGENSEN, D. W. Do personality and social psychologists study men more than women? *Representative Research in Social Psychology*, 1971, *2*, 71–76.

HOMANS, G. C. *The human group*. New York: Harcourt, Brace & World, 1950.

HORNER, M. *Sex differences in achievement motivation and performance in competitive and noncompetitive situations*. Unpublished doctoral dissertation, University of Michigan, 1968.

HORNER, M. Femininity and successful achievement: A basic inconsistency. In J. Bardwick, E. Douvan, M. Horner, & D. Guttman (Eds.), *Feminine personality & conflict*. Belmont, Calif.: Brooks/Cole, 1970.

HORNEY, K. The flight from womanhood (1926). Reprinted in J. B. Miller (Ed.), *Psychoanalysis and women*. Baltimore, Md.: Penguin Books, 1973, 5–20.

HUNT, M. *Sexual behavior in the 1970s*. Chicago, Ill.: Playboy Press, 1974.

HUTT, C. *Males and females*. Harmondsworth, Middlesex, England: Penguin Education, 1972.

HYDE, J. S., & SCHUCK, J. R. *The development of sex differences in aggression: A revised model.* Paper presented at the American Psychological Association meetings, San Francisco, August 1977.

IVEY, M. E., & BARDWICK, J. M. Patterns of affective fluctuation in the menstrual cycle. *Psychosomatic Medicine,* 1968, *30,* 336–345.

"J". *The sensuous woman.* New York: Stuart, 1969.

JANEWAY, E. On "female sexuality." In J. Strouse (Ed.), *Woman & analysis.* New York: Dell, 1974.

JOHNSON, C. A., SMITH, D. E., WHATLEY, J. L., & DEVOGE, T. The effects of sex and personalism factors on subjects' responses to hypnotic suggestions. *Proceedings of the 81st Annual Convention of the American Psychological Association,* Montreal, 1973, *8,* 1077–1078.

JOHNSON, P. Women and power: Toward a theory of effectiveness. *Journal of Social Issues,* 1976, *32*(3), 99–110.

JOHNSON, P. B., & GOODCHILDS, J. D. "How women get their way." *Psychology Today,* October 1976, *10,* 69–70.

JOHNSON, R. *Aggression in man and animals.* Philadelphia: W. B. Saunders Co., 1972.

JOHNSON, W. *Stuttering and what you can do about it.* Minneapolis: University of Minnesota Press, 1961.

JOHNSON, W. Stuttering: How the problem develops. In B. J. Franklin & F. J. Kohout (Eds.), *Social psychology and everyday life.* New York: David McKay Company, 1973, pp. 202–211.

JONES, E. E., & DAVIS, K. E. From acts to dispositions: The attribution process in person perception. In L. Berkowitz (Ed.), *Advances in experimental social psychology* (Vol. 2). New York: Academic Press, 1965.

JOURARD, S. *The transparent self.* Cincinnati: D. Van Nostrand and Reinhold, 1971.

JULTY, S. A case of "sexual dysfunction." *Ms.,* 1972, *1*(5), pp. 18; 20–21.

JUNG, C. G. Two essays on analytical psychology. In *Collected works* (Vol. 7). New York: Pantheon Press, 1953.

KALLMAN, F. J. Comparative twin study on the genetic aspects of male homosexuality. *Journal of Nervous and Mental Disorders,* 1952, *115,* 283–298.

KANTER, R. M. Women and the structure of organizations: Explorations in theory and behavior. In M. Millman & R. M. Kanter (Eds.), *Another voice*. New York: Anchor Press, 1975.

KANTER, R. M. Why bosses turn bitchy. *Psychology Today*, 1976, *9*(2), 56–59, 88–91.

KENKEL, W. F. Influence differentiation in family decision-making. *Sociology and Social Research*, 1957, *42*, 18–25.

KENNICKE, L. *Self profiles of highly skilled female athletes participating in two types of activities: Structured and creative.* Unpublished manuscript, Pennsylvania State University, 1972.

KINSEY, A. C., POMEROY, W. B., MARTIN, C. E., & GEBBARD, P. H. *Sexual behavior in the human female.* Philadelphia: W. B. Saunders, 1953.

KIPNIS, D. The powerholder. In J. T. Tedeschi (Ed)., *Perspectives on social power.* Chicago: Aldine, 1974.

KLEIN, V. *The feminine character: History of an ideology* (2nd ed.). Urbana: University of Illinois Press, 1971.

KOENIGSKNECHT, R. A., & FRIEDMAN, P. Syntax development in boys and girls. *Child Development*, 1976, *47*, 1109–1115.

KOESKE, R., & KOESKE, G. An attributional approach to moods and the menstrual cycle. *Journal of Personality and Social Psychology*, 1975, *31*(3), 473–478.

KOHLBERG, L. A cognitive–developmental analysis of children's sex-role concepts and attitudes. In E. E. Maccoby (Ed.), *The development of sex differences.* Stanford, Calif.: Stanford University Press, 1966.

LALONDE, M. *The media image.* An address by the Minister responsible for the Status of Women to the Ottawa's Women's Canadian Club, September 17, 1975 (Health and Welfare publication).

ANN LANDERS, *The Winnipeg Tribune*, July 28, 1977, p. 30.

LANDRETH, C. Four-year-old's notions about sex appropriateness of parental care and companionship activities. *Merrill–Palmer Quarterly*, 1963, *9*, 175–183.

LANSKY, L. M. The family structure also affects the model: Sex-role, attitudes in parents of preschool children. *Merrill–Palmer Quarterly*, 1967, *13*, 139–150.

LAWS, J. L., & SCHWARTZ, P. *Sexual scripts: The social construction of female sexuality.* Hinsdale, Ill.: The Dryden Press, 1977.

LAZOWICH, L. M. On the nature of identification. *Journal of Abnormal Psychology*, 1955, *51*, 175–183.

LEHNE, G. K. Homophobia among men. In D. S. David & R. Brannon (Eds.), *The Forty-nine percent majority*. Reading, Mass.: Addison–Wesley Publishing Company, 1976.

LERNER, R. M. *Concepts and theories of human development*. Reading, Mass.: Addison–Wesley Publishing Company, 1976.

LESTER, J. Being a boy. In D. S. David & R. Brannon (Eds.), *The forty-nine percent majority*. Reading, Mass.: Addison–Wesley Publishing Company, 1976.

LEVENSON, H., BURFORD, B., BONNO, B., & DAVIS, L. Are women still prejudiced against women? A replication and extension of Goldberg's study. *Journal of Psychology*, 1975, *89*, 67–71.

LEVINE, S. Sex differences in the brain. *Scientific American*, 1966, *214*(4), 84–90.

LEVY, B. L. The school's role in the sex-role stereotyping of girls: A feminist review. *Feminist Studies*, 1975, *1*, 5–23.

LEVY, J. Lateral specialization of the human brain: Behavioral manifestations and possible evolutionary basis. In John A. Kiger (Ed.), *The biology of behavior*. Corvallis: Oregon State University Press, 1972.

LEWIS, L. Parents and children: Sex-role development. *School Review*, 1972, *80*, 229–240.

LEWIS, M., & ROSENBLUM, L. A. (Eds.). *The effect of the infant on its caregiver*. New York: Wiley, 1974.

LIEBENBERG, B. *Expectant fathers*. Paper presented at the annual meeting of the American Orthopsychiatric Association, Washington, D.C., March 1967.

LINDESMITH, A. R., & STRAUSS, A. L. (Eds.). *Social psychology*. New York: Holt, Rinehart and Winston, 1968.

LINTON, S. Primate studies and sex differences. In A. S. Skolnick and J. H. Skolnick (Eds.), *Family in transition*. Boston: Little, Brown and Company, 1971, pp. 194–197.

LISSEY, F. J., KLODIN, V., & MATSUYAMA, S. S. Human aggression and the extra Y chomosome: Fact or fantasy? *American Psychologist*, 1973, *28*, 674–682.

LOCKHEED, M. E., & HALL, K. P. Conceptualizing sex as a status characteristic: Applications to leadership training strategies. *Journal of Social Issues*, 1976, *32*(3), 111–124.

LOPATA, H. Z. *Occupation: Housewife.* New York: Oxford University Press, 1971.

LOPICCOLO, J. Case study: Systematic desensitization of homosexuality. *Behavior Therapy,* 1971, *2*, 394–399.

LUCE, S. Women's athletic potential. *Atlantis,* 1976, *2*(1), 4–13.

LYNN, D. B. The process of learning parental and sex-role identification. *The Journal of Marriage and the Family,* 1966, *28*, 466–470.

LYNN, D. B. *The father: His role in child development.* Monterey, Calif.: Brooks/ Cole Publishing Company, 1974.

MACCOBY, E. E. The meaning of being female. *Contemporary Psychology,* 1972, *17*, 369–372.

MACCOBY, E. E., & JACKLIN, C. N. *The psychology of sex differences.* Stanford, Calif.: Stanford University Press, 1974.

MACLEAN, P. D., & PLOOG, D. W. Cerebral representation of penile erection. *Journal of Neurophysiology,* 1962, *25*, 29–55.

MAINARDI, P. The politics of housework. In R. Morgan (Ed.), *Sisterhood is powerful.* New York: Vintage Books, 1970.

MAKOSKY, V. P. Sex-role compatibility of task and competitor, and fear of success as variables affecting women's performance. *Sex Roles,* 1976, *2*(3), 237–248.

MALAMUTH, N. M., FESHBACH, S., & JAFFE, Y. Sexual arousal and aggression: Recent experiments and theoretical issues. *Journal of Social Issues,* 1977, *33*, 110–133.

MALINOWSKI, B. *The sexual lives of savages.* New York: Routledge, 1932.

MANLEY, R. O. Parental warmth and hostility as related to sex differences in children's achievement orientation. *Psychology of Women Quarterly,* 1977, *1*(3), 229–246.

MANN, T., & LUTWAK-MANN, C. Secretory function of male accessory organs of reproduction in mammals. *Physiological Zoology,* 1951, *31*, 17–55.

MANN W. E. *Society behind bars.* Toronto: Social Science Publishers, 1967.

MARQUIS, J. N. Orgasmic reconditioning: Changing sexual object choice through controlling masturbation fantasies. *Journal of Behavior Therapy and Experimental Psychiatry,* 1970, *1*, 263–271.

MARTIN, G., & PEAR, J. *Behavior modification: What it is and how to do it.* Englewood Cliffs, N.J.: Prentice-Hall, 1978.

MARTIN, M. F., GELFAND, D. M., & HARTMAN, D. P. Effects of adult and peer observers on boys' and girls' responses to an aggressive model. *Child Development*, 1971, *42*, 1271–1275.

MASLOW, A. H. Self-esteem (dominance feeling) and sexuality in women. *Journal of Social Psychology*, 1942, *16*, 259–294.

MASLOW, A. H. *Motivation and personality.* New York: Harper & Row, 1954.

MASTERS, W. H., & JOHNSON, V. E. *Human sexual response.* Boston: Little, Brown, 1966.

MASTERS, W. H. & JOHNSON, V. E. *Human sexual inadequacy.* Boston: Little, Brown, 1970.

MASTERS, W. H., & JOHNSON, V. E. *The pleasure bond.* Boston: Little, Brown, 1974.

MATTHEWS, A. M. The case of the migrant wife: Looking at the world from the underdog perspective. *The Occasional Papers of The McMaster Sociology of Women Programme*, 1977, Spring, 165–194.

MAY, R. B., & HUTT, C. Modality and sex differences in recall and recognition memory. *Child Development*, 1974, *45*, 228–231.

McCLELLAND, D. C. *The achieving society.* Princeton, N. J.: Van Nostrand, 1961.

McCLELLAND, D. C., ATKINSON, J. W., CLARK, R. A., & LOWELL, E. L. *The achievement motive.* New York: Appleton, 1953.

McGINLEY, P. *Sixpence in her shoe.* New York: Macmillan, 1964.

McMAHAN, I. D. *Sex differences in expectancy of success as a function of task.* Paper presented at the meeting of the Eastern Psychological Association, April 1972.

MEAD, G. H. *Mind, self and society.* Chicago: Phoenix Books, 1934.

MEAD, G. H. *George Herbert Mead on social psychology.* Chicago: University of Chicago Press, 1956.

MEAD, G. H. *Selected writings.* New York: Bobbs–Merrill, 1964.

MEAD, M. *Sex and temperament.* New York: William Morrow, and Mentor, 1935.

MEISSNER, M. Sexual division of labour and inequality: Labour and leisure. In M. L. Stephenson (Ed.), *Women in Canada.* Don Mills, Canada: General Publishing Company, 1977, 160–180.

MELGES, F. T. Postpartum psychiatric syndromes. *Psychoanalytic Medicine*, January–February 1968, *30* 95–108.

MELTZER, B. N., & PETRAS, J. W. The Chicago and Iowa schools of symbolic interactionism. In J. C. Manis & B. N. Meltzer (Eds.), *Symbolic interaction, a reader in social psychology*. Boston: Allyn and Bacon, 1972, 43–56.

MILTON, G. A. The effects of sex-role identification upon problem-solving skill. *Journal of Abnormal and Social Psychology*, 1957, *55*, 208–212.

MISCHEL, W. Sex-typing and socialization. In P. H. Mussen (Ed.), *Charmichael's manual of child psychology*. New York: Wiley, 1970.

MISCHEL, W. *Introduction to personality*. New York: Holt, Rinehart and Winston, Inc., 1971.

MITCHEL, G. D. Paternalistic behavior in primates. *Psychological Bulletin*, 1969, *71*, 399–417.

MITCHELL, J. On Freud and the distinction between the sexes. In J. Strouse (Ed.), *Women & analysis*. New York: Dell, 1974.

MONAHAN, L., KUHN, D., & SHAVER, P. Intrapsychic versus cultural explanations for the "Fear of Success" motive. *Journal of Personality and Social Psychology*, 1974, *29*, 60–64.

MONEY, J., & EHRHARDT, A. A. *Man and woman, boy and girl*. Baltimore, Md.: The Johns Hopkins University Press, 1972.

MONTAGU, A. *The natural superiority of women*. New York: Macmillan, 1952. Rev. ed., New York: Collier Books, 1968.

MOOS, R. H. The development of a menstrual distress questionnaire. *Psychosomatic Medicine*, 1968, *30*, 853–867.

MORGAN, M. *The total woman*. Old Tappan, N.J.: Revell, 1973.

MORGAN,R. (Ed.). *Sisterhood is powerful*. New York: Vintage Books, 1970.

MORRIS, C. W. Introduction: George H. Mead as social psychologist and social philosopher. In C. W. Morris (Ed.), *Mind, self and society*. Chicago: University of Chicago Press, 1962, ix–xxxv.

MORRIS, J. *Conundrum*. Scarborough, Ontario: New American Library of Canada, 1974.

MOYER, K. E. The physiology of violence: Allergy and aggression. *Psychology Today*, 1975, *9*(2), 77–79.

MUNDY, J. Women in rage: A psychological look at the helpless heroine. In R. K. Unger, & F. L. Denmark (Eds.), *Woman: Dependent or independent variable?* New York: Psychological Dimensions Inc., 1975.

MUSSEN, P. H. Some antecedents and consequences of masculine sex-typing in adolescent boys. *Psychological Monographs*, 1961, *75*, No. 506.

MUSSEN, P. H., & DISTLER, L. Masculinity, identification, and father–son relationships. *Journal of Abnormal and Social Psychology*, 1959, *59* 350–356.

MUSSEN, P., & DISTLER, L. Child-rearing antecedents of masculine identification in kindergarten boys. *Child Development*, 1960, *31*, 89–100.

MUSSEN, P., & RUTHERFORD, E. Parent–child relations and parental personality in relation to young childrens' sex-role preference. *Child Development*, 1963, *34*, 589–607.

MYERS, A. *Cognitive functioning and sex-typing in children.* Paper presented at the annual meeting of the Association for Women in Psychology, St. Louis, February 1977. (a)

MYERS, A. *Situational-flexibility in field-dependence–independence.* Paper presented at the annual meeting of the Canadian Psychological Association, Vancouver, June 1977. (b)

MYERS, A., & LIPS, H. Participation in competitive amateur sports as a function of psychological androgyny. *Sex Roles*, 1978, *4*(4), 571–578.

NEWTON, N. Trebly sensuous woman. *Psychology Today*, 1971, *5*, pp. 68–71; 98–99.

NOCHLIN, L. Why have there been no great women artists? In T. B. Hess & E. C. Baker (Eds.). *Art and sexual politics.* New York: Collier Books, 1973.

NUNES, M., & WHITE, D. *The lace ghetto.* Toronto, Canada: New Press, 1973.

NYE, F. I. Sociocultural context. In L. W. Hoffman & F. I. Nye (Eds.), *Working mothers.* San Francisco: Jossey–Bass Publishers, 1975, 1–31.

OAKLEY, A. *Sex, gender and society.* New York: Harper and Row, 1972.

O'LEARY, K., & WILSON, G. T. *Behavior therapy: Application and outcome.* Englewood Cliffs, N.J.: Prentice-Hall, 1975.

O'NEILL, N., & O'NEILL, G. *Open marriage: A new lifestyle for couples.* New York: M. Evans and Company, Inc., 1972.

OWEN, D. The 47XYY male: A review. *Psychological Bulletin*, 1972, *78*, 209–233.

PAIGE, K. E. Effects of oral contraceptives on affective fluctuations associated with the menstrual cycle. *Psychosomatic Medicine*, 1971, *33*, 515–537.

PAIGE, K. E. Women learn to sing the menstrual blues. *Psychology Today*, 1973, *7*(4), 41–46.

PARLEE, M. B. Comments on D. M. Broverman, E. L. Klaiber, Y. Kobayashi, and W. Vogel: Roles of activation and inhibition in sex differences in cognitive abilities. *Psychological Review*, 1972, *79*, 180–184.

PARLEE, M. B. The premenstrual syndrome. *Psychological Bulletin*, 1973, *80*, 454–465.

PAVLOV, I. P. [Conditional reflexes: An investigation of the physiological activity of the cerebral cortex.] (G. V. Anrep, trans.). London: Oxford University Press, 1927.

PERLMAN, D. The premarital sexual standards of Canadians. In K. Ishwaran (Ed.), *Marriage and divorce in Canada*. Toronto: McGraw–Hill Ryerson, in press.

PESKIN, H. The duration of normal menses as a psychosomatic phenomenon. *Psychosomatic Medicine*, 1968, *30*, 378–389.

PHETERSON, G. I., KIESLER, S. B., & GOLDBERG, P. A. Evaluation of the performance of women as a function of their sex, achievement and personal history. *Journal of Personality and Social Psychology*, 1971, *19*, 114–118.

PHOENIX, C. H. Prenatal testosterone in the nonhuman primate and its consequences for behavior. In R. C. Friedman, R. M. Richart, & R. L. VandeWiele (Eds.), *Sex differences in behavior*. New York: Wiley, 1974.

PHOENIX, C. H., GOY, R. W., GERALL, A. A., & YOUNG, W. C. Organizing action of prenatally-administered testosterone propionate on the tissues mediating mating behavior in the female guinea pig. *Endocrinology*, 1959, *65*, 369–382.

PIAGET, J. *The psychology of intelligence*. London: Routledge & Kegan Paul, 1947.

PLECK, J. Male threat from female competence. *Journal of Consulting and Clinical Psychology*, 1976, *44*(4), 608–613.

PLECK, J. My male sex role—and ours. In D. David & R. Brannon (Eds.), *The forty-nine percent majority*. Menlo Park, Calif.: Addison–Wesley, 1976.

PORTER, J. *The vertical mosaic*. Toronto: University of Toronto Press, 1965.

PRICE, W. H., & WHATMORE, P. B. Criminal behavior and the XYY male. *Nature*, 1967, *213*, 815. (a)

PRICE, W. H., & WHATMORE, P. B. Behavior disorders and pattern of crime among XYY males identified at a maximum security prison. *British Medical Journal*, 1967, *1*, 533–536 (b)

RACHMAN, S. Sexual fetishism: An experimental analogue. *The Psychological Record*, 1966, *16*, 293–296.

RACHMAN, S., & HODGSON, R. J. Experimentally-induced "sexual fetishism": replication and development. *The Psychological Record*, 1968, *18*, 25–27.

RADIN, N. Father–child interactions and the intellectual functioning of four-year-old boys. *Developmental Psychology*, 1972, *6*, 353–361.

RAMEY, E. Men's cycles. *Ms.*, 1972, *1* (8), pp. 8; 11–12; 14–15.

RASMUSSEN, L., RASMUSSEN, L., SAVAGE, C., & WHEELER, A. *A harvest yet to reap: A history of prairie women.* Toronto: The Women's Press, 1976.

RAYMOND, M. J. Case of fetishism treated by aversion therapy. *British Medical Journal*, 1956, *2*, 854–857.

REBECCA, M., HEFNER, R. & OLESHANSKY, B. A model of sex-role transcendence. *Journal of Social Issues*, 1976, *32*(3), 197–206.

RECK, A. J. Introduction. In A. J. Reck (Ed.), *Selected writings.* New York: Bobbs–Merrill, 1964, xiii–lxii.

REISS, I. *Premarital sexual standards in America.* New York: The Free Press, 1960.

Report of the Royal Commission on the Status of Women in Canada. Ottawa: Information Canada, 1970.

RIMM, D. C., & MASTERS, J. C. *Behavior therapy: Techniques and empirical findings.* New York: Academic Press, 1974.

RODIN, J. Menstruation, reattribution and competence. *Journal of Personality and Social Psychology*, 1976, *33*, 345–353.

ROLLIN, B. Motherhood: Who needs it? *Look*, 1970, *34* (19), 15–17.

ROSALDO, M. Z. Woman, culture and society: A theoretical overview. In M. Z. Rosaldo & L. Lamphere (Eds.), *Woman, culture and society.* Stanford, Calif.: Stanford University Press, 1974, 1–16.

ROSENTHAL, D. *Genetic theory and abnormal behavior.* New York: McGraw–Hill, 1970.

ROSENTHAL, R. *Experimenter effects in behavioral research.* New York: Appleton-Century-Crofts, 1966.

ROSENTHAL, R., ARCHER, D., DiMATTEO, M. R. KOWUMAKI, J. H., & ROGERS, P. O. Body talk and tone of voice: The language without words. *Psychology Today*, 1974, *8* (September), 64–68.

ROSENTHAL, R., PERSINGER, G. W., MULRY, R. C., VIKAN-KLINE, L., & GROTHE, M. Changes in experimental hypotheses as determinants of experimental results. *Journal of Projective Techniques and Personality Assessments*, 1964, 28, 465–469.

ROSENZWEIG, S. The experimental situation as a psychological problem. *Psychological Review*, 1933, *40*, 337–354.

ROSSI, A. S. Transition to parenthood. *Journal of Marriage and the Family*, 1968, *30*, 26–39.

ROSSI, A. S. (Ed.). *The feminist papers*. New York: Bantam Books, 1974.

ROTKIN, K. F. The phallacy of our sexual norm. In A. G. Kaplan & J. P. Bean (Eds.), *Beyond sex-role stereotypes: Readings toward a psychology of androgyny*. Boston: Little, Brown and Company, 1976.

RUBIN, Z. *Liking and loving: An invitation to social psychology*. New York: Holt, Rinehart & Winston, 1973.

RUSSELL, D. E. *The politics of rape*. New York: Stein & Day, 1975.

SCHACTER, S., & SINGER, J. E. Cognitive, social, and physiological determinants of emotional state. *Psychological Review*, 1962, *69*, 379–399.

SCHEFF, T. Negotiating reality: Notes on power in the assessment of responsibility. In B. J. Franklin & F. J. Kohout (Eds.), *Social psychology and everyday life*. New York: David McKay, 1973, 55–72.

SCHIMEL, J. L. Some practical considerations in treating male sexual inadequacy. *Medical Aspects of Human Sexuality*, 1971, *5*, 24, 29–31.

SCHRODER, H. M., DRIVER, M. J., & STREUFERT, S. *Human information processing*. New York: Holt, Rinehart and Winston, 1967.

SEARS, R. R. Comparison of interviews with questionnaires for measuring mother's attitudes towards sex and aggression. *Journal of Personality and Social Psychology*, 1965, *2*, 37–44.

SEARS, R. R. Relation of early socialization experiences to self-concept and gender roles in middle childhood. *Child Development*, 1970, *41*, 267–289.

SEARS, R. R., MACCOBY, E. E., & LEVIN, H. *Patterns of child rearing*. New York: Harper & Row, 1957.

SECHREST, L., & FAY, T. L. *The dimensionality of masculinity–femininity*. Paper presented at meeting of the Midwestern Psychological Association, Chicago, May 1973.

SELIGMAN, M. F. P. Phobias and preparedness. *Behavior Therapy*, 1971, *2*, 307–320.

SERMAT, V., & SMYTH, M. Content analysis of verbal communication in the development of a relationship: Conditions influencing self-disclosure. *Journal of Personality and Social Psychology*, 1973, *26*, 332–346.

SHAVER, P. Questions concerning fear of success and its conceptual relatives. *Sex Roles*, 1976, *2* (3), 305–320.

SHERFEY, M. J. *The nature and evolution of female sexuality.* New York: Vintage Books, 1966.

SHERMAN, J. Problem of sex differences in space perception and aspects of intellectual functioning. *Psychological Review*, 1967, *74*, 290–299.

SHERMAN, J. *On the psychology of women: A survey of empirical studies.* Springfield, Ill.: Charles C Thomas, 1971.

SHERMAN, J. Social values, femininity, and the development of a female competence. *Journal of Social Issues*, 1976, *32* (3), 181–195.

SHIELDS, S. A. Functionalism, Darwinism and the psychology of women: A study in social myth. *American Psychologist*, 1975, *30* (7), 739–754.

SKINNER, B. F. *The behavior of organisms.* New York: Appleton, 1938.

SKOLNICK, A. Families can be unhealthy for children and other living things. *Psychology Today*, 1971, *5*, 18–22.

SKOLNICK, A. S., & SKOLNICK, J. H. *Family in transition.* Boston: Little, Brown and Company, 1971.

SLAVIN, M. *Themes of feminine evil.* Unpublished doctoral dissertation, Harvard University, 1971.

SOMMER, B. *Mood and the menstrual cycle.* Paper presented at the Eighty-Third Annual Convention of the American Psychological Association, Chicago, 1975.

SPENCE, J. T., HELMREICH, R., & STAPP, J. Likability, sex-role congruence of interest, and competence: It all depends on how you ask. *Journal of Applied Social Psychology*, 1975, *5* (2), 93–109.

STAFFORD, R. E. Sex differences in spatial visualization as evidence of sex-linked inheritance. *Perceptual & Motor Skills*, 1961, *13*, 428.

STEIN, A. H. The effects of maternal employment and educational attainment on the sex-typed attributes of college females. *Social Behavior and Personality*, 1973, *1* (2), 111–114.

STEIN, A. H., & BAILEY, M. M. The socialization of achievement orientation in females. *Psychological Bulletin*, 1973, *80* (5), 345–366.

STEIN, A. H., POHLY, S. R., & MUELLER, E. The influence of masculine, feminine and neutral tasks on children's achievement behavior, expectancies of success, and attainment values. *Child Development*, 1971, *42*, 195–207.

STERN, K. *The flight from woman.* New York: The Noonday Press, 1965.

STEWART, A. J. *Power arousal and thematic apperception in women.* Paper presented at the meeting of the American Psychological Association, Chicago, September 1975.

STEWART, A. J., & RUBIN, Z. The power motive in the dating couple. *Journal of Personality and Social Psychology*, 1976, *34* (2), 305–309.

STOLL, C. S. *Female & male.* Dubuque, Iowa: William C. Brown Company, Publishers, 1974.

STRAUS, M. A., GELLES, R. J., & STEINMETZ, S. K. Theories, methods and controversies in the study of violence between family members. In S. K. Steinmetz & M. A. Straus (Eds.), *Violence in the family.* New York: Dodd, Mead, 1974.

STRONG, E. K. Interests of men and women. *Journal of Social Psychology*, 1936, *13*, 49–67.

SWANSON, H. H., & CROSSLEY, D. A. Sexual behavior in the golden hamster and its modification by neonatal administration of testosterone propionate. In M. Hamburgh & E. J. W. Barrington (Eds.), *Hormones in development.* New York: Appleton–Century–Crofts, 1971.

TAVRIS, C., & OFFIR, C. *The longest war: Sex differences in perspective.* New York: Harcourt Brace Jovanovich Inc., 1977.

TAYLOR, S. E., & LANGER, E. J. Pregnancy: A social stigma? *Sex Roles*, 1977, *3*, 27–35.

TEATHER, L. The feminist mosaic. In G. Matheson (Ed.), *Women in the Canadian mosaic.* Toronto: Peter Martin Associates, 1976, 301–346.

TENNOV, D. *Psychotherapy: The hazardous cure.* New York: Anchor Press, 1976.

TERMAN, L., & MILES, C. C. *Sex and personality.* New York: McGraw–Hill, 1936.

TERMAN, L. M. & TYLER, L. E. Psychological sex differences. In L. Carmichael (Ed.), *Manual of child psychology* (2nd ed.). New York: John Wiley & Sons, Inc., 1954, pp. 1064–1114.

THIBAUT, J., & KELLEY, H. *The social psychology of groups.* New York: John Wiley and Sons, Inc., 1959.

THOMPSON, C. "Penis envy" in women (1943). Reprinted in J. B. Miller (Ed.), *Psychoanalysis and women.* Baltimore, MD.: Penguin Books, 1973.

TIDBALL, M. E. Perspective on academic women and affirmative action. *Educational Record*, 1973, *54*, 130–135.

TIGER, L. *Men in groups.* New York: Random House, 1969.

TOBIAS, S. Math anxiety, *Ms.*, 1976, *5*(3), pp. 56–59; 92.

TREIMAN, D. J., & TERRELL, K. Sex and the process of status attainment: A comparison of working women and men. *American Sociological Review*, 1975, *40*, 174–200.

TRESMER, D. Do women fear success? *Signs*, Summer 1976, *1* (4), 863–874.

TRETHOWAN, W. H. The Couvade syndrome. In J. G. Howells (Ed.), *Modern perspectives in psycho-obstetrics.* New York: Brunner/Mazel Publishers, 1972.

TURNER, M. *Career planning workshops for women: Assessment of critical factors related to outcomes.* Unpublished master's thesis, College of Education, University of Saskatchewan at Saskatoon, 1977.

TYLER, S. J. *Differences in social and sport self-perceptions between female varsity athletes.* Unpublished manuscript, Pennsylvania State University, 1973.

UDRY, J. R. *The social context of marriage* (2nd ed.) Philadelphia: J. B. Lippincott Company, 1971.

ULLMANN, L. P., & KRASNER, L. *A psychological approach to abnormal behavior* (2nd ed.) Englewood Cliffs, N. J.: Prentice-Hall 1975.

ULRICH, R. E., & AZRIN, N. H. Reflexive fighting in response to aversive stimulation. *Journal of the Experimental Analysis of Behavior*, 1962, *5*, 511–520.

VALINS, S. Emotionality and information concerning internal reactions. *Journal of Personality and Social Psychology*, 1967, *6*, 458–463.

VAUGHAN, T. R., & REYNOLDS, L. T. The sociology of symbolic interaction. *American Sociologist*, 1968, *3*, 208–214.

VEEVERS, J. E. The child-free alternative: Rejection of the motherhood mystique. In M. L. Stephenson (Ed.), *Women in Canada.* Toronto: New Press, 1973, 183–200.

VERNON, W., & ULRICH, R. Classical conditioning of pain-elicited aggression. *Science*, 1966, *152*, 668–669.

VEROFF, J. Process vs. impact in men's and women's achievement motivation. *Psychology of Women Quarterly*, 1977, *1* (3), 283–293.

VICKERS, J. Women in the universities. In G. Matheson (Ed.), *Women in the Canadian mosaic.* Toronto: Peter Martin Associates, 1976, 199–240.

VROEGH, K. Masculinity and femininity in the elementary and junior high school years. *Developmental Psychology*, 1971, *4*, 254–261.

WABER, D. P. Sex differences in mental abilities, hemispheric lateralization, and rate of physical growth at adolescence. *Developmental Psychology*, 1977, *13* (1), 29–38.

WALLACE, C. Changes in the churches. In G. Matheson (Ed.), *Women in the Canadian mosaic*. Toronto: Peter Martin Associates, 1976, 93–130.

WALSTER, E. Passionate love. In Z. Rubin (Ed.), *Doing unto others*. Englewood Cliffs, N.J.: Prentice–Hall, 1974, 150–162.

WARDLE, M. G. Women's physiological reactions to physically demanding work. *Psychology of Women Quarterly*, 1976, *1* (2), 151–159.

WARME, G. Childhood development problems. In P. D. Steinhauer & Q. Rae–Grant (Eds.), *Psychological problems of the child and his family*. Toronto: Macmillan of Canada, 1977, 100–125.

WARNER, R., & IHARA, T. A lover's guide to living together legally. *Ms.*, 1977, *6*, pp. 54–56; 83–84.

WATSON, J. A., & KIVETT, V. R. Influences on the life satisfaction of older fathers. *The Family Coordinator*, 1976, *25*, 482–488.

WATSON, J. B. *Behaviorism*. Chicago, Ill.: The University of Chicago Press, 1930.

WEIDEGER, P. *Menstruation and menopause*. New York: Dell, 1977.

WEINER, B., FRIEZE, I., KUKLA, A., REED, L., REST, S., & ROSENBAUM, R. M. *Perceiving the causes of success and failure*. Morristown, N. J.: General Learning, 1971.

WEISSTEIN, N. Kinder, kuche, kirche as scientific law. In R. Morgan (Ed.), *Sisterhood is powerful*. New York: Vintage, 1970, 205–220.

WEISSTEIN, N. *Psychology constructs the female or, the fantasy life of the male psychologist*. Boston: New England Free Press, 1971.

WEITZ, S. Sex differences in nonverbal communication. *Sex Roles*, 1976, *2* (2), 175–184.

WELLS, T. *Woman—Which includes man, of course: An experience in awareness*, Newsletter of the Association for Humanistic Psychology, 1970. Reprinted by Theodora Wells, P.O. Box 3392, Beverly Hills, CA 90212.

WHITBECK, C. Theories of sex difference. In C. C. Gould & M. W. Wartofsky (Eds.), *Women and philosophy: Toward a theory of liberation*. New York: G. P. Putnam's Sons, 1976, 54–80.

WIGGINGS, J. S., RENNER, K., CLORE, G. L., & ROSE, R. J. *The psychology of personality*. Boston: New England Free Press, 1971.

WILLIAMS, J. M. *Psychology of women: Behavior in a biosocial context.* New York: W. W. Norton & Company, Inc., 1977.

WILSON, R. *Feminine forever.* New York: M. Evans and Co., 1966.

WINTER, D. G. *The power motive.* New York: Free Press, 1973.

WINTER, D. G. *Power motives and power behavior in women.* Paper presented at the meeting of the American Psychological Association, Chicago, September 1975.

WINTER, D. G., & STEWART, A. J. Power motivation. In H. London & J. Exner (Eds.), *Dimensions of personality.* New York: Wiley, in press.

WITKIN, H. A. Individual differences in ease of perception of embedded figures. *Journal of Personality,* 1950, *19,* 1–15.

WITKIN, H. A., BIRNBAUM, J., LOMONACO, S., LEHR, S., & HERMAN, J. L. Cognitive patterning in congenitally totally blind children. *Child Development,* 1968, *39,* 768–786.

WITKIN, H. A., DYK, R. B., FATERSON, H. F., GOODENOUGH, D. R., & KARP, S. A. *Psychological differentiation.* New York: Wiley, 1962.

WITKIN, H. A., & GOODENOUGH, D. R. *Field dependence revisited.* Research bulletin, Educational Testing Service, Princeton, N. J., 1976.

The Wolfenden Report. New York: Lancer Books, 1964.

WOLPE, J. *The practice of behavior therapy* (2nd ed.) New York: Pergamon Press, 1973.

WOLPE, J. Behavior therapy and its malcontents: II. Multimodal Eclecticism, Cognitive Exclusivism and "Exposure Empiricism." *Journal of Behavior Therapy and Experimental Psychiatry,* 1976, *7,* 109–116.

WOOLF, V. *A room of one's own.* New York: Harcourt Brace & World, Inc., 1929.

WRIGHTSMAN, L. *Social psychology* (2nd ed.) Monterey, Calif.: Brooks/Cole, 1977.

ZILLMAN, D. Excitation transfer in communication-mediated aggressive behavior. *Journal of Experimental Social Psychology,* 1971, *7,* 419–434.

Index